African Youth and the Persistence of Marginalization

The much heralded growth and transformation of many economies in sub-Saharan Africa over the last decade continues to receive prominent attention in academic scholarship and among policy practitioners. An apparent feature about this transformation, however, is that Africa's youth appear to have been left out. This book critically examines the extent and consequences of the marginalization of African youth. It questions conventional wisdoms about data trends, aspirational goals, and common policy interventions surrounding Africa's youth that have been variously propagated in both the development studies literature and in mainstream donor policy reports.

The book explores macro trends from both a temporal and cross-regional perspective in order to highlight what is distinct about contemporary African youth and whether their prospects and behaviours do actually vary from their counterparts in other regions of the world or from previous generations of African youth. Such studies include cross-country analyses of youth employment patterns and modes of political participation, in-depth examination of the behaviours and aspirations of the urban youth, and critical reflections on the impact of rural employment initiatives, vocational education, and learnership programmes.

The incorporation of multiple methods and disciplines, as well as its attention to policy issues, ensures that the book will be of great interest to graduate students, researchers, and professional researchers whose work lies at the intersection of African area studies and development studies as well as those focused on development economics, political science, and public policy and administration.

Danielle Resnick is a Research Fellow in the Development Strategies and Governance Division at the International Food Policy Research Institute (IFPRI), USA.

James Thurlow is a Senior Research Fellow in the Development Strategies and Governance Division at the International Food Policy Research Institute (IFPRI), USA.

UNU World Institute for Development Economics Research (UNU-WIDER) was established by the United Nations University as its first research and training centre and started work in Helsinki, Finland, in 1985. The Institute undertakes applied research and policy analysis on structural changes affecting the developing and transitional economies, provides a forum for the advocacy of policies leading to robust, equitable and environmentally sustainable growth, and promotes capacity strengthening and training in the field of economic and social policy-making. Its work is carried out by staff researchers and visiting scholars in Helsinki and through networks of collaborating scholars and institutions around the world.

United Nations University
World Institute for Development Economics Research (UNU-WIDER)
Katajanokanlaituri 6B, 00160 Helsinki, Finland
www.wider.unu.edu

Routledge Studies in African Development

Self-Determination and Secession in Africa
The post-colonial state
Edited by Redie Bereketeab

Economic Growth and Development in Africa
Understanding global trends and prospects
Horman Chitonge

African Youth and the Persistence of Marginalization
Employment, politics, and prospects for change
Edited by Danielle Resnick and James Thurlow

African Youth and the Persistence of Marginalization

Employment, politics, and prospects
for change

**Edited by Danielle Resnick
and James Thurlow**

Routledge
Taylor & Francis Group

LONDON AND NEW YORK

UNITED NATIONS
UNIVERSITY
UNU-WIDER

First published 2015
by Routledge
2 Park Square, Milton Park, Abingdon, Oxfordshire OX14 4RN

and by Routledge
711 Third Avenue, New York, NY 10017

First issued in paperback 2016

Routledge is an imprint of the Taylor & Francis Group, an informa business

British Library Cataloguing-in-Publication Data
A catalogue record for this book is available from the British Library

Library of Congress Cataloging-in-Publication Data
African youth and the persistence of marginalization : employment, politics,
    and prospects for change / edited by Danielle Resnick and James Thurlow.
        pages cm
    Includes bibliographical references and index.
    1. Youth—Africa—Social conditions.   2. Youth—Africa—Economic
conditions.   3. Youth—Employment—Africa.   4. Marginality,
Social—Africa.   I. Resnick, Danielle, 1980– editor of compilation.
II. Thurlow, James (Development economist), editor of compilation.
    HQ799.A35A375 2015
    305.235096—dc23
    2014041827

ISBN: 978-1-138-63045-1 (pbk)
ISBN: 978-1-138-82947-3 (hbk)

Typeset in Goudy
by Apex CoVantage, LLC

Contents

Figures

Tables

Boxes

Acknowledgements

This edited volume is the product of a three year project on 'Prospects for Africa's Youth' supported by the United Nations University-World Institute for Development Economics Research (UNU-WIDER). The contributors to this volume are all established experts in the areas of urban studies, geography, education policy, development and labor economics, agricultural policy, and political science. However, as Africanists, each recognized the importance of applying a youth lens to their area of specialty given current demographic trajectories on the continent. In doing so, this volume has a more theoretically and methodologically eclectic range of contributions than traditional scholarship found on youth studies. We are especially grateful to each of the contributors for collaborating on this initiative, traveling long distances to a workshop in Helsinki, Finland in mid-2013 to help elucidate key findings from case studies, and remaining committed to the project despite many other pressing commitments.

As major donors to UNU-WIDER's research program, we are also thankful for financial assistance from the governments of Denmark, Finland, Sweden, and the United Kingdom. In addition, we are grateful for the initial support for this project by UNU-WIDER's current director, Professor Finn Tarp and appreciative of the efforts by UNU-WIDER's administrative staff for helping to keep this work moving forward. In particular, Lorraine Telfer-Taivainen and Lisa Winkler were instrumental in editing the chapters and pushing the manuscript toward completion. Dr. Peter Wobst of the United Nation's Food and Agricultural Organization (FAO) deserves a special thanks as well for engaging in initial discussions on this project and pushing us to consider more the policy implications of our collective contributions. Finally, we would like to thank Khanam Virjee and Helen Bell at Routledge for their enthusiasm for this project and continued patience with the finalization of the manuscript.

We hope this volume will be a welcome addition to the already rich and nuanced literature on African youth and help inform both scholarly and practitioner thinking about this important constituency as we move into a post-2015 world.

Abbreviations

ACLD	Armed Conflict Location and Event Data
GLLAMM	Generalized Linear Latent and Mixed Models
HLP	High Level Panel
HSRC	Human Sciences Research Council
JSS	Junior Secondary School
LMES	Labour Market Entry Survey
LPI	Lived Poverty Index
MARDEF	Malawi Rural Development Fund
MDGs	Millennium Development Goals
NQF	National Qualifications Framework
NYEP	National Youth Employment Programme
PSM	Propensity Score Matching
SETAs	Sector Education and Training Authorities
SSA	Sub-Saharan Africa
SSS	Senior Secondary School
TVET	Technical, Vocational Education, and Training
UPE	Universal Primary Education
UPIMA	Urbanization and Poverty in Mining Africa
YEDF	Youth Enterprise Development Fund
YIAP	Youth in Agriculture Programme

Contributors

Nana Akua Anyidoho is a Senior Research Fellow at the Institute of Statistical, Social, and Economic Research (ISSER), University of Ghana, and co-convenor of the Young People and Agrifood Theme of the Future Agricultures Consortium. Her recent research focuses on economic empowerment pathways for Ghanaian youth; the work aspirations of university students; and young people's interaction with agricultural policy and the agrifood sector.

Deborah Fahy Bryceson is an Honorary Research Fellow at the Centre of African Studies, University of Edinburgh. Over the last 25 years she has published extensively on changing work patterns in Africa, exploring an array of labour practices, including those connected with smallholder agriculture, trade, alcohol production, and most recently artisanal mining. Her books on the latter topic include *Mining and African Urbanisation* (Routledge, 2013) and *Mining and Social Transformation in Africa* (Routledge, 2014).

Michael Chasukwa is a Senior Lecturer and former Head of the Department of Political and Administrative Studies, Chancellor College, University of Malawi. His research and teaching interests include governance, local government, decentralisation, politics of development, agricultural policies, agrarian transformation, youth and development, and political economy.

Blessings Chinsinga is an experienced academic, researcher and consultant currently based at the Department of Political and Administrative Studies, Chancellor College, University of Malawi as an Associate Professor specializing in political economy of development, governance and democracy, public policy analysis, rural livelihood, and local level politics. He is also the Deputy Director for the Centre for Social Research (CSR) which is the research arm of the Faculty of Social Science since January 2013.

Karen Tranberg Hansen is Professor Emerita of Anthropology at Northwestern University. As an urban and economic anthropologist, she has conducted extensive research in Zambia, she has published widely on urban life in Zambia, gender, housing, the informal economy, and work, and consumption. Among others, her books and co-edited volumes include *Keeping House in Lusaka* (Columbia University Press 1997), *Salaula: The World of Secondhand*

Clothing and Zambia (University of Chicago Press 2000), *Reconsidering Informality: Perspectives from Urban Africa* (Nordic Africa Institute 2004), *Youth and the City in the Global South* (Indiana University Press 2008), and *Street Economies in the Urban Global South* (SAR Press 2013).

Jennifer Leavy is an economist by training whose work centres on livelihoods of the poorest and most vulnerable people, mainly in rural areas. She has a strong interest in the intersection of economic, social, and cultural life. Recent work has focused on: youth aspirations, social mobility, and transitions out of poverty; wellbeing, vulnerability, and climate change adaptation. Jennifer is a Senior Research Fellow in the School of International Development at the University of East Africa.

Moses Oketch is a Reader at the Institute of Education, University of London. He has previously worked at Vanderbilt University. He has been Director of Research at African Population and Health Research Center, and a visiting professor at University of Pennsylvania. His research focuses on economics of education, educational policy analysis and impact evaluation, particularly in sub-Saharan Africa.

Neil Rankin is an Associate Professor in the Department of Economics, University of Stellenbosch. Most of his work is in four, often related, areas: microeconomic aspects of international trade; firms and firm dynamics; prices and pricing at a disaggregated level; and policy evaluation, and has focused mainly on sub-Saharan Africa. Between 2009 and 2013 he was the Principal Investigator of a large-scale impact evaluation project which investigated the impact of a wage subsidy on youth employment in South Africa.

Danielle Resnick is a Research Fellow in the Development Strategies and Governance Division at the International Food Policy Research Institute (IFPRI) and formerly a Research Fellow at the United Nations University World Institute for Development Economics Research (UNU-WIDER). As a political scientist, her research focuses on foreign aid and democracy, party politics, electoral behavior, and the political economy of development in urban and rural areas. In addition to a number of journal articles, she is the author of *Urban Poverty and Party Populism in African Democracies* (Cambridge University Press, 2013) and co-editor of *Democratic Trajectories in Africa: Unraveling the Impact of Foreign Aid* (Oxford University Press, 2013).

Gareth Roberts is a Researcher at the African Micro-Economic Research Unit (AMERU), School of Economic and Business Sciences, University of the Witwatersrand, South Africa. His primary interest is in youth unemployment and he was most recently part of a team that implemented an evaluation of a targeted youth wage-subsidy voucher for the National Treasury of South Africa. Gareth also has extensive experience managing data collection and is currently the Impact Evaluation coordinator in South Africa for the World Bank's Development Impact Evaluation Initiative (DIME).

Volker Schöer is the director of the African Micro-Economic Research Unit (AMERU) at the School of Economic and Business Sciences (SEBS) at the University of Witwatersrand, South Africa, which brings together South African, African, and other international researchers to conduct rigorous quantitative research on microeconomic issues related to firms, labour markets and education. His work has appeared in, among others, the *Journal of International Development, Review of Development Economics,* and the *South African Journal of Economics.*

James Sumberg is an agriculturalist by training and has over 30 years of experience working on small-scale farming systems and agricultural research policy, primarily in sub-Saharan Africa. A key research interest has been the dynamics of change within agricultural systems. He joined IDS as a Research Fellow in October 2009. Previously he served as Programme Director at The New Economics Foundation and Senior Lecturer in Natural Resource Management in the School of Development Studies, University of East Anglia. He has also held research positions at WADRA – the Africa Rice Centre, the International Livestock Centre for Africa, CARE International and the Gambian Livestock Department.

Getnet Tadele is an Associate Professor at the department of sociology, Addis Ababa University, Ethiopia. His publications include numerous articles in prestigious journals including Culture, Health and Sexuality, HIV/AIDS and Social Services, BMC public Health, International Health, American Journal of Tropic Medicine Hygiene, Ethiopian Journal of Health Development, and IDS and CODESRIA bulletin. He is also co-editor of *Vulnerabilities, Impacts and Responses to HIV/AIDS in Sub-Saharan Africa* (Palgrave Macmillan, 2013).

James Thurlow is a Senior Research Fellow in the Development Strategies and Governance Division of the International Food Policy Research Institute (IFPRI) and formerly a Research Fellow at the United Nations University World Institute for Development Economics Research (UNU-WIDER). His research focuses on the interactions between policies, economic growth, and poverty, primarily using computable general equilibrium and micro-simulation modeling. He has worked with governments and researchers throughout sub-Saharan Africa, and in Bangladesh, Peru, Tunisia, and Vietnam. Among other outlets, his work has appeared in *Agricultural Economics, American Journal of Agricultural Economics, Review of Development Economics, Review of Income and Wealth,* and *World Development.*

Stephen Whitfield is a Lecturer in Food Security and Climate Change in the Sustainability Research Institute at the University of Leeds. His research focuses on the socio-politics of climate change adaptation in African agriculture. This has involved work on a range agricultural innovations and strategies, from conservation agriculture to genetically modified crops.

Joseph Yaro is an associate professor of Human Geography at the University of Ghana, with a focus on Rural Development. He combines a rich background in development studies and rural geography with extensive rural research experience in northern Ghana. His specific research interests include sustainable development in rural areas, rural livelihoods, food security, climate change adaptation, land tenure, and transnational land deals/grabs.

Foreword

Today's youth in many countries across the world are viewed as creative new agents of change while simultaneously, and paradoxically, also a lost generation stymied by their economic vulnerability. Honing in on sub-Saharan Africa where this contradiction is highly apparent, UNU-WIDER launched a multi-disciplinary research project to uncover what could be the causes of this daunting social phenomenon, and what could be done to address it. Field experts on Africa were brought into the project team to ensure developing country perspectives and experiences, focusing on youth's participation in economic development, their modes of engagement with the state, and government policy interventions.

This book contains the essence of the project, which bridged three years of robust academic research – teasing out the nuanced social, economic, institutional, political, and policy constraints – for the reader to absorb and consider further.

I heartily thank the editors, Danielle Resnick and James Thurlow, former Research Fellows at UNU-WIDER, for undertaking this intellectual endeavor for the benefit of many people, not least sub-Saharan Africa's youth and the region's policy makers.

Finn Tarp
Director, UNU-WIDER
Helsinki, November 2014

1   Introduction

African youth at a crossroads

Danielle Resnick and James Thurlow

Introduction

Across the globe, today's youth are often paradoxically considered both 'agents of change' who are driven by their aspirations for a better life and 'a lost generation' who are trapped by their economic vulnerability. Nowhere is this contradiction more pronounced than in sub-Saharan Africa. Indeed, Africa's youth are frequently portrayed as having a bifurcated identity, emphasized by scholarly references to this diverse constituency as 'Hooligans and Heroes' (Perullo 2005), 'Heroes or Villains' (Seekings 1993), 'Vanguard or Vandals' (Abbink and van Kessel 2005), 'Makers and Breakers' (Honwana and De Boeck 2005), and 'Troublemakers or Peacemakers' (McEvoy-Levy 2013).

The singular attention accorded to African youth in a host of recent literature and policy reports (see Abbink and van Kessel 2005; Aguilar 1998; Filmer and Fox 2014; Honwana and De Boeck 2005; Honwana 2012; Sommers 2012) is, among other reasons, motivated by the region's sizeable youth bulge. Officially defined, a youth bulge refers to a surfeit of people, relative to the total population, who are 24 years old or younger. Globally, at least half the population is now below 25, with 1.5 billion between the ages of 12 and 24 (Sommers 2010). Since the phenomenon is driven by the confluence of lower child mortality in countries that still have relatively high fertility rates, a majority of those young people are concentrated in developing countries (see Garcia and Farès 2008). In Africa, approximately half of the entire region's population is below the age of 20 (Leahy et al. 2007). By way of comparison, the next 'youngest' region, the Middle East and North Africa, has approximately one-fifth of its population living in the 15–24 age category (Assaad and Roudi-Fahimi 2007). Yet, as highlighted in Chapter 2 of this volume, Africa not only has the world's highest share of young people relative to the total population, but also is the only region where this trend is expected to continue for the coming decades. In fact, of the top ten countries with the highest fertility rates, all ten are located in Africa (see PRB 2014).[1]

The prospects of such a youth bulge have sometimes invoked neo-Malthusian fears of increased resource scarcity, particularly linked to jobs, and in turn Hobbesian predictions for peace and stability. Reflecting the general relegation of women in studies of African youth, even though females constitute the majority of Africa's young population and have slightly higher unemployment rates (see

Abbink 2005; Gyimah-Brempong and Kimenyi 2013), the instability thesis is mostly focused on males. For instance, Fuller (1995) argues that a concentration of young men increases the likelihood of social unrest. Goldstone (2001; 2010) likewise claims that with fewer responsibilities and susceptible to radical ideas, young males are more likely to be instigators of violence, while Collier (2007) claims they may potentially be mobilized as soldiers in civil conflict.

Such fears have been echoed by the US National Intelligence Council in its predictions of de-stabilizing trends in the coming decades (see NIC 2012). Others have claimed that since youth bulges are associated with conflict, they may also be more likely to lead to authoritarian governments since violence and the lack of order result in state repression. According to Cincotta (2008), when the youth bulge begins to dissipate, countries become more stable, the business elite is less worried about a lack of order and a fear of property loss, and in turn, authoritarian regimes lose support from elites and political liberalization ensues. He finds that a region's number of liberal democracies grows as the average proportion of young people, aged 15–29, declines.

This alarmism has prompted African policymakers to respond with seemingly new initiatives to address a perceived youth crisis. Most notably, at its summit in The Gambia in 2006, the African Union issued an African Youth Charter, which is a guiding framework to encourage youth empowerment and development within the region. The Charter commits African governments to a wide-ranging list of approximately 25 broad goals, including promoting youth employment, helping with the psychological and social reintegration of youth involved in conflict, ensuring equal access to education and health care, and upholding freedom of movement, expression, and association (AU 2006). Subsequently, the AU declared 2009–2018 the Decade of Youth Development, and during its 2011 summit in Equatorial Guinea, it issued a document on 'Accelerating Youth Empowerment for Sustainable Development' that focused on financing the Youth Charter's implementation (see ILO 2012). Likewise, in the High-Level Panel (HLP) report on the Post-2015 Development Agenda, youth are given specific attention, emphasizing that 'Young people must be subjects, not objects, of the post-2015 development agenda' (UN 2013: 17). Toward this end, one of the eleven goals promoted by the HLP is economic transformation that results in job creation and inclusive growth, with a particular emphasis on youth.

Yet, the importance of youth is not a new phenomenon in Africa, nor is the prominence of generational conflict. Iliffe (1995: 95) even noted that 'conflict between . . . generations [has been] one of the most dynamic and enduring forces in African history.' Disputes with traditional elders over access to cattle and land, conflicts with colonial authorities over the legitimacy of colonial rule, and even pro-democracy movements against geriatric presidents have all highlighted the repeated tension between young and old over time (e.g. Burgess 2005a; McKittrick 2002).

This introductory chapter therefore places the challenges faced by the youth in historical perspective, while also distinguishing what is different for today's youth compared with previous generations. In doing so, attention is given to the region's economic growth over the last decade, rapid urbanization, and greater political liberalization. These processes undoubtedly have generated new opportunities for the youth. But, the chapter highlights that they also have often exacerbated underlying power asymmetries faced by this constituency, pinpointing factors contributing to their ongoing marginalization. Subsequently, the organization of the book is discussed and the key aspects of each chapter summarized. In doing so, the main contribution of the collection is to question conventional wisdoms about both the youth's behaviours and preferences, as well as common public policy prescriptions promoted by the international community.

What is unique about today's African youth?

In the broader literature about age, an important distinction is frequently made between life cycle and generational effects. The main distinction is between whether age represents either 'a measure of accumulated life experience or a measure of the conditions prevailing during an individual's formative years' (Down and Wilson 2013: 433). More specifically, in the life cycle perspective, everyone undergoes behavioural and attitudinal changes linked to the passage of various life stages due to a different set of biological needs, cognitive abilities, and social characteristics as one ages (see O'Rand and Krecker 1990). For instance, younger people typically may be less risk-averse (due to fewer familial or job responsibilities) and tend to be less partisan (e.g. Converse 1976), less religious (Stolzenberg 1995), more democratic (Rose et al. 1998), and more likely to have cosmopolitan world views (e.g. Inglehart 1995). Moreover, they are deciding whether to further their education beyond the primary level, attempting to break into the labour market and learning how to exercise their citizenship via paying taxes and registering to vote (World Bank 2006). Difficulties encountered in these initial life stages can have cumulative effects over time.

In the generational perspective, there is something specific about a period of time that has a substantial impact on that cohort's views and identity. Economic crisis or boom, shifts in public welfare policies, technological innovation, political transition, or civil war are some of the factors that can influence the perceptions, preferences, and opportunities for a specific group of youth. According to Mannheim (1952: 291), one's 'common location in the social and historical process' during his/her formative years can lead to potentially categorical differences between both young and older people. For instance, Mishler and Rose (2007) find that Russia's *glasnost* generation, who were born in 1987 or later, demonstrate much less support for a communist regime than older Russians. In South Africa, there is frequent reference to the 'Born Free' generation who have grown up without ever experiencing apartheid (see Mattes 2012). Similarly, half of Rwanda's population today was not alive at the time of the 1994 genocide, meaning that their perceptions of the political landscape differ from those who have experienced that trauma and the social polarization that preceded it.

Both life-cycle and generation effects appear to be simultaneously at the root of the marginalization of African youth in multiple domains. By adopting a historical view, the following sections highlight that many of the problems facing today's youth in Africa are not new and are instead a by-product of the fragile transition from adolescence to adulthood. However, there are specific trends related to economic transformation, demographic shifts, and political transition in Africa that further contextualize the specific environment in which today's youth are operating vis-à-vis both other generations and their counterparts in other regions of the world.

Economic growth, employment, and educational attainment

Many of the alarmist fears discussed above related to the youth are particularly tied to concerns over *unemployed* youth. Kaplan (1996: 16) suggested that the youth bulge was on the verge of bursting, depicting Africa's youth as 'out of school, unemployed, loose molecules in an unstable social fluid that threatened to ignite.' Many case studies of civil war in Africa focus on the role played by unemployment, whether in driving young people to establish the Revolutionary United Front (RUF) in Sierra Leone (see Richards 1996) or to join the genocidal *Interahamwe* in Rwanda (see Roessler 2005) or to support the Mungiki cult violence in Kenya (see Kagwanja 2005a). Urdal (2006) also finds that youth bulges lead to a higher propensity for political violence, arguing that high unemployment creates low opportunity costs for this group (see also Leahy et al. 2007).

Opportunities for youth employment have waxed and waned in Africa over the last half century. Colonialism provided new employment options in some settings and the prospects for challenging patriarchal authority. In Uganda, Summers (2005) describes how the British colonial governor from the 1920s to 1940s focused on opening new jobs to young Africans in the civil service. In Southern Africa, Carton (2000: 136) notes that new access to wage labour, particularly through the mines, gave young men greater ability to challenge 'customary relations at home, especially with respect to personal freedom in work, play and courtship.' Labour migration enabled youth to accumulate resources independently from their fathers and thereby escape parental controls (see Waller 2006).

In the immediate post-colonial period in the 1960s, economic growth rates in Africa were at their highest (Ndulu and O'Connell 2008). At the same time, high levels of employment were facilitated by the practice of import-industrialization strategies that protected uncompetitive industries and by jobs in the public service. For instance, Hart (1976) notes that as of 1960, more than one-third of the labour force in Ghana worked for the government. Consumer subsidies also ensured that even low-wage employment was broadly tolerable. As is well known by now, these same policies became unsustainable and began unraveling in the mid-1970s, when Africa's descent into economic decline began (Ndulo and O'Connell 2008). Around this time, the term 'informal economy' was coined by Hart (1973) in his investigation of the challenges faced by unskilled rural migrants arriving in urban areas of Southern Ghana. Barchiesi (1996) similarly noted that increasingly, public servants relied on the informal sector to supplement their dwindling incomes. O'Brien (1996) highlighted that West African youth concentrated into the informal sector faced qualitatively different economic conditions in the 1980s than in the more prosperous 1960s and 1970s.

While the structural adjustment period of the 1980s and 1990s continued to be a period of sluggish growth in most of the region, the period since the 2000s is often heralded in the media as a time of 'Africa Rising' (see Economist 2011; Perry 2012). On average, GDP growth has been about five percent a year since 2000 and is not simply limited to those countries with sizeable natural resource commodities (Devarajan and Fengler 2013). The African Development Bank has even claimed that as a consequence of the growth, the region's middle class has grown by 300 million people since 2000 (AfDB 2011). However, much of this economic growth has been driven by the services sector rather than more labour-intensive manufacturing (McMillan et al. 2014). As of 2010, only about 8 percent of employment is provided by manufacturing, which is a marginal increase over the 7.8 percent that the sector contributed back in 1975 (see deVries et al. 2013). As Filmer and Fox (2014: 32) note, 'Africa's decade of growth was not "jobless," but patterns of employment growth differed across countries.' In places such as South Africa, for instance, youth unemployment has remained high, increasing from 49 to 52 percent of the population between 2009 and 2012.[2] By contrast, Chapter 2 of this volume shows that youth unemployment is much lower in West and Central Africa.

From a subjective perspective, unemployment also remains a key concern. As seen in Figure 1.1, evidence from the Afrobarometer public opinion survey

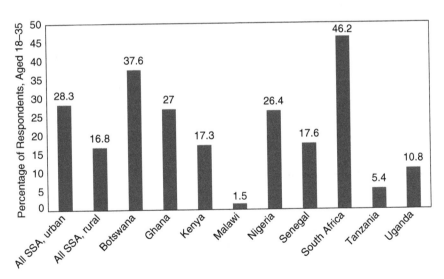

Figure 1.1 Share of African youth who believe unemployment is country's most important problem, by urban/rural residence and selected countries

Source: Afrobarometer, Round 5 (2012/2014)

Notes: Round 5 contains 28 sub-Saharan African countries with 45,991 observations. Results here are weighted by survey weights.

database shows that insufficient jobs are the overarching priority that the youth believes needs to be addressed by their respective governments, with the problem perceived to be more pronounced in urban than in rural areas. Interestingly, there is vast variation across the region, with those in Southern African countries, such as Botswana and South Africa, identifying unemployment as more of a problem than countries such as Malawi, Tanzania, or Uganda.

Compared to previous generations, the challenge of finding suitable jobs for today's African youth is complicated by the fact that they are better educated, not to mention healthier, than ever before (World Bank 2006). At the dawn of independence in the 1960s, the expansion of the school system to the broader African populace represented an initial critical juncture in expanding youth skills beyond farming and petty trade (see Last 2005). A second and even more dramatic juncture has occurred since the 1990s as the result of at least two factors. One factor was the Millennium Development Goals, which were instrumental at mobilizing donor support and resources for addressing deficiencies in primary education (see UNU-WIDER 2014).[3] At the same time, a number of African governments since the 1990s have abolished fees for primary education, which some have argued has been part of a drive to garner more votes in rural areas in the wake of democratization (see Harding and Stasavage 2014; Stasavage 2005). In some African countries, secondary school fees have also been abolished, particularly in the wake of campaign promises toward this end (see Ohba 2011).

Although the quality of education still remains a significant concern (see Pritchett 2013) and Africa's rates of secondary school enrolment are lower than elsewhere (see Chapter 2 of this volume), there is no doubt that a far larger set of African youth are completing primary and secondary schooling than ever before. In turn, the dearth of jobs is more problematic since a larger share of youth today are less inclined to work in unskilled employment, such as in the informal sector or in agriculture. For instance, Resnick and Thurlow (2014) find that in Zambia, unemployment rates among those aged 18–34 increased from 13.9 percent in 2002 to 21.1 percent in 2010. Furthermore, 26 percent of those who had completed secondary school were unemployed in 2010 while the equivalent rate for those who had only completed primary school was 14 percent.

Rural-urban transformation(s)

Besides persistent employment challenges in the wake of substantial education improvements, African youth are grappling with living in the fastest urbanizing region of the world. By 2030, this traditionally agrarian region is predicted to reach the urban inflection point whereby at least half of the region's population will live in urban areas (Kessides 2006). The youth in particular are believed to be at the forefront of this demographic shift. In fact, according to the World Bank (2006), the youth are 40 percent more likely than their older counterparts to move from rural to urban areas, or within urban areas. Typically, as a part of a life cycle trend, migration rates peak between ages 15–24, when young people are more risk-seeking and move away from families in search of employment (UNDESA 2005).

Historically, colonial authorities were concerned about the implications of rural–urban migration and were particularly suspicious about the growing presence of large numbers of young people who lacked regular industrial employment and who were perceived as potential criminals (see Clapham 2006). Waller (2006:91) notes that although rural guerrilla movements have probably been more destabilizing than urban youth gangs in Africa, 'Constructions of delinquency drew on a presumed and morally weighted dichotomy between town and country.' Burgess (2005b) likewise observes that British colonial authorities viewed towns as morally inferior to rural areas and worried about the emergence of a consumption-driven youth who disrespected elders and the rule of law (see also Burton 2001). In turn, 'It also became common for the British to correlate youth, the city, and nationalism, and to construe willingness to question the authority of seniors as a willingness also to challenge the legitimacy of colonialism' (Burgess 2005b: xiv).

Many of these same concerns continued to linger during the nationalist era, particularly as independence leaders began to consolidate one-party states. Rustication exercises were not an uncommon means of addressing the perceived threat of young, urban masses. Perhaps best known was Julius Nyerere's effort in Tanzania to expel urbanites to rural *Ujamaa* villages in the 1970s (Maro and Mlay 1982). In 1983, the *Nguzi Kazi* ('hard work') campaign again tried to relocate un- and underemployed youth who migrated to Tanzania's cities back to their rural homes (Sawers 1989). In the waning days of his regime, Houphouët Boigny also carried out a *rétour à la terre* campaign in Côte d'Ivoire that focused on urban youth (see Babo 2010).

Most of these urban containment policies have not succeeded. In fact, today estimates suggest that 7 out of 10 residents in African cities are 30 years old or younger, and that in the slums of megacities of Lagos or Kinshasa, the figure is closer to 80 percent (Smith 2011). Poor urban planning is at the root of the dismal conditions in many of Africa's slums, which can be characterized by poor services, substandard housing, fierce competition for low-paid jobs, and the threat of sexual violence. As Hansen and Vaa (2004) point out, colonial legal frameworks for urban development remain relatively unchanged, aimed at limiting containment rather than confronting growth. African governments have often approached urban development in a rather piecemeal way, focused on individual projects (Mabogunje 1994). While government support for low-income housing remains scarce, private investment has been growing for high-end luxury developments, such as Nigeria's Eko Atlantic and the Cité du Fleuve in the Democratic Republic of the Congo (DRC) (see Skelton 2014).

But, despite the hardships faced in these cities, many youth are not easily dissuaded from migrating to urban areas or completely discouraged by the inequalities they encounter in such settings (see Sommers 2010). For instance, 75 percent of Kenyan youth in Nairobi's slums had high aspirations that included gaining financial independence, owning their home, looking after aging parents, and having a good job (Kabiru et al. 2013). In Burundi, Sommers and Uvin (2011) found many of the youth who migrated to the capital of Bujumbura from rural areas were happy with their decision, and about half of those living in the city's slums believe their lives were better than those of their parents. For many, there is a distinct urban identity that develops, which makes returning to rural areas more difficult. Sommers (2010) notes that despite housing demolitions by the Sudanese government of internally displaced persons (IDPs) in Khartoum, young IDPs had no desire to leave the city. Similarly, a survey of youth who were pushed by civil conflict into the city of Butembo in the eastern DRC revealed that they did not plan to return to their homes or their agricultural livelihoods even after conditions became more secure in rural areas (Raeymaekers 2010).

Yet, this trend is not uniformly true across the region. Return migration to the countryside, often prompted by economic decline in urban areas, has also occurred. In the 1980s, the collapse of copper mining prompted Zambians to migrate from the Copperbelt back to rural areas (Ferguson 1999) and in Benin, disillusioned, unemployed graduates returned to their villages as job opportunities in the civil service became increasingly scarce (Bierschenk and de Sardan 2003).

But, in areas of land scarcity and high youth bulges, land inheritance in rural areas becomes a central problem, especially among those whose parents may only be in their 50s and not yet willing to 'retire' (Jayne et al. 2014). Some youth return to the countryside and find that land has been bequeathed to migrants in the interim. This has long been a problem in Africa, as Boone's (2014) work on youth in the Asante areas of Ghana in the 1950s illustrates and Le Meur's (2006) research on conflicts over land rights among youth and traditional authorities in Benin. The problem became particularly pronounced in Côte d'Ivoire when economic decline prompted unemployed youths to migrate from cities to the arable rural areas in the west of the country in the 1990s. Returning to their villages, young Ivoirians found that their parents had rented or ceded their land to migrants who often had a different ethnicity and religion. This stoked ethnic and intergenerational tensions that became key factors in that country's subsequent civil war (see Banégas 2006; Chauveau and Richards 2008).

Political transition without sufficient representation

A majority of Africa's youth are navigating these demographic shifts and employment constraints in more democratic political settings than youth cohorts of the past. Political scientists often point to Africa benefitting from the third wave of democratization in the early 1990s, with approximately 29 African countries holding multi-party elections between 1989 and 1994 (e.g. Bratton and van de Walle 1997). A further wave of liberalization emerged in the early 2000s with the end of civil wars in Sierra Leone and Liberia and the allowance of multi-party competition in Uganda. While autocratic and hybrid regimes are still present in the region, most of Africa's youth have access to more independent media outlets, greater freedom of association and fora for civic engagement, and more political parties to represent their interests than ever before.

Even in earlier eras, the numerical significance of the youth was recognized as a political opportunity. Nationalist era leaders saw the youth as a symbol of liberation and often mobilized youths against colonial rule. For instance, Kwame Nkrumah of Ghana rallied unemployed youths in Accra, known as 'veranda boys' because they slept outside on verandas, to support his Convention Peoples Party in the 1950s (Austin 1964). Leopold Senghor of Senegal launched a well-known radio programme titled 'Youth, Hope of the World' in the 1960s (Diouf 2003). Burgess (2001) notes that Tanzania's Julius Nyerere advised Kenyan nationalists to promote youth within their ranks because they were more willing to take risks and had more progressive views. In his 'Second Scramble' speech, Nyerere (1966:204) noted that Africa was in an advantageous position because of its large, youthful population: 'The young have had an education which is a present-day education; their ideas are present-day ideas.' The youth, in turn, saw nationalist movements as a chance to challenge the authority of their elders (Burgess 2005b).

However, this often turned out to be a false expectation and belied a fundamental asymmetry in these relations: the youth were seen as instrumental to advancing the goals of older leaders but not necessarily given the option to become leaders themselves. As Schatzberg's (2001) notes, the 'paternal metaphor' whereby African leaders use a discourse that portrays them as fatherly benefactors for their citizens has been pronounced for much of Africa's post-colonial history, and this became especially true as one-party rule began to take root in much of the region. Due to their lack of resources, the youth were often manipulated by their elders (O'Brien 1996). At worst, promising youth leaders were targeted for assassination, as happened too often in the 1960s and 1970s in Kenya (Kagwanja 2005b). At best, aging autocrats co-opted young people into youth leagues or wings, such as Hastings Banda's Young Pioneers in Malawi, Daniel Arap Moi's *Jeshi la Mzee* ('old man's army'), Robert Mugabe's 'war veterans,' or more recently Laurent Gbagbo's Young Patriots in Côte d'Ivoire. These organizations were often tantamount to private militias used against opposition movements that were mobilizing for democratization (see Abbink 2005; Laasko 2007).

Democratization has offered an opportunity for the youth to exert a greater voice, especially since the size of this constituency implies that they cannot be ignored. In Liberia, for example, 40 percent of all registered voters are 29 years old or younger (Gavin 2008). Consequently, throughout the region, there have been active attempts by sexa-, septua-, and octogenarian presidential candidates to woo the youth to the voting booth through appeals to theatrics and pop culture. In his blue marches during his presidential campaigns of the 2000s in Senegal, Abdoulaye Wade blasted reggae and rap music through the streets of Dakar (Foucher 2007). Jacob Zuma's 'ride n'braai' parties in his 2009 campaign involved politicians from the African National Congress (ANC) playing *kwaito* music by popular disc jockeys and handing out meat and beer to young attendees (Butler 2009). In 2011, President Yoweri Museveni of Uganda famously released a rap song to convince his young populace why he should receive yet another term even after already being in office for 24 years (see de Torrenté 2013). The late Michael Sata of Zambia similarly had a well-known rapper, Dandy Krazy, record the campaign tune *Donchi Kubemba* for his 2011 presidential campaign. Such tactics may be somewhat effective in keeping young Africans interested in the electoral process. Following expectations of life cycle effects, African youth do tend to vote less than older Africans. But, at the absolute level, they vote in higher proportions than their counterparts in other areas of the world (see Resnick and Casale forthcoming).

The main challenge though remains: how to best bring the youth into the political and policy arenas in a more meaningful and consistent manner besides electoral mobilization every four or five years. Current mechanisms are not deemed very effective. As Smith (2011) notes, party youth wings are geared more toward advocating for leaders from a particular homeland, rather than mobilizing on behalf of youth issues. Despite the African Union's Youth Charter, non-partisan youth groups in Africa are only granted observer status within the pan-African organization.[4] And even though a majority of African governments have cabinet ministries devoted to youth issues, Table 1.1 reveals that there is an overwhelming tendency to either categorize the youth as either a constituency closely intertwined with leisure activities, such as sport and arts, or as a residual group, along with women and children. As Gavin (2008: 223) notes, such ministries are often 'marginal and marginalized.'

The above discussion therefore acknowledges that all young people are vulnerable due to the fragile life-cycle transition from adolescence to adulthood.

Table 1.1 Popularity of Youth Ministries in Africa (selected countries)

Country	Youth-related cabinet Ministry?	If so, name of Ministry
Angola	Yes	Ministry of Youth and Sports
Benin	Yes	Ministry of Youth and Sports
Botswana	Yes	Ministry of Youth, Sport, and Culture
Burkina Faso	Yes	Ministry of Employment, Professional Development, and Youth
Burundi	Yes	Ministry of Youth, Sports, and Culture
DRC	Yes	Ministry of Youth, Sports, Leisure, Culture, and Arts
Ethiopia	Yes	Ministry of Women, Children, and Youth Affairs
Ghana	Yes	Ministry of Youth and Sport
Kenya	No	——
Lesotho	Yes	Ministry of Gender, Youth, Sports, and Recreation
Liberia	Yes	Ministry of Youth and Sport
Madagascar	Yes	Ministry of Youth and Sport
Malawi	Yes	Ministry of Youth, Sports, and Culture
Mali	Yes	Ministry of Youth and Civic Reconstruction
Mauritius	Yes	Ministry of Youth and Sports
Mozambique	Yes	Ministry of Youth and Sport
Namibia	Yes	Ministry of Youth, National Service, Sport, and Culture
Nigeria	Yes	Ministry of Youth Development
Rwanda	Yes	Ministry of Youth and ICT

(Continued)

Table 1.1 (Continued)

Country	Youth-related cabinet Ministry?	If so, name of Ministry
Senegal	Yes	Ministry of Youth, Employment, and Promotion of Civic Values
Sierra Leone	Yes	Ministry of Youth Affairs
South Africa	No	——
Tanzania	Yes	Ministry for Information, Youth, Culture, and Sports
Togo	Yes	Ministry of Grassroots Development, Crafts, Youth, and Youth Employment
Uganda	Yes	Ministry of State for Youth and Children's Affairs
Zambia	Yes	Ministry of Youth and Sport
Zimbabwe	No	——

Source: https://www.cia.gov/library/publications/world-leaders-1/index.html. These are updated as of October 2014.

But, the range of contemporary forces occurring in Africa in the economic, demographic, and political domains, in interaction with shifting global dynamics, reconfigure the range of opportunities available to today's youth, while also creating the basis for new grievances. Importantly, these forces have strong historical lineages, whether related to the region's longstanding inability to generate labour-intensive growth, adherence to colonial-era urban planning patterns, fragile rural property rights, and asymmetric relations between leaders and citizens. In other words, the youth bulge has magnified and increased the urgency of addressing more long-standing social, economic, and political challenges that are relevant to an even broader set of Africans beyond the youth.

Organization of book

The following chapters touch on different dynamics of the above three trends with the aim of also unpacking conventional wisdoms on African youth. The definition of youth employed in the volume is necessarily broad, ranging from 15–35, depending on the context specificities of each chapter. Unlike other volumes on the youth, the contributions here are truly interdisciplinary, spanning anthropology, economics, geography, political science, public policy, and sociology. They also encompass a diverse range of methodologies, including participant observation, comparative case studies, and statistical analyses, and straddle different levels of analysis, from the community- to the cross-country level.

The substantive chapters are organized into three main sections. In Part I, attention is given to cross-country analyses of economic and political trends among African youth. Given that a great deal of work on African youth is based on detailed case studies, Part I aims to provide a more macro perspective to highlight differences across countries and vis-à-vis other developing regions of the world. Chapter 2 does this by focusing on the overriding concern related to the youth: employment. James Thurlow critically examines the common belief, discussed earlier in this introduction, that Africa's youth bulge will overwhelm the absorptive capacity of many economies and lead to runaway unemployment. Drawing on current and historical data, Thurlow finds that Africa's youth bulge has already reached its peak and that youth unemployment rates in Africa are similar to those of other developing regions. The exception, as noted above, is Southern Africa. He concludes that Africa's youth bulge is similar to those experienced by other developing regions in the late-1970s. Moreover, he finds some cause for optimism over Africa's future unemployment trajectory. By estimating rates of job creation based on countries' historical economic growth patterns, and then combining this information with future growth and population projections, he concludes that youth unemployment rates until 2030 will rise, but not dramatically. However, if economic growth and falling fertility rates do not meet expectations, then youth unemployment rates could as much as double by 2030. Thurlow concludes that while the concerns about future youth unemployment are not unwarranted, the uniqueness of Africa's youth bulge is often overstated.

Chapter 3 focuses on the nature of political participation among African youth and the implications for social unrest. Around the world, it is broadly believed that due to life-cycle effects, younger people have a greater propensity to protest because they have fewer commitments, less access to formal modes of influence, and may be more likely to oppose traditional norms and authority structures (see Braungart 1975; Jarvikoski 1993; Marsh 1974). Similarly, in Africa, media emphasis on high-profile protest events suggests that the youth are disproportionately engaged in this behaviour. Using data from the Armed Conflict and Event Database (ACLED) and the Afrobarometer public opinion survey database, Resnick empirically analyses how common protest is among the youth and investigates why some youth protest while others do not. Through a multi-level statistical model that incorporates micro-level, behavioural data with macro-level, country characteristics, she finds that only a small share of youth engage in protests and this has been declining over time. Furthermore, she highlights that instead of material grievances related to unemployment or deprivation, the youth are more likely to protest when they are better educated, follow the news more, and have broader social capital networks. Even though restrictive civil liberties tend to reduce the likelihood of protest among older Africans, they appear to be less of a constraint among the youth.

Part II then proceeds with more in-depth, case studies set in East and Southern Africa that focus on the youth's aspirations and prospects for social mobility with a particular emphasis on urban settings. In Chapter 4, Karen Tranberg Hansen expands on the fact that, as noted earlier in this chapter, a majority of Africa's youth are concentrating in cities. Hansen questions a prominent view that Africa's urban youth are essentially 'stuck' in a period of 'waithood' between adolescence and adulthood (Honwana 2012; Sommers 2012) and that urban youth are a 'lumpen' class who are driven to criminality as a result of idleness and unemployment (see Abdullah 1997; Clapham 2006). Contrary to the view that the youth are simply waiting around for a better tomorrow, Hansen's chapter details how proactive male and female urban youth are, with a particular emphasis on

South Africa, Zambia, and Zimbabwe. She highlights several forms of sociality that bring young women and men together around music, religion, and recreation. The solidarities and networks that result from such interactions help young people situate themselves in relation to others at the present and in relationship to the future, shaping the urban dynamic in the process.

In Chapter 5, Bryceson provides a complementary critique to the waithood perspective by focusing on artisanal gold mining in northwestern Tanzania. The contribution of her chapter is threefold. First, she contextualizes the experience of African youth, including again both males and females, in a broader transformative process related to natural resource extraction in the region. Over the last fifteen years, many African countries have experienced a 'mining take-off.' Mining activities have bifurcated into two sectors: large-scale, capital-intensive production generating the bulk of the exported minerals, and small-scale, labour-intensive artisanal mining, which, at present, is catalyzing far greater immediate primary, secondary and tertiary employment opportunities for unskilled African labourers. Secondly, she provides a useful reminder that a great deal of Africa's urbanization is also occurring in secondary towns and not just in megacities, which is a point that much of the literature on *urban* youth has not sufficiently recognized. The impact of mining on economic and social life in secondary town communities in Tanzania is contextualized within the uneasy transitions from an agrarian to a mining-based country, from rural to urban lifestyles, and the growing scope and power of foreign-directed, capital-intensive, corporate mining relative to local labour-intensive artisanal mining. Thirdly and most importantly, she addresses Sommers' (2011: 296) lament that the youth scholarship has been characterized by 'the limited nature (or complete absence) of information about how youth view their own situation and what motivates them to make life-altering choices.' Specifically, her fieldwork delves into the attitudes of secondary school students toward mining as a form of employment and in turn, questions the perceived wisdom that the agency of youth remains stifled by older generations.

Part III encompasses critical reflections on existing policy responses to Africa's perceived youth employment crisis. In Chapter 6, James Sumberg and his co-authors assess the impact of a longstanding approach to dealing with the urban youth unemployment dilemma, which is to enhance opportunities in rural areas to encourage reverse migration. Despite little empirical analysis, this idea has long been prominent in the donor community (see Rhoda 1983). In fact, in its 1995 World Programme for Action for Youth, the UN General Assembly emphasized that governments should make farming more attractive to young people in rural areas (see UN-DESA 2005). Sumberg et al. first adopt a Transformative Work and Opportunity Space framework around the concepts of transitions and mobilities. The framework privileges difference and diversity among work opportunities, rural areas and young people. The authors argue that policy and programmes that seek to engage young people with agriculture must be more realistic, rooted in more context-specific social and economic analysis, and appreciative of the variety of ways that rural men and women use agriculture to serve their needs and interests. They illustrate these arguments using cases of rural youth employment programmes in Ethiopia, Ghana, and Malawi.

Chapter 7 addresses an even more widely advocated approach to grappling with the youth employment challenge, which is to promote technical and vocational education (TVET). For instance, as part of its Decade of Youth Action, the AU emphasizes the benefits of TVET, noting it 'will be important in helping African policymakers determine what skills their young people need to gain employment, become better entrepreneurs, or more successful farmers' (Agbor et al. 2012: 10). In fact, approximately 17 African countries have education plans for TVET and the African Development Bank is a major endorser of such education. Yet, Moses Oketch highlights that thus far, most TVET programmes have not been able to address the mismatch between skills and labour market needs and have failed to prepare the youth adequately for the specific occupations associated with it. Instead, general education has the promise of better career mobility and higher wages than vocational streams. Using case studies from Botswana, Ghana, and Kenya, this chapter examines when, why, and under what conditions TVET has been more or less successful.

In Chapter 8, Neil Rankin, Gareth Roberts, and Volker Schöer build on Oketch's skepticism about the general ineffectiveness of TVET by looking at South Africa's learnership programme, which combines classroom learning with on-the-job training. In theory, this programme is intended to create skills, transition young people into jobs more quickly, and reduce one of Africa's highest rates of youth unemployment. By drawing on a unique, longitudinal dataset of young people between 2009 and 2012 and combining it with firm level data, the chapter assesses whether the programme meets its objectives and, based on the findings, draws lessons for similar programmes in other countries. The results are disappointing: young people completing learnerships are more likely to be employed immediately after programme completion, but in the long-term, their employment prospects do not differ from those who did not complete the programme. In addition, the largest beneficiaries of learnerships are those who had higher skills and education in the first place. Importantly, Rankin, Roberts, and Schöer also pay heed to the way in which learnerships are funded and find that its design actually results in the redistribution of resources from smaller to larger firms and from more to less labour-intensive firms. The authors therefore provide caution about importing models from Europe, where these types of learnerships and TVET more broadly are quite popular, without better refining key design features to local contexts.

In sum, this volume operates at two levels. On the one level, it situates the youth challenge within Africa's broader developmental trajectory, both historically and globally. At another level, the contributions collectively probe a number of conventional wisdoms that have been advanced in the literature regarding the breadth of the problems faced by African youth and their resultant responses. The alarmist perspectives related to youth instability, apathy, and lack of agency find little support in the range of countries examined here. At the same time, common policy prescriptions advanced by major international organizations and the donor community are questioned for being based on a rather mechanistic understanding of youth preferences and behaviours. As a consequence, the concluding chapter briefly touches on the implications of these findings for better integrating African youth into the post-2015 world.

Notes

1 These are, in order, Niger, South Sudan, Somalia, Chad, Democratic Republic of Congo, Central African Republic, Angola, Mali, Burundi, and Zambia (see PRB 2014).
2 See the World Bank's World Development Indicators database (http://databank.world bank.org/data/). The figures cited here are based on the International Labour Organization's definition of youth unemployment as the share of the labour force between the ages of 15–24 who do not have work but are looking for it.
3 The second target of the MDGs was to achieve universal primary education by increasing enrolments at the primary level and narrowing gender gaps in youth literacy rates.
4 See http://www.afrimap.org/fr/newsarticle.php?id=2525.

References

Abbink, J. (2005). 'Being young in Africa: The politics of despair and renewal.' In J. Abbink and I. van Kessel (eds.), *Vanguard or Vandals: Youth Politics and Conflict in Africa*. Leiden, The Netherlands: Brill.

Abbink, J. and I. van Kessel (eds.). (2005). *Vanguard or Vandals: Youth Politics and Conflict in Africa*. Leiden, The Netherlands: Brill.

Abdullah, I. (1997). 'Lumpen Youth Culture and Political Violence: Sierra Leoneans Debate the RUF and the Civil War.' *Africa Development*, 22 (3/4): 171–215.

African Development Bank (AfDB). 2011. 'Middle of the Pyramid: Dynamics of the Middle Class in Africa.' Market Brief. Tunis, Tunisia: AfDB.

African Union (AU). (2006). *African Youth Charter*. Adopted by the Seventh Ordinary Session of the Assembly, Banjul, The Gambia, 2 July.

Agbor, J., O. Taiwo, and J. Smith. (2012). 'Sub-Saharan Africa's Youth Bulge: A Demographic Dividend or Disaster?' Chapter In *Foresight Africa: Top Priorities for the Continent in 2012*. Washington, DC: Brookings Institution.

Aguilar, M. (1998). *The Politics of Age and Gerontocracy in Africa: Ethnographies of the Past and Memories of the Present*. Trenton, NJ: Africa World Press.

Assaad, R. and F. Roudi-Fahimi. (2007). 'Youth in the Middle East and North Africa: Demographic Opportunity or Challenge?' *Policy Brief*, April. Washington, DC: Population Reference Bureau.

Austin, D. (1964). *Politics in Ghana 1946–1960*. London, UK: Oxford University Press.

Babo, A. (2010). *Les jeunes, la terre et les changements sociaux en pays Baoulé*. Paris, France: Editions Karthala.

Banégas, R. (2006). 'Côte d'Ivoire: Patriotism, ethnonationalism and other African modes of self-writing.' *African Affairs*, 105(421): 535–552.

Barchiesi, F. (1996). 'The Social Construction of Labour in the Struggle for Democracy: The Case of Post-independence Nigeria.' *Review of African Political Economy*, 23(69): 349–369.

Bierschenk, T. and J-P Olivier de Sardan. (2003). 'Powers in the Village: Rural Benin between Democratization and Decentralization.' *Africa*, 73(2): 145–173.

Boone, Catherine. (2014). *Property Rights and Political Order*. New York, NY: Cambridge University Press.

Bratton, M. and N. van de Walle. (1997). *Democratic Experiments in Africa: Regime Transitions in Comparative Perspective*. New York, NY: Cambridge University Press.

Braungart, R. G. (1975). 'Youth and Social Movements.' In Sigmund E. Dragastin and Glen H. Elder, Jr. (eds.), *Adolescence in the Life Cycle: Psychological Change and Social Context*. Washington, DC: Hemisphere.

Burgess, T. (2001). 'African Youth and the Colonial State.' Paper presented at the Conference of the Historical Association of Tanzania, University of Dar es Salaam, Tanzania.

Burgess, T. (2005a). 'Imagined Generations: Constructing Youth in Revolutionary Zanzibar.' In J. Abbink and I. van Kessel (eds.), *Vanguard or Vandals: Youth Politics and Conflict in Africa*. Leiden, The Netherlands: Brill.

Burgess, T. (2005b). 'Introduction to Youth and Citizenship in East Africa.' *Africa Today*, 51(3): vi–xxiv.

Burton, A. (2001). 'Urchins, Loafers and the Cult of the Cowboy: Urbanization and Delinquency in Dar es Salaam, 1919–1961.' *Journal of African History*, 42: 199–216.

Butler, A. (2009). 'The ANC's National Election Campaign of 2009: Siyanqoba!' Chapter 4 in Roger Southall and John Daniel (eds.), *Zunami! The 2009 South African Elections*. Auckland Park, South Africa: Jacana Media Ltd.

Carton, B. (2000). *Blood from Your Children: The Colonial Origins of Generational Conflict in South Africa*. Charlottesville: University Press of Virginia.

Chauveau, J. P. and P. Richards. (2008). 'West African Insurgencies in Agrarian Perspective: Côte d'Ivoire and Sierra Leone Compared.' *Journal of Agrarian Change*, 8(4): 525, 531.

Cincotta, R. (2008). 'How democracies grow up: Countries with too many young people may not have a fighting chance for freedom.' *Foreign Policy*, 165: 80–82.

Clapham, C. (2006). 'The Political Economy of African Population Change.' *Population and Development Review*, 32(S1): 96–114.

Collier, P. (2007). *The Bottom Billion: Why the Poorest Countries are Failing and What Can be Done About It*. Oxford, UK: Oxford University Press.

Converse, P. (1976). *The Dynamics of Party Support: Cohort-Analyzing Party Identification*. Beverly Hills, CA: Sage.

de Torrenté, N. (2013). 'Understanding the 2011 Ugandan Elections: The Contribution of Public Opinion Surveys.' *Journal of Eastern African Studies*, 7(3): 530–548.

Devarajan, S. and W. Fengler. (2013). 'Africa's Economic Boom: Why the Pessimists and Optimists are Both Right.' *Foreign Affairs*, May/June: 68–81.

de Vries, K., M. Timmer, and G. de Vries. (2013). 'Structural Transformation in Africa: Static gains, Dynamic losses.' Groningen Growth and Development Centre Research Memorandum #136. Groningen, The Netherlands: University of Groningen.

Diouf, M. (2003). 'Engaging Postcolonial Cultures: African Youth and Public Space.' *African Studies Review*, 46 (2):1–12.

Down, I. and C. Wilson (2013). 'A rising generation of Europeans? Life-cycle and cohort effects on support for "Europe".' *European Journal of Political Research*, 52(4): 431–456.

The Economist. (2011). 'Africa's hopeful economies: The sun shines bright.' 3 December: 68–70.

Ferguson, J. (1999). *Expectations of Modernity: Myths and Meanings of Urban Life on the Zambian Copperbelt*. Berkeley and Los Angeles: University of California Press.

Filmer, D. and L. Fox. (2014). *Youth Employment in Sub-Saharan Africa*, with K. Brooks, A. Goyal, T. Mengistae, P. Premand, D. Ringold, S. Sharma, and S. Zorya. Paris and Washington, DC: Agence Française de Développement and World Bank.

Foucher, V. (2007). '"Blue Marches': Public Performance and Political Turnover in Senegal.' In J. Strauss and D.C. O'Brien (eds.), *Staging Politics: Power and Performance in Asia and Africa*. New York, NY: I.B. Tauris & Co Ltd.

Fuller, G. (1995). 'The Demographic Backdrop to Ethnic Conflict: A Geographic Overview.' In CIA (ed.), *The Challenge of Ethnic Conflict to National and International Order in the 1990s*. Washington, DC: Central Intelligence Agency.

Garcia, M. and J. Farès. (2008). *Youth in Africa's Labor Market*. Washington, DC: The World Bank.

Gavin, M. (2008). 'Africa's Restless Youth.' *Current History* 106(700): 220–226.

Goldstone, J. (2001). 'Demography, Environment, and Security: An Overview.' In M. Weiner and S. Russell (eds.), *Demography and National Security*. Oxford, UK: Berghahn Books.

Goldstone, J. (2010). 'The New Population Bomb: The Four Megatrends that Will Change the World.' *Foreign Affairs*, January/February: 31–43.

Gyimah-Brempong, K. and M. Kimenyi. (2013). *Youth Policy and the Future of African Development*. Washington, DC: Brookings Institution.

Harding, R. and D. Stasavage. (2014). 'What Democracy Does (and Doesn't Do) for Basic Services: School Fees, School Inputs, and African Elections.' *The Journal of Politics*, 76(1): 229–245.

Hansen, K. and M. Vaa. (2004). 'Introduction.' In K. T. Hansen and M. Vaa (eds.), *Reconsidering Informality: Perspectives from Urban Africa*. Uppsala, Sweden: Nordiska Afrikainstitutet.

Hart, K. (1973). 'Informal Income Opportunities and Urban Employment in Ghana.' *The Journal of Modern African Studies*, 11(1): 61–89.

Hart, K. (1976). 'The Politics of Unemployment in Ghana'. *African Affairs*, 75(301): 488–497.

Honwana, A. (2012). *The Time of Youth: Work, Social Change, and Politics in Africa*. Boulder, CO: Lynne Rienner Publishers.

Honwana, A. and F. De Boeck (eds.). (2005). *Makers and Breakers: Children and Youth in Postcolonial Africa*. Trenton, NJ: Africa World Press.

Iliffe, J. (1995). *Africans: The History of a Continent*. Cambridge: Cambridge University Press.

Inglehart, R. (1995). 'Changing values, economic development and political change.' *International Social Science Journal*, 47: 379–403.

International Labor Organization (ILO). (2012). *Global Employment Trends 2012: Preventing a deeper jobs crisis*. Geneva, Switzerland.

Jarvikoski, T. (1993). 'Young People as Actors in the Environmental Movement.' *Young*, 3(3): 80–93.

Jayne, T., J. Chamberlin, and D. Headey. (2014). 'Land pressures, the evolution of farming systems, and development strategies in Africa: A synthesis.' *Food Policy*, 48: 1–17.

Kabiru, C., D. Beguy, S. Mojola, and C. Okigbo. (2013). 'Growing up at the "margins": Concerns, Aspirations, and Expectations of Young People Living in Nairobi's Slums.' *Journal of Research on Adolescence*, 23(1): 81–94.

Kagwanja, P. (2005a). '"Power to *Uhuru*": Youth Identity and Generational Politics in Kenya's 2002 Elections.' *African Affairs*, 105 (418): 51–75.

Kagwanja, P. (2005b). 'Clash of Generations? Youth Identity, violence, and the politics of transitions in Kenya.' In J. Abbink and I. van Kessel (eds.), *Vanguard or Vandals: Youth Politics and Conflict in Africa*. Leiden, The Netherlands: Brill.

Kaplan, R. (1996). The Ends of the Earth: From Togo to Turkmenistan, from Iran to Cambodia, a Journey to the Frontiers of Anarchy. New York, NY: Random House.

Kessides, C. (2006). *The Urban Transition in Sub-Saharan Africa: Implications for Economic Growth and Poverty Reduction*. Washington, D.C.: The World Bank.

Laasko, L. (2007). 'Insights into Electoral Violence in Africa.' In M. Basedau, G. Erdmann, and A. Mehler (eds.) *Votes, Money, and Violence: Political Parties and Elections in Sub-Saharan Africa*. Sweden and South Africa: Nordiska Afrikainstitutet and University of Kwa-Zulu Natal.

Last, M. (2005). 'Towards a political history of youth in Muslim northern Nigeria, 1750–2000.' Chapter 2 in J. Abbink and I. van Kessel (eds.), *Vanguard or Vandals: Youth Politics and Conflict in Africa*. Leiden, The Netherlands: Brill.

Leahy, E. with R. Engelman, C. Vogel, S. Haddock, and T. Preston. (2007). *The Shape of Things to Come: Why Age Structure Matters to a Safer, More Equitable World*. Washington, DC: Population Action Council.

Le Meur, P. Y. (2006). 'Droits & Conflits Fonciers en Afrique: le cas du Bénin. Étude de Politique Foncière.' Rapport de recherche Mission de terrain. Copenhagen, Denmark: Danish Institute for International Studies.

Mabogunje, A. (1994). 'Overview of Research Priorities in Africa.' In R. Stren, *Urban Research in the Development World, Vol.2-Africa*. Toronto, CA: University of Toronto Press.

Mannheim, K. [1927] (1952). 'The Problem of Generations.' In K. Mannheim (ed.), *Essays on the Sociology of Knowledge*, London: Routledge and Kegan Paul.

Maro, P. S., and W. Mlay. (1982). 'Population Redistribution in Tanzania.' In J. Clarke and L. Kosinski (eds.), *Redistribution of Population in Africa*. Heinemann, London.

Marsh, A. (1974). 'Explorations in Unorthodox Political Behaviour: A Scale to Measure Protest Potential.' *European Journal of Political Research*, 2: 107–29.

Mattes, R. (2012). 'The "Born Frees": The Prospects for Generational Change in Post-apartheid South Africa.' *Australian Journal of Political Science*, 47(1): 133–153.

McEvoy-Levy, S. (ed) (2013). *Troublemakers or Peacemakers? Youth and Post-Accord Peace Building*. South Bend, IN: University of Notre Dame Press.

McKittrick, M. (2002). *To Dwell Secure: Generation, Christianity, and Colonialism in Ovamboland*. Oxford: James Currey.

McMillan, M., D. Rodrik, and I. Verduzco-Gallo. (2014). 'Globalization, Structural Change, and Productivity Growth, with an Update on Africa.' *World Development*, 63(November): 11–32.

Mishler, W. and R. Rose. (2007). 'Generation, Age, and Time: The Dynamics of Political Learning during Russia's Transformation.' *American Journal of Political Science*, 51(4): 822–834.

National Intelligence Council (NIC). (2012). *Global Trends 2030: Alternative Worlds*. Washington, DC: Office of the Director of National Intelligence.

Ndulu, B. and S. O'Connell. (2008). 'Policy plus: African growth performance, 1960–200.' In B. Ndulu, S. O'Connell, R. Bates, P. Collier, and C. Soludo (eds.), *The Political Economy of Economic Growth in Africa, 1960–2000, Volume 1*. Cambridge, UK: Cambridge University Press.

Nyerere, J. (1966). *Freedom and Unity: A selection of writings and speeches, 1952–1965, Vol. 1*. London, UK: Oxford University Press.

Ohba, A. (2011). 'The abolition of secondary school fees in Kenya: Responses by the poor.' *International Journal of Educational Development*, 31: 402–408.

O'Brien, D.C. (1996). 'A Lost Generation? Youth Identity and State Decay in West Africa.' In R. Werbner and T. Ranger (eds.), *Postcolonial Identities in Africa*. London: Zed Books.

O'Rand, A. and M. Krecker (1990). 'Concepts of the Life Cycle: Their History, Meanings, and Uses in the Social Sciences.' *Annual Review of Sociology*, 16: 241–262.

Perry, A. (2012). 'Africa Rising.' *Time*, 180(23): 48–52.

Perullo, A. (2005). 'Hooligans and Heroes: Youth Identity and Hip-Hop in Dar es Salaam, Tanzania.' *Africa Today*, 51(4): 75–101.

Population Reference Bureau (PRB). (2014). *World Population Data Sheet*. Washington, DC: PRB. Accessed at www.prb.org.

Pritchett, L. (2013). *The Rebirth of Education*. Washington, DC: Center for Global Development.

Raeymaekers, T. (2010). 'Not going home: displace youth after war.' *Forced Migration Review*, 36 (November): 21–22.

Resnick, D. and D. Casale. (forthcoming). 'Young populations in young democracies: generational voting behavior in sub-Saharan Africa,' *Democratization*. doi:10.1080/13510347. 2013.793673

Resnick, D. and J. Thurlow. (2014). 'The Political Economy of Zambia's Recovery: Structural Change without Transformation?' *IFPRI Discussion Paper 1320*. Washington, DC: International Food Policy Research Institute (IFPRI).

Rhoda, R. (1983). 'Rural Development and Urban Migration: Can we keep them down on the farm?' *International Migration Review*, 17(1): 34–64.

Richards, P. (1996). *Fighting for the Rain Forest: War, Youth and Resources in Sierra Leone*. Oxford: James Currey.

Roessler, P. (2005). 'Donor-Induced Democratization and the Privatization of State Violence in Kenya and Rwanda.' *Comparative Politics*, 37(2): 207–227.

Rose, R., W. Mishler and C. Haerpfer (1998). *Democracy and its Alternatives: Understanding Post-Communist Societies*. Baltimore, MD: Johns Hopkins University Press.

Sawers, L. (1989). 'Urban primacy in Tanzania.' *Economic Development and Cultural Change*, 37(4): 841–859.

Schatzberg, M. (2001). *Political Legitimacy in Middle Africa: Father, Family, Food*. Bloomington, IN: Indiana University Press.

Seekings, J. (1993). *Heroes or Villains? Youth Politics in the 1980s*. Johannesburg: Ravan Press.

Skelton, R. (2014). 'Architecture: Africa in the making.' *The Africa Report*. May. http://www.theafricareport.com/North-Africa/architecture-africa-in-the-making.html

Smith, S. (2011). 'Youth in Africa: Rebels without a Cause but not without Effect.' *SAIS Review vol. XXXI, No. 2*: 97–109.

Sommers, M. (2010). 'Urban youth in Africa.' *Environment and Urbanization*, 22(2): 317–322.

Sommers, M. (2011). 'Governance, Security and Culture: Assessing Africa's Youth Bulge.' *International Journal of Conflict and Violence*, 5(2): 292–303.

Sommers, M. (2012). *Stuck: Rwandan Youth and the Struggle for Adulthood*. Athens: University of Georgia Press.

Sommers, M. and P. Uvin. (2011). 'Youth in Rwanda and Burundi: Contrasting Visions.' *USIP Special Report 293*, October. Washington, DC: United States Institute of Peace.

Stasavage, D. (2005). 'Democracy and Education Spending in Africa.' *American Journal of Political Science*, 49(2): 343–358.

Stolzenberg, R. (1995). 'Religious Participation in Early Adulthood.' *American Sociological Review*, 60: 84–103.

Summers, C. (2005). 'Young Buganda and Old Boys: Youth, Generational Transition and Ideas of Leadership in Buganda, 1920–1949.' *Africa Today*, 51(3): 109–128.

United Nations (UN) (2013). *A New Global Partnership: Eradicate Poverty and Transform Economies through Sustainable Development*. New York, NY: UN.

United Nations Department of Economic and Social Affairs (UN-DESA). (2005). *World Youth Report 2005: Young people today, and in 2015*. New York, NY: UN-DESA.

United Nations University-World Institute for Development Economics Research (UNU-WIDER). (2014). *ReCOM Position Paper: Aid and the Social Sectors*. Helsinki, Finland: UNU-WIDER.

Urdal, H. (2006). 'A Clash of Generations? Youth Bulges and Political Violence.' *International Studies Quarterly*, 50: 607–629.

Waller, R. (2006). 'Rebellious Youth in Colonial Africa.' *Journal of African History*, 47:77–92.

World Bank. (2006). *World Development Report 2007: Development and the Next Generation*. Washington, DC: World Bank.

Part I

Cross-country analyses of economic and political trends

2 Youth employment prospects in Africa

James Thurlow

Introduction

The 2000s were an unprecedented and much heralded time of economic growth and poverty reduction in sub-Saharan Africa.[1] Rising worker productivity within sectors was bolstered by a move away from agriculture toward more productive jobs (McMillan et al. 2014). This period of rapid growth, coupled with 'positive structural change,' contrasts sharply with the poor performance of the 1990s, when Africa lagged behind other developing regions. Yet, despite the subcontinent's apparent turnaround, there is concern that even a continuation of recent economic growth may not generate enough decent job opportunities to absorb the growing number of young job seekers entering the labour market. As discussed in Chapter 1, many view rising youth unemployment as a major threat to future social and economic development in Africa (see, for example, AfDB et al. 2012; Filmer and Fox 2014; and World Bank 2012).

Yet Africa is not the first region to experience a 'youth bulge' in its population. Nor is it alone in its concern over the long-term implications of youth unemployment. In this chapter we examine global employment trends and ask whether there is something *quantitatively* unique about youth unemployment in Africa today. We find that Africa has much in common with other developing regions when they experienced their youth bulges three decades ago. Moreover, youth unemployment in Africa appears to be no more pronounced than it is in the broader developing world, even though Africa's youth bulge has only recently started to recede.

Of course, favourable conditions today do not guarantee that the future prospects of young job seekers are positive. We examine these prospects using a simple projection model that measures, in broad terms, the implications of alternative demographic and economic scenarios. In light of Africa's recent resurgence, we ask whether concerns over rising youth unemployment are warranted. We find some evidence for optimism. If the pace and pattern of economic growth from the 2000s continues, then youth unemployment rates are likely to remain constant until 2030, after which time they should begin to fall as the youth bulge recedes and population growth slows. There are, however, risks associated with this more optimistic scenario. If fertility rates exceed expectations or economic growth returns to a more modest trajectory, then youth unemployment rates could more than double by 2030. This would put Africa beyond the experiences of other developing regions and could place substantial downward pressure on the returns to labour, with implications for social welfare and mobility.

The next section reviews historical cross-country data on population and economic growth and youth unemployment. This is followed by a description of the projection model and its data sources. We then present the model results and conclude by summarising our main findings.

Placing Africa in the global context

Population growth

The youth bulge in Africa has received considerable attention in the international development community (see Filmer and Fox 2014). The main information base for gauging historical and future demographic changes are the global population projections produced by the United Nations Department of Economic and Social Affairs (UNDESA 2013). Drawing on these projections, Figure 2.1 reports Africa's share of the global youth and adult populations from 1950 to 2100. We follow the United Nations by defining 'youth' as people between 15 and 24 years of age, and 'adults' as those aged 25 years or older.

The figure shows how Africa's share of the global youth population remained constant until the early 1990s, and then began to rise. This gradual concentration of youth in Africa is expected to accelerate from 2010 onwards. A major reason for this is a continuation of Africa's high fertility rates at a time when these rates are falling elsewhere in the world. High fertility means that sub-Saharan Africa's

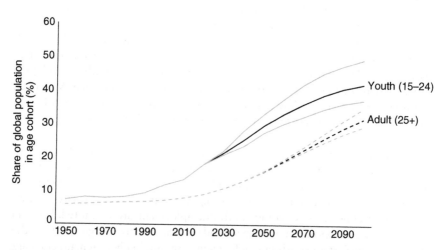

Figure 2.1 Sub-Saharan Africa's projected share of global youth and adult populations

Source: Own calculations using population projections from UNDESA (2013).

Notes: Black lines are medium fertility rate scenarios; top and bottom grey lines are low and high fertility rate scenarios, respectively.

population is projected to more than double between 2010 and 2050, i.e., from 0.8 billion to 2.1 billion people. Africa will account for one-third of the world's population expansion during 2010–2030 and two-thirds of the expansion during 2030–2050. By 2050, Africans will comprise 30 percent of the world's population, up from 12 percent in 2010.

Assumptions about how fertility rates will evolve after 2010 lead to different population projections. Figure 2.1 reports UNDESA's lower and upper bound fertility scenarios, which are used later in our analysis. Depending on the fertility scenario, the figure indicates that, by 2100, somewhere between a third and a half of the world's youth will live in Africa. Lowering fertility rates reduces the number of children born today. It therefore takes 15 years for changes in fertility rates to alter the youth population projections and 25 years to influence adult projections. It is inevitable then that Africa's youth population will continue to grow rapidly until after 2030, even if fertility rates were dramatically reduced today.

Table 2.1 reports the share of youth in the total working age population, i.e., all people aged 15 years or older. This measure provides the clearest indication of a 'youth bulge' in the workforce. The table indicates that youth make up a larger share of the workforce in Africa than in other developing regions, i.e., 35 percent in Africa compared to 26 percent in developing countries as a whole. This is because other regions have already experienced their youth bulges. Whereas Africa's youth share peaked in 2003, the youth shares of other developing regions peaked in the late 1970s. Moreover, Africa's peak shares were only slightly higher than those of other developing regions, i.e., 36 percent in Africa in 2003 compared to 33 percent

Table 2.1 Youth (15–24 years) share of potential labour force (15+ years)

	Youth share (%)		Historical peak share	
	2010	2050	%	Year
World	24.1	17.5	29.7	1975
Developing countries	26.4	18.2	33.0	1975
East Asia, Pacific	22.5	13.2	32.7	1974
Europe, Central Asia	26.3	15.4	33.3	1978
Latin America	25.1	15.1	33.9	1979
Middle East, North Africa	29.3	17.8	35.3	1979
South Asia	28.2	17.3	33.2	1980
Sub-Saharan Africa	35.1	28.4	36.4	2003
East Africa	36.5	27.4	38.3	2003
Central Africa	36.3	29.0	36.8	2007
Southern Africa	29.2	19.5	34.5	1976
excluding South Africa	36.2	21.9	37.2	2003
West Africa	34.5	30.2	36.3	1998

Source: Own calculations using population data from UNDESA (2013).

Notes: Potential labour force is the total population aged 15 years and older.

for all developing countries in 1975. Africa's current youth bulge therefore appears to be quite similar to those experienced by other regions three decades ago.

Four key observations emerge from the table. First, had we adopted the African Union's broader definition of youth, i.e., 15–35 years, Africa's youth bulge probably peaked nearer to 2010 instead of in 2003. The definition of 'youth' does not, therefore, alter the fact that Africa's youth bulge is receding, albeit gradually. Secondly, South Africa's youth bulge peaked in the mid-1970s along with other developing regions, making the country an outlier in sub-Saharan Africa. Once South Africa is removed, then the remaining group of Southern African countries conform to the broader African experience.[2] Thirdly, while West Africa's peak youth bulge in 1998 also preceded that of other African regions, the share of youth in its workforce has remained high at 35 percent. Finally, while this chapter focuses on sub-Saharan Africa, it is interesting to note that, like the Middle East, North Africa's youth bulge peaked in 1979, making the region similar to South Africa and therefore quite distinct from the rest of Africa.

Labour force participation

Population growth does not directly affect unemployment levels unless it leads to an increase in the number of people participating in the labour force. For example, an increase in the youth population could lead to higher school enrolment rather than more young people searching for work. Table 2.2 reports labour force

Table 2.2 Labour force participation rates, 2010

	Total	Youth		Adults	
		Male	Female	Male	Female
World	64.3	56.5	41.3	84.0	54.4
Developed countries	60.4	49.1	43.9	71.9	54.8
Developing countries	65.2	57.6	40.9	87.4	54.3
East Asia, Pacific	72.7	59.5	57.0	86.6	67.1
Europe, Central Asia	57.1	52.3	31.7	80.6	45.8
Latin America	66.1	62.9	42.5	85.8	56.5
Middle East, North Africa	48.4	47.0	16.2	84.6	23.8
South Asia	57.1	57.8	23.6	90.7	34.9
Sub-Saharan Africa	70.2	55.9	51.5	87.3	71.2
East Africa	81.0	68.7	66.4	94.0	83.8
Central Africa	71.2	48.1	49.0	90.9	77.7
Southern Africa	53.4	32.4	26.5	75.0	53.1
excluding South Africa	66.8	51.9	42.9	87.7	68.8
West Africa	62.2	49.5	40.6	82.2	60.4

Source: Own calculations using population data from UNDESA (2013) and labour force labour force trends data from ILO (2012).

Notes: Youth are between 15 and 24 years of age; adults are 25 years and older.

participation rates, which are the share of the working age population (aged 15 or older) who are looking for or have found employment. Participation rates are usually less than 100 percent because at least some of the working age population are either retired or attending school. Others may be discouraged and no longer searching for jobs, or be working within the household, which is not usually treated as employment in official statistics.

The table shows how total participation rates are higher for sub-Saharan Africa than for most other developing regions. This is due to female participation rates, which are particularly high in Africa. Participation rates are lower for youth than for adults, which is consistent with a larger share of youth enrolled in school. This youth–adult gap is narrower for women, probably because women in most countries are more likely to be responsible for child rearing and thus unavailable for work outside of the household. Youth participation rates are particularly high in Africa, reflecting low secondary school enrolment. There is considerable variation across countries within Africa. Youth participation is lowest in Southern Africa, where school enrolment is higher and where widespread unemployment often discourages young job seekers (see below).

Table 2.3 shows how youth participation rates fell throughout the developing world over the last two decades, due in large part to higher secondary and tertiary school enrolment. The decline in Africa's average participation rate was fairly small, but this was mainly due to rising participation rates in Nigeria and only modest declines in South Africa. Removing these two populous countries reveals declining participation rates in the rest of Africa. This is consistent with substantial improvements in secondary school enrolment, mainly during the 2000s. Despite

Table 2.3 Changing youth labour force participation and school enrolment rates, 1995–2010

	Change in rate (%-point)		
	Labour force participation	School enrolment	
		Secondary	Tertiary
World	−7.4	14.7	13.8
Developed countries	−5.6	4.3	21.4
Developing countries	−7.8	–	–
East Asia, Pacific	−10.6	28.6	17.4
Europe, Central Asia	−6.1	10.9	20.9
Latin America	−3.4	19.4	23.1
Middle East, North Africa	−3.7	12.9	15.3
South Asia	−8.7	17.1	10.9
Sub-Saharan Africa	−0.3	15.8	4.0

Source: Own calculations using population data from UNDESA (2013), labour force trends data from ILO (2012), and enrolment data from World Bank (2014).

Notes: Youth are between 15 and 24 years of age.

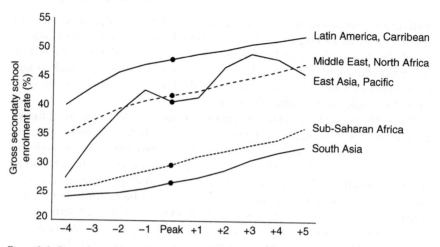

Figure 2.2 Secondary school enrolment rates during developing regions' youth bulge periods

Source: Own calculations using World Bank (2014).

Notes: Measures the ratio of total enrolment, regardless of age, to the population of the age group that officially corresponds to secondary schooling. The peak year of the youth bulge is the year when the youth share of the total working age population was at its highest (see Table 2.1).

these improvements, secondary school enrolment in Africa is low by international standards, i.e., 40 percent in 2010 compared to a global average of 71 percent (World Bank 2014). Africa's tertiary school enrolment is extremely low, i.e., 8 per-cent compared to 29 percent globally, and has not noticeably improved over the last two decades.

It is perhaps more relevant to compare Africa's secondary school enrolment rates to those of other developing regions during the period of their youth bulges. Figure 2.2 shows gross enrolment rates in the peak year of other regions' youth bulges (see Table 2.1) and for the four preceding and five subsequent years. Afri-ca's enrolment rates are slightly higher than what South Asia's were around 1980, but they are well below the enrolment rates of the other developing regions dur-ing their youth bulges. The pace at which Africa is raising its enrolment rates is similar to that of other regions three decades ago. Thus while Africa currently lags behind other regions, it appears to be on a similar trajectory.

Population levels interact with labour force participation rates to determine the supply of young job seekers. Gradually closing the school enrolment gap between Africa and developed countries is one of the scenarios considered later in this chapter. A lower youth participation rate would dampen the effects of rapid population growth on total labour supply.

Economic growth

Economic growth is the major determinant of long-run labour demand. Table 2.4 reports average annual growth in total value-added or gross domestic product

Table 2.4 Economic growth, 1990–2010

	Average annual GDP growth rate (%)			Share of world GDP (%)	
	1990–2010	1990–2000	2000–2010	1990	2010
World	1.57	2.99	0.18	100	100
Developed countries	0.11	2.31	−2.04	85.15	63.70
Developing countries	6.21	6.26	6.16	14.85	36.30
East Asia, Pacific	8.12	7.83	8.40	5.06	17.64
Europe, Central Asia	3.47	2.24	4.72	1.23	1.78
Latin America	5.09	7.08	3.13	4.28	8.44
Middle East, North Africa	4.54	4.37	4.72	1.45	2.57
South Asia	6.30	5.46	7.15	1.60	3.99
Sub-Saharan Africa	3.72	2.30	5.15	1.24	1.88
East Africa	3.97	2.82	5.14	0.20	0.32
Central Africa	4.55	1.08	8.13	0.11	0.20
Southern Africa	2.79	2.27	3.32	0.60	0.76
excluding South Africa	3.71	3.85	3.58	0.04	0.06
West Africa	4.71	2.42	7.06	0.33	0.60

Source: Own calculations using data from World Bank (2014).

Notes: GDP is gross domestic product measured at factor cost and in constant 2005 US dollars (unadjusted for cross-country differences in purchasing power).

(GDP). Regional GDP is measured at factor cost and in constant 2005 US dollars, using historical data compiled by the World Bank (2014). African growth during 1990–2010 was 3.7 percent per year, which was well below the developing country average of 6.2 percent. However, as discussed earlier, the 2000s marked a turning point for Africa, with GDP growth rates more than doubling after the 1990s. The subcontinent's share of world GDP rose from 1.2 percent in 2000 to 1.9 percent in 2010, after remaining constant throughout the 1990s. In fact, Africa's recent resurgence offset a slowdown in Latin America, leaving GDP in developing countries growing steadily over the last two decades. This contrasts sharply with the GDP contraction in developed countries in the late 2000s.

Most African sub-regions improved their economic performance in the 2000s. One possible exception is Southern Africa, where growth increased only modestly, and slowed slightly if South Africa is excluded. Other sub-regions experienced large accelerations in GDP growth, such that African GDP grew at 5.2 percent per year during the 2000s. This was much closer to the developing country average of 6.2 percent and was only exceeded by East Asia (China) and South Asia (India). Even a return to the average growth rates over the last two decades, instead of the fast growth of the 2000s, would place Africa on a much firmer long-run trajectory. Later in this chapter we explore the implications of alternative growth scenarios.

Unemployment

Finally, we consider how unemployment rates vary across the world. An unemployment rate is the share of the population who participate in the labour force but are unable to find work. Table 2.5 reports unemployment rates calculated using labour force data from the International Labour Organisation (ILO 2012). The ILO uses labour force surveys and other data to estimate a continuous annual time series of country-level labour force statistics, including youth and adult employment. Note that no distinction is made between part-time and full-time workers. A low unemployment rate might therefore hide the fact that some people are not working as many hours or months in the year as they would like to, i.e., they are underemployed. What constitutes work can also vary across countries. For example, subsistence farming is treated as employment in most developing countries, but not in developed countries. This is subsumed under the broader issue that many jobs in developing countries, particularly in Africa, may not be considered 'decent' employment (see AfDB et al. 2012).

Caveats aside, the table shows that unemployment rates in Africa in 2010 were higher than the average for all developing countries, i.e., 7.6 percent compared to 5.4 percent. There are three reasons for this. First, Southern Africa has particularly high unemployment, both within and beyond South Africa.[3] Second, unemployment rates are typically higher for women in developing countries. High female labour force participation rates in Africa therefore lead to higher

Table 2.5 Unemployment rates, 2010

	Total	Youth		Adults	
		Male	*Female*	*Male*	*Female*
World	6.0	12.4	12.7	4.3	4.9
Developed countries	8.7	19.4	16.8	7.7	7.1
Developing countries	5.4	11.6	12.1	3.5	4.2
East Asia, Pacific	4.4	11.2	8.9	3.4	2.8
Europe, Central Asia	10.8	18.9	19.9	8.6	9.1
Latin America	7.2	11.8	18.5	4.3	6.8
Middle East, North Africa	9.7	19.9	35.8	4.9	11.4
South Asia	3.9	9.9	11.4	1.9	3.3
Sub-Saharan Africa	7.6	10.7	12.2	5.9	6.5
East Africa	6.9	8.9	11.5	4.6	6.3
Central Africa	6.0	10.1	10.4	5.1	4.2
Southern Africa	24.9	45.5	53.9	18.2	22.8
excluding South Africa	25.5	37.0	49.9	17.5	22.0
West Africa	5.7	9.3	8.9	5.0	4.0

Source: Own calculations using population data from UNDESA (2013) and labour force trends data from ILO (2012).

Notes: Youth are between 15 and 24 years of age; adults are 25 years and older.

overall unemployment rates for the subcontinent. Finally, unemployment rates for youth are higher than for adults in all regions. The narrower youth–adult gap in Africa is because adult unemployment rates are higher than the average for developing countries, which pushes up overall unemployment rates. In contrast, youth unemployment rates in Africa are often lower than the developing country average, particularly in West Africa. With the exception of Southern Africa, youth unemployment rates during Africa's youth bulge are similar to prevailing unemployment rates in other developing regions.

Five stylized facts emerged from our examination of the global context. First, it appears that Africa's youth bulge has already begun to recede and what remains is the more general challenge posed by rapid population growth. Second, Africa's youth bulge, measured by the share of youth in the working age population, is similar in magnitude to the youth bulges that other developing regions experienced three decades ago. Third, Africa has not raised school enrolment rates by as much as other regions have, and so labour force participation rates remain high. Fourth, youth unemployment rates in Africa are similar to those in other developing regions, at least according to the data used here. Finally, there is large variation across sub-regions within Africa, especially between Southern and West Africa.

Together, these insights suggest that there is nothing *quantitatively* unique about youth unemployment in Africa today, except for the region's low school enrolment rates and its delayed youth bulge. This assessment is, however, based on historical trends and cross-country comparisons. The rest of this chapter adopts a forward-looking approach and asks whether demographic and economic trends warrant greater concern for the future of Africa's young job seekers.

Projecting youth employment

Projection model

A simple projection model is used to estimate future labour supply and demand in order to gauge the extent of unemployment. The model's single equation (or identity) is shown below

$$U_t = S_t - D_t = P_t \cdot r_t - b \cdot (1 + G \cdot \varepsilon)^t \qquad \textit{where } t = 0, 1, \ldots, n$$

where S, D, and U are the quantity of labour supply, demand and unemployment, respectively, in year t. Labour supply S is equal to the population P multiplied by the labour force participation rate r, where r lies between 0 and 1. Labour demand is projected using the number of employed people in the base year b (2010); the average annual GDP growth rate G for the simulation period; and an employment-to-growth elasticity ε. This elasticity indicates the percentage change in employment given a one percent change in national GDP. While not shown, the model includes one equation for each of the four population groups (i.e., male/female and youth/adult combinations) in each of the four African sub-regions (i.e., East, Central, Southern, and West). The model is run over the period 2010–2050.

Most of the information used to calibrate the model was discussed in the previous section. Future populations P are from UNDESA (2013). We compare outcomes across median, low and high fertility scenarios (see Figure 2.1). Labour force participation rates r and employment levels b are initially assigned 2010 values as reported in ILO (2012) (see Table 2.2). In our analysis we will lower participation rates over time to reflect improvements in school enrolment. Annual GDP growth rates G remain constant over the simulation period and are calculated using data from the World Bank (2014) (see Table 2.4). Finally, the employment-growth elasticity is econometrically estimated – a process described next.

Employment-growth elasticities

In estimating the model's elasticities, we adopt the approach described in Kapsos (2005), which was later adapted by Crivelli et al. (2012). We employ the following multivariate log-linear regression model

$$ln(e_{it}) = \alpha + \beta_1 ln(y_{it}) + \beta_2 C_i ln(y_{it}) + \beta_3 C_i + w_{it}$$

where e is the number of employed persons in country i and year t, and y is the level of GDP. The model includes country dummies C which are interacted with logged GDP. The point elasticity of employment with respect to growth for country i is the sum of the two estimated coefficients on GDP, as shown below

$$\varepsilon = \beta_1 + \beta_2$$

The elasticity ε reflects the employment intensity of growth. An elasticity of 0.7, for example, implies that a one percent increase in GDP generates a 0.7 percent increase in employment. If labour productivity is measured as GDP per worker, then an elasticity between zero and one implies an increase in both employment and productivity as GDP grows. In our example, one percent GDP growth generates 0.3 percent labour productivity growth (i.e., 1.0–0.7=0.3). An elasticity greater than one implies that growth in employment exceeds growth in GDP causing average labour productivity to decline. The reverse is true for an elasticity below zero.

It is worth noting that long-term economic development and positive structural change are normally associated with rising labour productivity (see McMillan et al. 2014) and therefore an elasticity less than one. Moreover, elasticities are generally smaller when unemployment rates and population growth rates are low, or when economic growth rates are high. In an extreme case, for example, when no one is unemployed and the population is constant, then an increase in employment is not possible and so all economic growth must come from rising worker productivity. In this case, the employment-growth elasticity is zero.

Data on GDP growth comes from World Bank (2014) and on employment quantities from ILO (2012). Information is available for 168 countries spanning the period 1991–2010, although some countries lack GDP data for the full 20-year period. The countries included in the sample and the regions to which they belong is shown in Table 2.A2 in the appendix to this chapter. Separate regressions are run for each gender and age group. The employment variable e has different values in each of the regressions, but the level of national GDP y remains the same, since this is neither age nor gender specific.

Figure 2.3 reports the estimated country-level elasticities. The figure uses a box-and-whisker plot to report the 168 countries' elasticities. These plots are a useful way of representing not only the range of elasticities but also how these are distributed within this range. The box in each plot shows the elasticity values for the 84 countries (half the sample) falling in the middle of the distribution. For example, half of the countries have adult elasticities between 0.44 and 0.95. The long and short bars dividing the box indicate the median and mean elasticities, respectively. The median adult elasticity (0.66) is higher than the mean (0.71), implying that the distribution is skewed towards higher elasticities. Finally, the lines (or whiskers) on either side of the box indicate the highest and lowest elasticities in the sample of 168 countries. The lowest adult elasticity is –0.22 for Moldova, and the highest is 1.58 for Algeria.

Globally, elasticities tend to be lower for youth than for adults. The median youth elasticity is only 0.31 and a much larger share of countries have negative elasticities suggesting that economic growth in these countries over the last two decades did not increase the level of youth employment. Elasticities are also

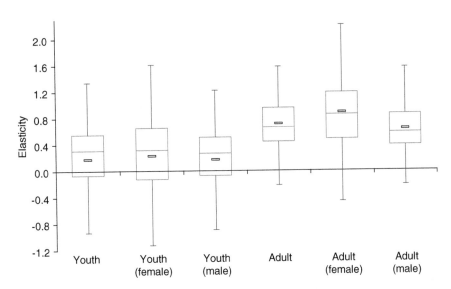

Figure 2.3 Distribution of employment-growth elasticities for all countries
Source: Own estimates using employment data from ILO (2012) and GDP data from World Bank (2014).

higher for women than for men amongst both youth and adults. Overall, however, the age gap is much more pronounced than the gender gap.

Table 2.6 reports average elasticities for different regions of the world. Africa shares two key characteristics with the rest of the world. First, youth elasticities are lower than those of adults. Second, elasticities are higher for women than for men, although this gap is narrower in Africa. Africa also has two distinctive features. First, youth elasticities in Africa are well above the developing country average. Second, there is considerable variation in elasticities across sub-regions. Southern Africa has the lowest elasticities for youth, but not for adults. The reverse is true for Central Africa. Only West Africa has relatively high elasticities across gender and age groups. These elasticities, when combined with the rate of economic growth, will determine the level of labour demand in each of the African sub-regions in the projection model.

In the next section we use the model to project youth unemployment in Africa based on a range of assumptions about population growth, school enrolment, and the pace and pattern of economic growth. The model does not include any behavioural responses beyond the employment-growth elasticity. We do not attempt to model labour market dynamics and wage determination. Instead we assume that the estimated elasticities remain constant over time. The model can therefore only provide an approximation of youth employment prospects in Africa. The model's strength lies in its transparency and its ability to compare alternative future scenarios across a diverse set of countries.

Table 2.6 Regional employment-growth elasticities

	Total	Youth		Adults	
		Male	Female	Male	Female
World	0.60	0.17	0.23	0.63	0.89
Developed countries	0.34	−0.41	−0.44	0.36	0.61
Developing countries	0.68	0.37	0.46	0.72	0.98
East Asia, Pacific	0.61	0.11	0.15	0.66	0.91
Europe, Central Asia	0.27	0.18	0.04	0.30	0.33
Latin America	0.83	0.24	0.48	0.89	1.32
Middle East, North Africa	0.85	0.54	0.63	0.90	1.33
South Asia	0.54	0.32	0.57	0.54	0.82
Sub-Saharan Africa	0.67	0.52	0.56	0.70	0.80
East Africa	0.65	0.45	0.47	0.76	0.81
Central Africa	0.60	0.53	0.53	0.59	0.60
Southern Africa	0.65	0.39	0.22	0.68	0.86
West Africa	0.72	0.62	0.77	0.69	0.87

Source: Own calculations using population data from UNDESA (2013) and labour force trends data from ILO (2012).

Notes: Youth are between 15 and 24 years of age; adults are 25 years and older.

Future employment scenarios

We simulate a range of employment scenarios, as shown in Table 2.7. Each scenario tests the implications of alternative assumptions about the values of the model's parameters. On the labour supply side, these include population growth P and labour force participation rates r, and on the demand side, there is the pace of economic growth G and its employment intensity ε.

Baseline

We first establish a baseline scenario. The baseline adopts the median population projection from UNDESA (see Figure 2.1). We assume that labour force participation rates continue to decline at the slow pace observed during 1995–2010 (see Table 2.3). We maintain, until 2050, the average annual GDP growth rates from the period 1990–2010. This is a 'middle of the road' estimate of Africa's growth prospects, with baseline GDP growing at 3.7 percent per year (see Table 2.4). Overall, the baseline can be summarized as a continuation of the pace and pattern of economic growth from the last two decades.

It is worth emphasizing that, while we simulate unemployment rates for the period 2010–2050, results towards the end of this period should be treated with greater caution. Our model is calibrated to employment-growth elasticities that were estimated using data from 1991–2010. While the last 20 years might be considered an adequate basis for projecting the next 20 years, this assertion becomes more questionable as we move further into the future. As such, we place greater emphasis on the model's estimated unemployment rates for 2030 than for 2050. Conveniently, 2030 is also the target year for the post-2015 development goals

Table 2.7 Projection model scenarios

Scenario names		Assumptions and adjustments
Baseline		Median fertility rate projection
		Constant 2010 participiation rates
		Average GDP growth, 1990–2010
		Constant employment-growth elasticity from 1991–2010
Population	Lower	Lower bound fertility rate projections
	Upper	Upper bound fertility rate projections
Enrolment		Youth participation rate declines to developed country average by 2050
Growth	Slow	Average GDP growth rate, 1990–2000 (growth slows)
	Fast	Average GDP growth rate, 2000–2010 (growth accelerates)
Intensity	Low	Industry share of GDP growth rises by 25% (elasticity falls)
	High	Agriculture share of GDP growth rises by 25% (elasticity rises)

Source: Own description of projection model simulations.

and is therefore the likely planning horizon for the international development community.

Figure 2.4 shows the projected unemployment rates in the baseline scenario. Youth unemployment rates gradually increase from 12.2 percent in 2010 to 16.6 percent in 2030. This is broadly consistent with the small changes in Africa's youth unemployment rates observed during 1995–2010 (ILO 2012) and evidence suggesting that the employment-intensity of African growth may have started to decline at the start of this period (Kapsos 2005). In absolute terms, however, the number of unemployed youth in the baseline more than doubles from 10 million in 2010 to 24 million in 2030. This is despite economic growth in Africa being relatively more employment-intensive, and its declining share of youth in the working age population. Economic growth is simply not fast enough in the baseline to offset rapid population growth. Average GDP per worker increases at only 0.8 percent per year in the baseline – from $2,200 in 2010 to $2,600 in 2030. Similarly, average GDP per capita rises by only US$210 over two decades – from $810 to $1,020.

The increase in unemployment rates in the baseline is largest for young men, reaching 17.4 percent in 2030. Female unemployment rates peak at 15.6 percent. This unevenness is due to higher female employment-growth elasticities and lower female participation rates, which work together to reduce the gap between labour demand and supply.

Youth unemployment rates begin to fall after 2030, returning to 2010 levels by 2050. This is the result of slower population growth and declining labour force participation rates. Whereas population growth during 2010–2030 is projected to be 2.6 percent per year, this drops to 1.8 percent during 2030–2050. This causes labour supply growth to decelerate without affecting the rate of economic growth and hence projected labour demand. While the youth bulge had started to recede by 2010, its effect on youth unemployment may last for much longer.

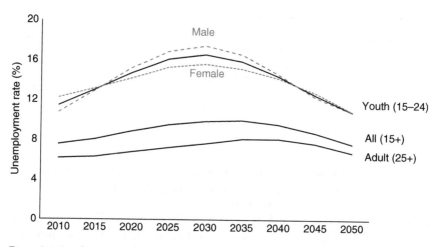

Figure 2.4 Baseline unemployment rates, 2010–2050
Source: Projection model results.

The adult unemployment rate increases only slightly in the baseline and remains well below the national average. As expected, the peak in adult unemployment occurs about ten years after the peak in youth unemployment. The youth bulge, while substantial within the narrow band of 15–24-year-olds, is relatively small compared to the total population. As such, the transition of unemployed youth to adulthood does not have an immediate impact on adult unemployment rates. These rates remain below eight percent throughout the simulation period.

The baseline is meant to reflect a 'middle of the road' growth and population trajectory for Africa. The projection model suggests that, while youth unemployment rates may rise under such a scenario, this increase is unlikely to be dramatic. In absolute terms, however, the number of unemployed youth in Africa more than doubles and does not begin to decline until the middle of the century. We now test the sensitivity of these baseline outcomes to alternative assumptions.

Fertility rates and school enrolment

Labour supply is determined by population growth and participation rates. We consider the effects of Africa experiencing either higher or lower than expected fertility rates. The median population projection that was used in the baseline is now replaced with new projections from UNDESA (2013). This alters the value of P in the model, but does not affect other parameters. The top panel in Table 2.8 shows how the share of youth in the total workforce in 2030 changes in the Upper and Lower Bound Population scenarios. As discussed earlier, adjusting fertility rates has little effect on the youth population until after 2025, because it takes time for changes in birth rates to affect the population aged 15 and older. As such, there is little difference between youth workforce shares in 2030 across the baseline and population scenarios (see the first three columns in the table). As was shown in Figure 2.1, the deviation in population levels between the baseline and alternative fertility scenarios only becomes significant towards 2050. Nevertheless, the table indicates that the share of youth in the workforce rises (falls) with higher (lower) fertility rates.

We also consider an alternative scenario in which youth participation rates decline more rapidly than they did in the baseline. More specifically, we assume that Africa is able to achieve the average youth participation rates of developed countries by 2050. We interpret this alternative scenario as Africa increasing school enrolment to the nearly universal levels achieved by developed countries today. The decline in youth participation rates is implemented smoothly over time, such that half of the gap between Africa and developed countries is closed by 2030. The lower panel in Table 2.8 shows how 49.6 percent of the youth population participates in the labour force by 2030 in the school enrolment scenario. This is below the baseline participation rate of 54.1 percent. Note that Southern Africa's participation rate was already below the developed country average in 2010 (see Table 2.2) and so we do not reduce these any further, i.e., they remain constant in all scenarios. Note also that each alternative assumption is modelled separately and so we use baseline population projections for the enrolment

Table 2.8 Youth population and labour force participation in the Population and Enrolment scenarios, 2030

	Baseline	Population scenarios		Enrolment scenario
		Lower	Upper	
Youth share of potential work force, 2030 (%)				
Sub-Saharan Africa	33.0	32.4	33.5	33.0
East Africa	32.9	32.3	33.5	32.9
Central Africa	34.0	33.5	34.6	34.0
Southern Africa	24.6	23.7	25.5	24.6
West Africa	34.0	33.4	34.5	34.0
Male	33.4	32.8	34.0	33.4
Female	32.5	31.9	33.1	32.5
Youth labour force participation rate, 2030 (%)				
Sub-Saharan Africa	54.1	54.1	54.1	49.6
East Africa	67.1	67.1	67.1	57.1
Central Africa	48.4	48.4	48.4	47.2
Southern Africa	28.6	28.6	28.6	28.6
West Africa	45.4	45.4	45.4	45.0
Male	56.3	56.3	56.3	52.3
Female	51.9	51.9	51.9	46.9

Source: Projection model results.

Notes: Youth are between 15 and 24 years of age.

scenarios and baseline participation rates for the population scenarios. We can therefore directly compare each scenario to the baseline in order to see to what extent changing model assumptions leads to different outcomes.

Figure 2.5 reports youth unemployment rates for the population and enrolment scenarios. There is no deviation in unemployment rates from baseline until after 2025, implying that lowering fertility rates is not a solution to Africa's immediate youth unemployment concerns. Beyond 2025, however, differences in fertility rates have major implications for youth unemployment. In the lower population scenario, the youth unemployment rate falls from 16.1 percent in 2025 to 3.2 percent in 2050. This is well below baseline unemployment rates in 2050. Conversely, if fertility rates are higher than expected, then unemployment rates in 2040 are almost double current rates, with one fifth of African youth searching for but unable to find work.

Increasing secondary school enrolment for youth reduces labour supply and unemployment rates relative to the baseline. The youth unemployment rate remains stable until 2025, because increased enrolment almost exactly offsets the effects of population growth. When population growth begins to slow down after 2025, participation rates continue to fall, leading to an accelerated decline in unemployment rates. This tapers off towards 2050 as unemployment

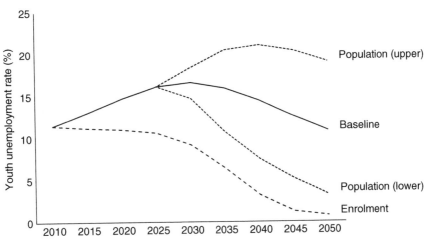

Figure 2.5 Youth unemployment in population and enrolment scenarios, 2010–2050
Source: Projection model results.
Notes: Youth are between 15 and 24 years of age.

rates approach zero. Increasing school enrolment is a more immediate means of reducing youth unemployment. However, unlike lowering fertility, higher school enrolment simply delays, rather than removes, the burden of finding jobs for a rapidly growing population. The youth unemployment problem might simply become an adult unemployment problem.

Table 2.9 reports average annual growth in GDP, GDP per worker, and GDP per capita for the period 2010–2030. Total GDP growth is fixed at baseline rates and is therefore the same for each scenario, i.e., 3.7 percent per year. Changes in the population growth rate lead to significant differences in GDP per capita. For example, annual growth in GDP per capita is 1.4 and 0.9 percent in the lower and upper population scenarios, respectively. Even small differences in annual growth rates can lead to large absolute differences by 2030. For example, GDP per capita in 2030 in the lower population scenario is 10 percent higher than in the upper population scenario, even though only half a percentage point separates their annual GDP growth rates. Similarly, youth unemployment rates are also almost four percentage points lower. Since employment levels are determined by labour demand, there is no difference in final year GDP per worker across the various scenarios.

Unemployment rates in all African sub-regions decline with lower fertility rates. Increasing school enrolment is most beneficial for East Africa, because its participation rates are currently the highest in Africa. Moving towards the participation rates of developed countries involves a larger reduction to labour supply in East Africa, and hence lower unemployment. The opposite is true for Southern Africa, whose participation rates are already below those of developed countries, and so therefore the sub-region does not experience any changes under the

Table 2.9 Worker productivity and youth unemployment in the population and enrolment scenarios, 2030

	Baseline	Population scenarios		Enrolment scenario
		Lower	Upper	
Average annual growth rate for Sub-Saharan Africa, 2010–30 (%)				
Total GDP	3.72	3.72	3.72	3.72
GDP per capita	1.17	1.41	0.93	1.17
GDP per worker	0.84	0.84	0.84	0.84
Youth unemployment rate, 2030 (%)				
Sub-Saharan Africa	16.6	14.7	18.4	9.2
East Africa	23.0	20.9	25.0	9.5
Central Africa	15.3	13.3	17.3	13.3
Southern Africa	39.4	36.2	42.3	39.4
West Africa	5.0	3.8	6.2	4.6
Male	17.4	15.2	19.5	11.1
Female	15.6	14.1	17.0	6.9

Source: Projection model results.

school enrolment scenario, i.e., youth unemployment rates remain at 39.4 percent. As with East Africa, women benefit the most in the school enrolment scenario because their participation rates are substantially higher than men's (see Table 2.2).

The population and enrolment scenarios test the sensitivity of our results to changes in the assumptions regarding the two labour supply parameters in the model. There are clear risks in the form of higher-than-expected fertility rates, but also opportunities though, for example, efforts to raise enrolment in secondary schools.

Pace and pattern of economic growth

We now consider changes to the parameters determining labour demand in the model. We reset the population and participation parameters to baseline values. As shown in Table 2.4, the 1990s was a period of slower economic growth, whereas the 2000s was a period of rapid growth. In the baseline set the growth parameter G, equal to the 1990–2010 average annual GDP growth rate. We now consider two alternative scenarios. The fast growth scenario accelerates annual GDP growth in the model from 3.7–5.2 percent per year, which matches the region's strong performance during the 2000s (see Table 2.4). In contrast, the slow growth scenario reduces growth to 2.3 percent, thus marking a return to the dismal 1990s.

The intensity scenarios consider how changes to the sectoral pattern of economic growth might affect youth unemployment. Crivelli et al. (2012) estimate employment-growth elasticities for agriculture, industry and services for 1991–2009. The authors find that agricultural GDP growth in Africa has a higher elasticity (0.47) than either industry (0.30) or services (0.34). Unfortunately, no elasticities were estimated for individual sub-regions in Africa. However, we use sectoral GDP data from the World Bank (2014) to measure the contribution of each sector to sub-regional economic growth during 1990–2010, i.e., the reference period for the baseline scenario. We find, for example, that agriculture accounted for 27.5 percent of the increase in total GDP in West Africa, but only 2.0 percent in Southern Africa. These shares are used to calculate weighted average employment-growth elasticities that are specific to each sub-region.

In the high intensity scenario we triple agriculture's contribution to total GDP growth and proportionally scale down the contributions of industry and services. Since agriculture's elasticity is the largest, this leads to an increase in the overall employment-growth elasticity. GDP growth now generates a larger increase in employment, but a smaller increase in labour productivity. Conversely, in the low intensity scenario we increase industry's contribution to GDP growth, leading to a smaller weighted elasticity. The bias towards employment rather than productivity is now reversed. It is worth noting that while we motivate changes to employment-growth elasticities based on broad agriculture versus industry, we are really comparing more and less labour-intensive sources of growth, hence the name of these scenarios.

Table 2.10 reports average annual growth in GDP, GDP per worker, and GDP per capita for the period 2010–2030. By design, total GDP growth is 2.3 and 5.2 percent per year in the slow and fast growth scenarios, respectively. This leads to differences in GDP per capita, even though population growth is identical in all scenarios. GDP per worker also varies across scenarios. This is not only due to the effects of economic growth on labour demand, but also changes in the employment intensity of growth. More labour-intensive growth in agriculture leads to more people being employed and therefore lower GDP per worker. This decline is offset when overall economic growth accelerates. The table highlights the trade-off between creating more jobs, and creating jobs that are more productive.

Figure 2.6 shows the evolution of youth unemployment under the growth and intensity scenarios. The baseline replicates what appeared in Figures 2.3 and 2.4.

Table 2.10 Worker productivity in the growth and intensity scenarios, 2010–2030

	Intensity scenarios	Average annual growth rate (%)		
		Growth scenarios		
		Slower	Baseline	Faster
Total GDP	–	2.30	3.72	5.15
GDP per capita	–	−0.22	1.17	2.57
GDP per worker	Low	0.75	1.12	1.88
	Baseline	0.58	0.84	1.82
	High	0.28	0.55	1.77

Source: Projection model results.

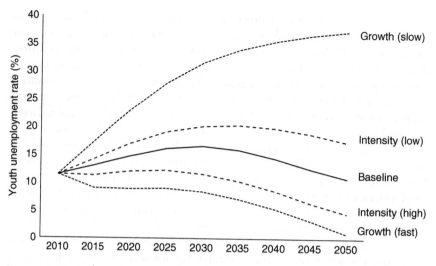

Figure 2.6 Youth unemployment in Growth and Intensity scenarios, 2010–2050
Source: Projection model results.
Notes: Youth are between 15 and 24 years of age.

A return to the slow GDP growth rates of the 1990s leads to a tremendous increase in youth unemployment, with rates in 2030 that are double what appears in the baseline. Conversely, if Africa can sustain the rapid growth of the 2000s, then unemployment rates are likely to remain fairly constant until 2030 and then begin decline.

Shifting the pattern of growth toward labour-intensive sectors can be nearly as effective as increasing the overall rate of growth. This is shown in Table 2.11, which reports unemployment rates in 2030. For youth as a whole, slower baseline growth driven by agriculture reduces unemployment to 11.5 percent, which is similar to the drop in unemployment rates when fast growth is led by industry.

We conclude by considering the effects of more rapid, labour-intensive growth on Africa's sub-regions. Unemployment rates in West Africa decline to zero by 2030 in our simple model. This is because unemployment rates in this sub-region were already low in 2010 (Table 2.5). West Africa also experienced one of the largest accelerations in economic growth from the 1990s to the 2000s (Table 2.4). This is more likely to lead to job creation since West Africa has high employment elasticities (Table 2.6). Finally, the large contribution of agriculture to GDP growth in West Africa means that the sub-region stands to benefit more under the high intensity scenario. Each of the above characteristics favours a more rapid decline in unemployment. In contrast, unemployment rates in Southern Africa remain virtually unchanged across the scenarios. This is due to slow economic growth, low employment-growth elasticities, and a small contribution to growth from agriculture – the exact opposite to West Africa. This heterogeneity across sub-regions cautions against general statements about past and future youth employment prospects in Africa.

Table 2.11 Youth unemployment in the growth and intensity scenarios, 2030

	Intensity scenarios	Youth unemployment rate, 2030 (%)		
		Growth scenarios		
		Slower	Baseline	Faster
Sub-Saharan Africa	Low	33.3	20.1	10.6
	Baseline	31.5	16.6	8.4
	High	28.3	11.5	4.4
East Africa	Low	32.3	25.6	18.2
	Baseline	30.6	23.0	14.5
	High	27.2	17.7	6.9
Central Africa	Low	42.8	25.4	2.2
	Baseline	41.0	15.3	0.0
	High	40.2	10.5	0.0
Southern Africa	Low	41.9	40.1	38.2
	Baseline	41.4	39.4	37.3
	High	41.2	39.2	37.1
West Africa	Low	30.2	7.5	0.0
	Baseline	28.2	5.0	0.0
	High	23.7	0.0	0.0

Source: Projection model results.

Notes: Youth are between 15 and 24 years of age.

Conclusions

In this chapter we asked whether there is something quantitatively unique about Africa's 'youth bulge.' Based on historical data, we find little evidence to suggest that Africa's youth bulge, which peaked in 2003, is significantly different from the youth bulges experienced in other developing regions three decades ago. The share of youth in the working age population is only slightly above what it was elsewhere. Current youth unemployment rates are also similar to what they are in the broader developing world. Labour force participation rates in Africa are, however, particularly high, reflecting low secondary school enrolment. However, enrolment rates in Africa today are similar to South Asia's in 1980. Moreover, while Africa is a late-starter, the pace at which it is raising school enrolment is similar to the pace of other developing regions during their youth bulges. In summary, Africa is undergoing a recognizable demographic transformation. What is different is the late stage at which this transformation is occurring. The absolute (not relative) scale of Africa's youth bulge is unprecedented, as is the more globalized context in which young workers must find employment.

In order to assess the employment prospects of Africa's youth, we developed a simple projection model that measures the gap between future labour supply and demand. We find that if Africa can maintain its current strong economic performance, then youth unemployment rates should remain fairly constant until

2030 and then start to decline. This gives some cause for optimism. However, if economic growth returns to a more modest trajectory or if fertility rates are higher than expected, then the model suggests that Africa's youth unemployment rate could more than double over the next two decades as the economy struggles to absorb a rapidly growing population. A spike in youth unemployment of this magnitude would put Africa beyond the experiences of other developing regions and could reasonably be expected to jeopardize future socioeconomic development.

The unevenness of past African growth suggests that greater youth unemployment in the future is a strong possibility, and thus requires a definite response from African governments and their international partners. Our analysis suggests that increasing secondary school enrolment and promoting labour-intensive sectors – even if it means slower structural change – would lessen the need to sustain rapid economic growth over the next two decades. These interventions, if successful, would increase the likelihood that youth unemployment does not become more of a hindrance to future development than it is today.

Notes

1 'Africa' and 'sub-Saharan Africa' will be used synonymously in this chapter.
2 We adopt the United Nations classification of African sub-regions (see Table 2.A2 in the Appendix).
3 Table 2.A2 in the Appendix to this chapter reports unemployment rates for individual African countries.

References

AfDB, OECD, UNDP, ECA. (2012). *African Economic Outlook 2012: Promoting Youth Employment*. African Development Bank, Organization for Economic Cooperation and Development, United Nations Development Programme, and Economic Commission for Africa. Available at: http://www.africaneconomicoutlook.org/en/theme/youth_employ ment (accessed 14 September 2014).
Crivelli, E., D. Furceri, J. Toujas-Bernaté. (2012). 'Can Policies Affect Employment Intensity of Growth? A Cross-Country Analysis.' *Working Paper WP/12/218*. Washington DC, USA: International Monetary Fund.
Filmer, D., and L. Fox. (2014). *Youth Employment in Sub-Saharan Africa*. Washington DC, USA: The World Bank.
ILO. (2012). *ILO Estimates of the Economically Active Population: 1990–2010 (Sixth Edition)*. Geneva, Switzerland: Employment Trends Unit, International Labour Organization.
Kapsos, S. (2005). 'The Employment Intensity of Growth: Trends and Macroeconomic Determinants.' *Employment Strategy Papers 2005/12*. Geneva, Switzerland: Employment Trends Unit, International Labour Organization.
McMillan, M., D. Rodrik, and I. Verduzco-Gallo. (2014). 'Globalization, Structural Change, and Productivity Growth, with an Update on Africa.' *World Development*, 63(November): 11–32.
UNDESA. (2013). *World Population Prospects: The 2012 Revision*. New York NY, USA: Department of Economic and Social Affairs, United Nations Secretariat.
World Bank. (2012). World Development Report 2013: Jobs. Washington DC, USA.
World Bank. (2014). World Development Indicators Online Database. Washington DC, USA.

Appendix

Table 2.A1 Youth unemployment rates for sub-Saharan African countries, 2010

Region/country	%	Region/country	%	Region/country	%
Eastern Africa	10.2	Central Africa	10.2	West Africa	9.1
Zambia	24.3	Gabon	41.4	Senegal	14.1
Mauritius	22.7	Equatorial Guinea	10.3	Mali	12.8
Kenya	18.0	D.R. Congo	10.2	Togo	10.3
Tanzania	14.6	Angola	10.2	Cape Verde	10.2
Malawi	13.7	C.A. Republic	10.2	Guinea-Bissau	10.2
Burundi	10.2	Chad	10.1	Gambia	10.2
Eritrea	10.2	Rep. Congo	10.1	Nigeria	10.2
Mozambique	10.2	Cameroon	9.2	Niger	7.3
Comoros	10.1	Southern Africa	49.3	Ghana	6.5
Somalia	10.1	Namibia	72.2	Cote d'Ivoire	6.4
Zimbabwe	8.0	South Africa	51.1	Liberia	5.8
Ethiopia	7.7	Swaziland	42.0	Burkina Faso	5.3
Uganda	7.3	Lesotho	32.7	Sierra Leone	5.2
Madagascar	2.3	Botswana	30.6	Guinea	4.9
Rwanda	0.7	Mauritania	52.6	Benin	0.9

Source: Own calculations using population data from UNDESA (2013) and labour force trends data from ILO (2012).

Notes: Youth are between 15 and 24 years of age.

Table 2.A2 Countries in sample, 1991–2010

Region [number of countries]	World Bank country codes (number of years of data if less than 20)
Developed [42]	alb, aus, aut, bel, bgr, bih (17), blr, can, che, cze, deu, dnk, esp, est (18), fin, fra, gbr, grc, hrv (16), hun, irl, isl, ita, jpn, ltu, lux, lva, mda, mkd, mlt, nld, nor, nzl, pol, prt, rom, rus, svk, svn, swe, ukr, usa
East Asia, Pacific [18]	brn, chn, fji, hkg, idn, khm (18), kor, lao, mac, mng, mys, phl, png, sgp, slb, tha, tmp (12), vnm
Europe, Central Asia [10]	arm, aze, cyp, geo, kaz, kgz, tjk, tkm, tur, uzb
Latin America [27]	arg, bhs, blz, bol, bra, brb, chl, col, cri, cub, dom, ecu, gtm, guy, hnd, hti (13), mex, nic, pan, per, pri, pry, slv, sur, tto, ury, ven
Middle East, North Africa [20]	are, bhr, dza, egy, irn, irq (11), isr, jor, kwt (19), lbn, lby (12), mar, omn, qat (11), sau, sdn, syr (17), tun, wbg (17), yem
South Asia [8]	afg (9), bgd, btn, ind, lka, mdv (10), npl, pak
East Africa [14]	bdi, com, eri (19), eth, ken, mdg, moz, mus, mwi, rwa, tza, uga, zmb, zwe
Central Africa [8]	ago, caf, cmr, cog, gab, gnq, tcd, zar
Southern Africa [5]	bwa, lso, nam, swz, zaf
West Africa [16]	ben, bfa, civ, cpv, gha, gin, gmb, gnb, lbr, mli, mrt, ner, nga, sen, sle, tgo

3   Protesting for a better tomorrow?

Youth mobilization in Africa

Danielle Resnick

Introduction

Since colonial times, young men and women have been identified as important players in Africa's major periods of political transition, ranging from the 1948 Accra Riots in Ghana to the Tanzanian nationalist movement of the 1950s (Allman 1990; Geiger 1997). By the 1970s, Nkinyangi (1991) notes that student protests were common in at least 29 countries in the region. By the time of the wave of democratic transitions in the late 1980s and 1990s, youth were, along with labour unions, religious organizations, and the professional classes, at the forefront of demands for political and economic reforms. For instance, in Senegal, the youth rioted in the wake of disputed elections in 1988 and abstained in subsequent elections in order to deprive President Abdou Diouf's regime of legitimacy (Diouf 1996; Villalón 1999). Student protests were also highly common in Côte d'Ivoire, Malawi, Kenya, and Zambia during this period, contributing to the end of one-party rule (see Bratton and van de Walle 1992). In South Africa, youth were closely intertwined with many pivotal moments in the anti-apartheid movement, from the Sharpeville massacre to the Soweto uprisings (see Clines 1994; Seekings 1993). More recently, the political power of Africa's youth has also been widely heralded. From the 'Fed Up' youth movements in Senegal and Sudan to Angola's Revolutionary Youth protest group and the Concerned Youth Groups in South Africa, Africa's young people have attracted widespread media attention by demonstrating against the abuses of incumbent regimes, poor service delivery, and high unemployment (see Alexander 2010; Hamilton 2010; Honwana 2013; Wonacott 2012).

Yet, analyses of these protests have been limited to either journalistic assessments or country-specific case studies, thereby inhibiting the ability to draw more comparative conclusions about the implications of this mobilization for the region's democratic consolidation. With a focus on contemporary African youth, this chapter therefore adopts a cross-country perspective to examine how common protest is as tool of political participation and why some individuals choose to protest while others do not. By combining data from the Armed Conflict and Event Database (ACLED) and the Afrobarometer public opinion survey database, the chapter highlights the youth's protest activities in comparative perspective while also probing individual-level determinants that influence their behaviour. In doing so, the analysis builds on a growing body of scholarship on political mobilization that emphasizes combining micro-level, behavioural data with macro-level, country characteristics to provide a more powerful understanding of the drivers of protest activity than examining either of those in isolation (see Dalton et al. 2010). The chapter's findings highlight that rather than material grievances, African youth are more likely to protest when they have access to particular resources, including education, media, and social capital. Moreover, the analysis suggests that while macro-level conditions, particularly the environment for civil liberties, constrains protest activities among older Africans, it is less significant for younger Africans.

Before elaborating on these results in more detail, the following section offers details on trends in protest activity across Africa, over time, and vis-à-vis other regions of the world. Attention is also given to the characteristics of African youth who claim to have recently participated in protests and demonstrations. Subsequently, the literature on protest is presented, detailing both the various individual- and country-level determinants of this mode of mobilization. Then, these hypotheses are tested empirically through a statistical analysis that relies on multi-level, logit modeling.

Protest trends across Africa

In order to gauge the involvement of African youth in protest activities, two key data sources were utilized: the Armed Conflict Location and Event Data (ACLED) database and Afrobarometer Round 5. ACLED offers disaggregated conflict data between 1997–2013 across 50 African countries by drawing on news reports, security updates from international organizations, and publications from non-governmental and human rights organizations.[1] By drawing on news reports from both international and local media, it provides the broadest coverage available on incidents of conflict. Various conflict event types are examined, including violence against civilians, military battles, non-violent territorial transfers, and protests and riots. The latter category encompasses both 'nonviolent spontaneous organizations of civilians for a political purpose' and 'violent disturbance of the public peace by three or more persons assembled for a common purpose' (see Raleigh et al. 2014; Raleigh et al. 2010).

Figure 3.1 illustrates the total number of riots and protests over time in sub-Saharan Africa in which youth were involved. This was determined by using the notes provided by ACLED that accompany each riot/protest event and isolating where there was a mention of 'youths,' 'young people,' or 'students' being among the main actors who participated. For purposes of comparison, trends are highlighted for the North African region as well. In both cases, there has been a substantial increase in riot and protest activities in recent years. The year 2008 represented a major upswing in activity south of the Sahara, specifically sparked by the global food price crisis (see Pinstrup-Anderson 2014). The Arab Spring in 2011 obviously was a key catalyst for protest activities in North Africa.

Yet, although these figures suggest that the youth may be increasingly likely to protest, Figure 3.2 highlights that youth south of the Sahara only constitute a small share of total protesters and that their participation has not significantly shifted since the late 1990s. A similar conclusion emerges from Figure 3.3, which shows

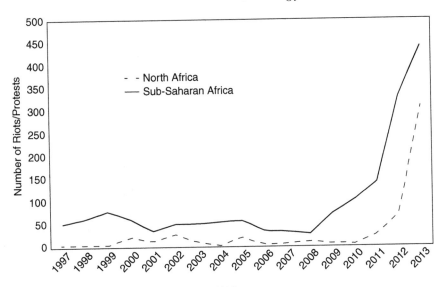

Figure 3.1 Youth protest over time, 1997–2013
Source: Calculated from the ACLED database (www.acleddata.com).

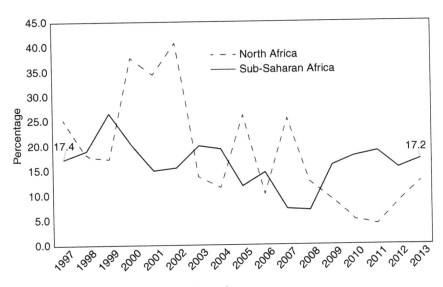

Figure 3.2 Youth protest compared with total protest
Source: Calculated from the ACLED database (www.acleddata.com).

by country the cumulative level of youth engagement in total protest activities
between 1997 and 2013. Countries such as Kenya, Nigeria, and South Africa have
had the region's largest total number of protests, which perhaps reflects that they
are among the most populous electoral democracies in Africa. However, even in
these countries, the youth represent the key participants in only one-third or less

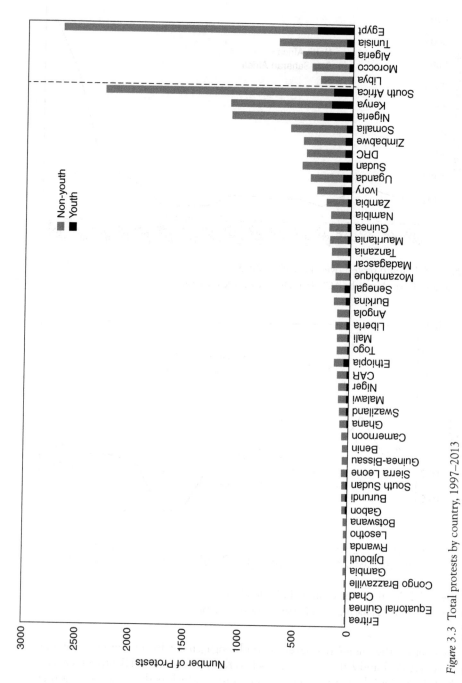

Figure 3.3 Total protests by country, 1997–2013

Source: Calculated from the ACLED database (www.acleddata.com).

Notes: CAR refers to Central African Republic. DRC refers to Democratic Republic of the Congo.

of these events. Notably, there are interesting temporal dynamics to these protests across countries. In South Africa, for example, there have been 176 youth protests but a majority of these have occurred in 2012 and 2013. Many of these protests have been associated with school-related issues, including substandard student accommodation, lack of textbooks, teacher shortages, and insufficient food and bursaries. However, some youths were involved in a spate of protesting in 2012 when Julius Malema was removed as the leader of the African National Congress (ANC) Youth League. In Kenya, youth protests were quite frequent in the late 1990s and early 2000s but were less common during much of the 2000s before spiking again in 2011.

While ACLED offers a perspective on the concentration of protest events, Afrobarometer provides more insight into the share of individuals who may be participating in protests across countries. Afrobarometer is a public opinion survey database that has now conducted five rounds of data collection since 2000. While the project was originally limited to Africa's electoral democracies, the fifth round was expanded to a broader range of regimes and also extended to include North Africa. In all, the data used here includes 28 sub-Saharan African countries and 4 North African countries with approximately 1,200 to 2,400 individuals surveyed in each country. Depending on the country, the surveys were conducted between 2011 and 2013.[2] 'Youth' has been divided into two cohorts: those who are between the ages of 18–24 and those who are 25–35. These two cohorts were chosen for a number of reasons. First, the United Nations defines the upper threshold of youth at 24, which is consistent with international conceptualizations of the youth and also includes the median age in Africa (i.e. 19). However, the African Union chooses 35 as its upper threshold, claiming that for many Africans, youth is delayed due the challenges of finding jobs, establishing a stable income, and starting a family (see AU 2006).[3] Secondly, this distinction enables for a more disaggregated examination of the priorities, characteristics, and behaviours of different youth cohorts.

What are the characteristics of these different youth cohorts compared with their older compatriots? Table 3.1 presents key demographic, socioeconomic, and political descriptive information across these three main groups. Compared with the older cohort, the youngest age cohort is more urbanized, more educated, and more likely to be unemployed. As noted below, geographic proximity has historically been viewed as an important correlate of protest activity, enabling large numbers of people to mobilize more quickly than in remote, rural areas (Walton and Ragin 1990). A number of observers have noted that due to the removal of primary and sometimes secondary school fees across Africa over the last two decades, school attendance has improved (Stasavage 2005; Filmer and Fox 2014). But the combination of high education with low employment prospects can be a catalyst for protest as young people have aspirations for social mobility that are thwarted by insufficient job opportunities.

Table 3.2 first contextualizes protest activity vis-à-vis other types of political mobilization and compares mobilization between Africans North and South of the Sahara. Respondents were asked whether they voted in the last national election.

Table 3.1 Descriptive characteristics of age cohorts

Characteristics	Aged 18–24 (%)	Aged 25–35 (%)	Aged 36 and older (%)
Male	44.6	46.4	54.6
Urban	42.1	38	32.7
No education	6.8	13.4	22.4
Primary education completed	10.1	12.4	14.3
Some secondary or completed	55.1	37.6	25.5
Unemployed	40.8	35.7	23

Source: Afrobarometer Round 5, sub-Saharan sample with 28 countries.

Notes: The percentages are weighted by within and cross-country survey weights.

Table 3.2 Political participation across age cohorts

Type of participation	Sub-Saharan Africans			North Africans		
	Ages 18–24 (%)	Ages 24–35 (%)	Ages 36 and above (%)	Ages 18–24 (%)	Ages 24–35 (%)	Ages 36 and above (%)
Used force or violence	2.6	3.1	2.9	1.0	1.5	0.7
Attended demonstration or protest march	10.2	9.5	7.8	12.5	9.6	6.8
Attended community meeting	47.2	61.1	68.3	16.6	17.1	19.8
Voted in last election	42.3	75.8	83.1	42	60.2	72

Source: Afrobarometer Round 5. Sub-Saharan sample includes 28 countries and North-African sample includes 4 countries.

Notes: The percentages are weighted by within and cross-country survey weights.

In addition, they responded to a variety of questions related to their activities over the course of the year prior to the survey taking place, including attending a community meeting, attending a demonstration or protest march, or using force or violence for a political cause.[4] Responses to these questions were coded as 'yes' if the respondent claimed that s/he had engaged in these activities 'once or twice,' 'several times,' or 'often.' As can be seen, the percentage of those in the two youth cohorts who protested is slightly higher than older Africans. However, the gap between young and old is even more pronounced in North Africa. In sub-Saharan Africa, voting and attending community meetings are still much more common modes of political participation than protesting. Only a small share of respondents from any of the cohorts in either region admitted to using violence.

Figure 3.4 helps to place the above trends in temporal perspective by comparing previous rounds of Afrobarometer data. In each time period, the share of 18–24-year-olds protesting is consistently higher than the other two age groups. However, overall, the share of Africans at all ages who were protesting over the last decade has gradually fallen. When compared with the protest event data from ACLED, this suggests that even though the absolute number of protests has increased since 2008, the share of individuals participating in them has decreased.

Yet, even though the participation of the youth has declined over time, the simple bivariate logit analysis presented in Table 3.3 indicates that they are still protesting at a statistically significant higher rate than their older counterparts. Based on odds ratios, those who are aged 18–24 are 34 percent more likely to protest than those who are 36 and older.[5]

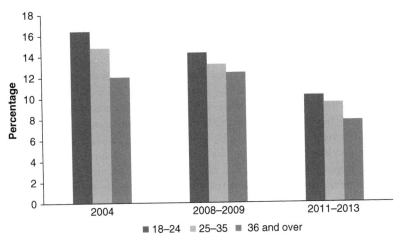

Figure 3.4 Share of the population protesting by age cohort

Sources: Calculated from Afrobarometer Rounds 3, 4, and 5.

Notes: These are weighted responses and only apply to the 28 sub-Saharan countries in the sample.

Table 3.3 Bivariate analysis of age and protest

Age Groups	Protest (coefficients)	Protest (odds ratios)
Ages 18–24	0.292*** (0.049)	1.339*** (0.066)
Ages 25–35	0.210*** (0.043)	1.234*** (0.053)
Constant	−2.466*** (0.029)	0.085*** (0.002)

Source: Afrobarometer Round 5, sub-Saharan African sample.

Notes: Number of observations is 45,553. Incorporates within and across country survey weights. The excluded reference group is those who are aged 36 and above. Linearized standard errors are in parentheses. ***Indicates statistical significance at the 0.010 level.

Micro-macro determinants of protest

The above trends affirm that while the youth do protest more than older Africans, protesters still tend to be a minority among African youth in absolute terms. This in turn raises a larger question regarding why do some young people decide to protest while others do not? Addressing this question requires a multi-level approach that takes into account both characteristics of individuals that may make them more likely to protest as well as the country context in which they are living. To do so, three main schools of thought prominent in the literature on protest movements are instrumental: grievance theory, resource mobilization theory, and political opportunity structures.[6]

As Gurr (1985) argued, demographic, economic, and ecological factors increasingly contribute to resource scarcity, which can exacerbate inequalities among individuals and even across communal groups. Grievance theory therefore suggests that the ensuing economic deprivation spurs protest and rebellion among those who are marginalized from opportunities that others enjoy (see Gurr 1970; Lipsky 1968). Dalton et al. (2010) claim that grievances are more likely to drive protest in low-income countries, such as those in Africa, than in more affluent ones. The reason is that in the former, dissatisfaction with economic conditions can reflect severe deprivation while in the latter, where living conditions are much higher, it may instead simply indicate disillusionment with quality of life. Indeed, many protests in Africa have been ostensibly linked to rises in the prices of basic goods and services, such as food, fuel, and transport, or water and electricity shortages. Nevertheless, the fact that many African countries have experienced similar price shocks and service delivery outages in recent years, but protests have been more sporadic, suggests that grievances alone are not a sufficient explanation.

Resource mobilization theory adopts a very different perspective by looking at the supply-side rather than the demand-side drivers of protest. More specifically, scholars in this school observe that sustained and organized protest requires resources in the form of money, educated protest leaders, access to an independent mass media, and infrastructure (Brady et al. 1995; Klandermans 1997; McCarthy and Zald 1977; Norris 2002). In addition, individuals are more likely to be recruited into protest activity, as well as other types of political mobilization, if they are embedded in social networks such as unions, churches, and political parties (Putnam 1993; Verba et al. 1995). In contrast to the grievance school, some studies of resource mobilization have found this theory to be less salient in the developing country context, with wealthier individuals less engaged in protest, and more powerful in industrialized countries (see Canache 2002).

In the African context, organizations such as labour unions and religious communities have historically been important drivers of protest movements, especially in the pro-democracy era. However, informalization of the labour force as a consequence of a declining manufacturing sector and structural adjustment has weakened the role of formal labour unions (see Croucher 2007). Political parties have though proved important institutional mechanisms for youth mobilization, especially via party youth leagues (Abbink 2005). Examples include the Young Democrats attached to the ruling Democratic Progressive Party (DPP) in Malawi, the Young Patriots who supported the former president of Côte d'Ivoire, Laurent Gbagbo, and the African National Congress Youth League. Depending on their affiliation with either opposition or incumbent parties, such youth leagues may be more or less likely to protest against the government. Philips' (2013) work on urban youth in Guinea further shows that well-established criminal gangs can also provide mobilizing structures to facilitate protest activities.

The nature of political opportunity structures constitutes a third school of thought. In this view, the macro political environment within which individuals are operating is the primary determinant of whether they protest or not. From one perspective, opportunities for protests and other types of extra-institutional activities often are greater in more open and liberalized environments where governments tolerate protests and thereby the costs to collective action are lower (see McAdam 1982; Tarrow 1998). In addition, greater political openness also suggests that policymakers may be more willing to consider protesters' demands, increasing perceptions that protest activities are an effective means of conveying grievances and achieving results.

Others, however, note that more circumscribed political environments with low levels of civil liberties and limited electoral democracy might be more conducive to protest. With limited means to access and influence policymakers through conventional means, people can only demonstrate their dissatisfaction through protest (see Kitschelt 1986; Brockett 1991).

A third perspective is that there is a curvilinear relationship such that protest levels are low in both closed and open systems but high in countries with more hybrid regimes (see Eisinger 1973). The reason is that in very open systems, there are other modalities for citizens to convey dissatisfaction. In very closed systems, the risks of and barriers to collective action may be too high and repression can undermine the capacity of protesters to mobilize. But in more hybrid contexts, 'there is a space of toleration by a polity and . . . claimants are neither sufficiently advantaged to obviate the need to use dramatic means to express their interests nor so completely repressed to prevent them from getting what they want' (Meyer 2004: 128). Tilly (1995) illustrated this relationship in research on Britain, illustrating how protest gradually became a more common means of political participation until Parliament became more democratic and protest politics were subsumed into parliamentary debate.

Ex-ante, from observing Figure 3.3, the relationship in the African context is not immediately clear. While some countries with repressive systems show low levels of protest, such as Eritrea and Equatorial Guinea, others have relatively high levels, including Sudan and Zimbabwe. Likewise, more democratic regimes span the entire spectrum, with low levels in Botswana but some of the highest protests in South Africa. Goodfellow's (2013) comparative work on urban protest in Uganda and Rwanda further highlights that two autocratic regimes can nonetheless demonstrate differing levels of tolerance for and accommodation of public protest. By utilizing a multi-level model that incorporates indicators reflecting these three main schools of thought, potential interactions between individual behaviours and country contexts can be further explored. For instance, closed political opportunities may be more likely to discourage potential protestors when they simultaneously face few resources in terms of money, education, or media access.

Empirical analysis

To test the above hypotheses about protest with respect to youth, the analysis here employs a multi-level, or hierarchical, modeling approach that integrates both variables relevant to individual behaviours and those describing country conditions. This modeling technique is becoming increasingly common to examining political participation (see Kittilson and Anderson 2011) and protest behaviour (see Dalton et al. 2010), including in the African context (see Mattes and Bratton 2007). In particular, the models here are estimated using the Generalized Linear Latent and Mixed Models (GLLAMM) technique. This technique introduces a random intercept term for countries, which controls for the likelihood that individual observations within countries are not independent of each other (see Rabe-Hesketh et al. 2005).

In particular, the analysis here focuses on explaining why a respondent in Afrobarometer has chosen to protest (often, several times, or once or twice) during the 12 months preceding the time that the survey was conducted. This was coded as a binomial outcome, equal to one if they responded in the affirmative and zero if they did not. Two demographic variables were then included. Gender was captured by assigning a one to those who were males and zero to females. Urban residence was also coded as a dummy variable. Age, which is traditionally included, was excluded here because the model is estimated separately across the three age groups discussed earlier: those between 18–24, 25–35, and 36 and older.

The other included individual level variables were proxies for the grievance and resource mobilization theories introduced in the preceding section. For grievances, factors that might highlight economic deprivation were taken into account. Specifically, respondents were considered unemployed if they stated that they do not have jobs but are looking for jobs. Another measure of deprivation is the Lived Poverty Index (LPI), which has been used frequently in analyses of Afrobarometer surveys (e.g. Mattes and Bratton 2009; Mattes 2008). The LPI captures how often over the previous year a respondent or his/her family has gone without enough food to eat, clean water, medicines or medical treatment, a cash income, or enough fuel to cook food. The index scores range along a five-point scale from zero to four with the former indicating no deprivation (e.g. the respondent did not go without any of those five goods and services) and the latter suggesting constant deprivation in all five domains. The average LPI for all of Africa is 1.26, with Mauritius and Togo having the lowest and highest average levels, respectively (Dulani et al. 2013).

Unfortunately, Afrobarometer does not ask about respondents' income or consumption expenditures and thus, an individual's material wealth is difficult to determine. However, other measures of resource mobilization are included. Education levels are along an ordinal scale that ranges from no schooling (zero) to post-graduate schooling (nine). In addition, a media access index was calculated that takes into account whether a respondent obtains news from radio, television, newspaper, and Internet, and how frequently such news is obtained (never, less than once a month, a few times a month, a few times a week, and every day). The index ranges from zero to four with higher values indicating that more media sources are accessed on a more frequent basis.

In order to assess a respondent's level of social capital, two measures are included that reflect their degree of participation in civic organizations, namely a religious organization or a voluntary association/community group. Membership referred to whether the respondent claimed to be an 'inactive member,' 'active member,' or 'official leader' while non-members were clearly identified as 'not a member.' Finally, a dummy variable was included for whether a respondent expressed that s/he had an affinity to a party that was in the opposition at the time of the survey. The reason for including this was because, as noted earlier, political parties can provide important mobilizing structures for protestors and opposition parties in particular are more likely to use protests as a means of indicating discontent.

At the country level, a measurement of the average real GDP per capita growth rate in the five years preceding the survey, calculated from the World Bank's World Development Indicators, was included to proxy for deprivation at the national level. Indeed, this indicator was used to test Gurr's (1968) claim that changes in the national economy, including inflation and growth rates, can also produce feelings of relative deprivation. In addition, the average of a country's ranking on Freedom House's civil liberties index in the five years before the survey was included to capture the level of political opportunities. The civil liberties index takes into account a number of factors that would presumably influence the potential for protest activity, including freedom of expression and belief, associational and organizational rights, rule of law, and personal autonomy and individual rights.[7] The index ranges from one to seven, with higher values indicating a more restrictive civil liberties environment. Finally, a dummy variable was included to capture whether elections (either presidential, legislative, or both) had occurred during the 12-month period prior to the survey collection.[8] Since protest activities in Africa tend to be higher around elections, including this dummy variable helps to control for any potential bias in the over-reporting of protest activity that may have otherwise been driven by the timing of the survey.

The results in Table 3.4 reveal four key findings. First, while individual factors tend to be associated with a majority of the variance related to the propensity to protest, country-level factors are not negligible. In fact, the country-level variables were statistically significant at explaining 13–24 percent of the variance in protest behaviour between the 36 and above and 18–24 year-old cohort, respectively. Although changes in GDP per capita do not appear to be relevant, individuals are less likely to protest in countries with worse rankings on the civil liberties index. However, this is only significant for the 25–35 and 36 and above cohorts, suggesting that the youngest cohort is less risk-averse. For the youngest

Table 3.4 Multi-level logit analysis of protest behaviour by age cohort

Variable	Ages 18–24	Ages 25–35	Ages 36 and above
Individual level			
Live in urban area	−0.051	0.009	−0.039
	(0.118)	(0.077)	(0.081)
Male	0.272***	0.297***	0.245***
	(0.101)	(0.069)	(0.073)
Member of religious group	0.277***	0.182**	0.197***
	(0.084)	(0.080)	(0.070)
Member of voluntary group	0.781***	0.716***	0.708***
	(0.103)	(0.105)	(0.083)
Unemployed	0.062	0.111	0.273***
	(0.080)	(0.077)	(0.092)
Level of education attained	0.095***	0.095***	0.055*
	(0.036)	(0.035)	(0.029)
Media index	0.295***	0.313***	0.357***
	(0.061)	(0.045)	(0.043)
Household deprivation index	0.080	0.171**	0.160**
	(0.072)	(0.072)	(0.064)
Close to opposition party	0.041	0.250**	0.331**
	(0.084)	(0.105)	(0.133)
Country level			
Civil liberties ranking (five-year average)	−0.115	−0.162*	−0.123**
	(0.095)	(0.086)	(0.059)
GDP per capita growth rate (five-year average)	−0.022	−0.048	−0.011
	(0.049)	(0.050)	(0.035)
Elections occurred in year prior to survey	0.509***	0.453**	0.287
	(0.193)	(0.227)	(0.176)
Constant	−3.512***	−3.610***	−3.858***
	(0.434)	(0.346)	(0.278)
Share of variance explained by country level	23.7%*	20.9%*	13%**
Number of individuals	8,401	13,644	18,244
Number of countries	28	28	28

Source: Afrobarometer Round 5, sub-Saharan African sample.

Notes: Coefficients are from multilevel random intercept models that are estimated using *gllamm* technique and incorporated both within and across country survey weights. Standard errors are in parentheses. Significant at the ***0.010, **0.05, and *0.10 levels.

cohort, however, having an election at any point during the 12 months prior to the survey was strongly associated with protest, hinting that elections served as a possible rallying point for their protest behaviour.

Secondly, grievance theory appears to have less explanatory power for understanding the protest behaviour of the youth. In fact, only among those aged 36 and above was being unemployed associated with protest. Based on the descriptive analysis in Table 2, one reason for this discrepancy could be that the youngest cohort has much higher unemployment and therefore it is less of a distinguishing feature for explaining disparities in mobilization within this cohort. In addition, household deprivation is not significantly associated with protest among 18–24-year-olds, though it is for the other age cohorts. While other studies using Afrobarometer have also found little support for the grievance theory (see Bratton et al. 2005), the present analysis highlights that this finding might be dependent on generational identity.

Thirdly and relatedly, the resource mobilization school has greater association with protest. This is evident across various measures of resources, including accessing the news more, being a member of a religious or voluntary group, and having higher levels of education. All of these variables are strongly substantively and statistically significant for all the age groups. This suggests that regardless of age, those who are already more engaged in their communities and aware of current events through the news and more education are more likely to mobilize via protest on behalf of their interests. As noted earlier, political parties can also be important sources of protest mobilization, and the opposition in particular is more likely to encourage protest than ruling parties. However, this appears to be less of an influence for 18–24-year-olds than for the older age cohorts.

Lastly, with respect to demographics, weak significance is attributed to urban residence. This is somewhat unexpected due to the longstanding scholarship emphasizing the importance of geographic proximity for protest (see Weiner 1967), and the fact that Africa's pro-democracy protests in the 1980s and 1990s were almost exclusively in urban areas (Bratton and van de Walle 1992). Yet, since proximity essentially facilitates information sharing about economic and political issues as well as when and where protests are expected to occur, the effects of this variable may be dampened when other factors that serve the same information sharing role (e.g. access to news, engagement in civic associations) are taken into account.

Conclusions

'Within each political generation – whether colonial, postcolonial, or multiparty – protest action is a prerogative of youth' (Bratton et al. 2005: 300). Indeed, African youth have historically played an important role in broader contestations over economic and political circumstances. This chapter has illustrated that even in more recent times, the youth are still the most likely to engage in protest. Over subsequent rounds of Afrobarometer surveys, African youth have continued to protest at higher rates than their older counterparts and, based on Round 5 of Afrobarometer, they are statistically more likely to protest than other age groups. These findings reflect those from other regions of the world (e.g. Bunce and Wolchik 2006; Valenzuela et al. 2012). Young people may be more likely to protest because they have more time for such activities due to a lack of career and familial responsibilities (see Barnes et al. 1979) or because they have more at stake and therefore a greater interest in influencing change in the short-term (Bloom 2012).

Nevertheless, it is important to keep in mind that this chapter also illustrated that only a small share of total African youth do actually protest while many more choose alternative modes of mobilization, including voting and participating in community meetings. In addition, the share of African youth protesting has declined over time and remains lower than in other regions of the world, such as North Africa. Moreover, the ACLED data revealed that only a small share of total protest events in Africa are exclusively led by young people and/or students.

Among those who do protest, the chapter revealed that rather than relative deprivation, access to requisite resources that facilitate information sharing and organization are more substantive predictors of protest activity. This is an important finding given the level of attention accorded to youth unemployment in Africa and dire predictions that grievances related to jobs, food, and water scarcity in the coming decades will be a catalyst for unrest spurred by this constituency (see NIC 2012). These grievances, especially among Africa's 18–24-year-olds, are necessary but not sufficient to engage in protests. Moreover, context is also important, with the youngest cohort less affected than older Africans by more restrictive civil liberties but more strongly associated with protest engagement during electoral periods.

This chapter concludes with two potential areas for further research. One relates to the recognition that protest activities are not only limited to demonstrations in the street but also increasingly involve the use of social media via computers and cell phones. This type of protest is not sufficiently captured in the Afrobarometer surveys and therefore could not be systematically explored here. Consequently, the true level of protest, across all age groups, may be understated here, especially among middle class African youth with computers, stable electricity, and internet connections. Future research could be done to validate in Africa the claims made in Latin America and North Africa that social media acts as an antecedent to, rather than substitute for, street protest by providing youth the tools to organize, create group identities, and find powerful mobilization frames (see de Zúñiga and Valenzuela 2011; Tufekci and Wilson 2012).

Secondly, this chapter was unable to systematically explore the underlying reasons why the youth choose to protest. The range of potential grievances is large, encompassing among other issues lack of decent jobs, poor quality schooling, high food and fuel prices, frequent service outages, prescriptions of foreign donors, constitutional infringements, and autocratic leadership. As a result, it is difficult to disentangle whether the youth employ protest to achieve broader economic, social, and political transformation or to meet narrower, more self-serving goals. Therefore, further exploration of the youth's motivations for protest, and how strongly they vary and interact within a specific country context, is essential for understanding what kind of progressive force youth protest actually represents.

Notes

1 See http://www.acleddata.com/.
2 Please see http://www.afrobarometer.org for more information. At the time of writing, the datasets for three countries (Ethiopia, South Sudan, and Sudan) had not yet been released. As such, the findings discussed here, and the statistical analyses presented

later in this chapter, exclude those countries. Moreover, Swaziland is also excluded because of too many missing variables on some of the key variables included in the subsequent statistical analysis, particularly affiliation to political party.

3 For both the UN and the AU, the lower threshold is 15. However, for ethical purposes, Afrobarometer only interviews individuals who are aged 18 and above, which is why that is the lower threshold.

4 See questions Q26A, Q26D, and Q26E in Afrobarometer Round 5.

5 This was calculated from the exponentiated coefficients from Table 3.

6 A fourth school of thought focuses on ideology and political values. One stream focuses on post-material and self-expressive values, especially in developed countries, whereby individuals are motivated by a desire to challenge authority and elites over issues about which they are passionate (e.g. climate change, gender equality, nuclear power) (Inglehart and Welzel 2005). Another looks at ideological extremism, finding that protests are more likely among those who adhere more closely with extremist views at either end of the ideological spectrum (see Powell 1982). However this school of thought cannot be explored in any detail in the current chapter because the Afrobarometer survey does not ask about post-material values and most parties in Africa are lacking readily distinguishable ideological content (see van de Walle 2003).

7 For more information, see http://www.freedomhouse.org/.

8 The dates for the most recent election that occurred prior to the Afrobarometer survey were determined by using the following source: www.electionguide.org.

References

Abbink, J. (2005). 'Being young in Africa: The politics of despair and renewal.' In J. Abbink and I. van Kessel (eds.), *Vanguard or Vandals: Youth, Politics, and Conflict in Africa*. Leiden, The Netherlands: Brill: 1–34.

African Union (AU). (2006). *African Youth Charter*. Adopted by the Seventh Ordinary Session of the Assembly, Bajul, The Gambia, 2 July.

Alexander, P. (2010). 'Rebellion of the poor: South Africa's service delivery protests – a preliminary analysis.' *Review of African Political Economy*, 37(123): 25–40.

Allman, J. (1990). 'The youngmen and the porcupine: class, nationalism and Asante's struggle for self-determination, 1954–1957.' *Journal of African History*, 31: 263–79.

Barnes, S., M. Kaase, and K. Allerback (1979). *Political Action: Mass Participation in Five Western Democracies*. Beverly Hills, CA: Sage Publications.

Bloom, D. (2012). 'Youth in the Balance.' *Finance and Development*, March: 6–11.

Brady, H., S. Verba, and K. Lehman Schlozman (1995). 'Beyond SES: A Resource Model of Political Participation.' *American Political Science Review* 89 (2): 271–94.

Bratton, M., R. Mattes and E. Gyimah-Boadi (2005). *Public Opinion, Democracy, and Market Reform in Africa*. Cambridge: Cambridge University Press.

Bratton, M., and N. van de Walle (1992). 'Popular Protest and Political Reform in Africa.' *Comparative Politics*, 24 (4): 419–42.

Brockett, C. (1991). 'The Structure of Political Opportunities and Peasant Mobilization in Central America.' *Comparative Politics*, 23(3): 253–274.

Bunce, V. and S. Wolchik (2006). 'Youth and Electoral Revolutions in Slovakia, Serbia, and Georgia.' *SAIS Review*, 26(2): 55–65.

Canache, D. (2002). *Venezuela: Public Opinion and Protest in a Fragile Democracy*. University of Miami: North-South Center Press.

Clines, F. (1994). 'New South Africa is Hoping to Channel its Youth Power.' *New York Times*, 23 April: 5.

Croucher, R. (2007). 'Organizing the Informal Economy: Results and Prospects-The Case of Ghana in Comparative Perspective.' In G. Wood and C. Brewster (eds.), *Industrial Relations in Africa*. New York, NY: Palgrave Macmillan

Dalton, R., A. van Sickle, and S. Weldon (2010). 'The Individual-Institutional Nexus of Protest Behaviour.' *British Journal of Political Science*, 40(1): 51–73.

de Zúñiga, G. and S. Valenzuela. (2011). 'The mediating path to a stronger citizenship: Online and offline networks, weak ties and civic engagement.' *Communication Research*, 38: 397–421.

Diouf, M. (1996). 'Urban Youth and Senegalese Politics: Dakar 1988–1994'. *Public Culture*, 8: 225–49.

Dulani, B., R. Mattes, and C. Logan (2013). 'After a Decade of Growth in Africa, Little Change in Poverty at the Grassroots.' *Afrobarometer Policy Brief No.1*.

Eisinger, P. (1973). 'The Conditions of Protest in American Cities.' *American Political Science Review*, 81: 11–28.

Filmer, D. and L. Fox (2014). *Youth Employment in Sub-Saharan Africa*. Washington, DC and Paris, France: World Bank and French Development Agency.

Geiger, S. (1997). *TANU women: gender and culture in the making of Tanganyikan nationalism, 1955–1965*. London, UK: Heinemann.

Goodfellow, T. (2013). 'The Institutionalisation of "Noise" and "Silence" in Urban Politics: Riots and Compliance in Uganda and Rwanda.' *Oxford Development Studies*, 41(4): 436–454.

Gurr, T. (1968). 'A Causal Model of Civil Strife: A Comparative Analysis Using New Indices.' *American Political Science Review*, 62: 1104–1124.

———. (1970). *Why Men Rebel*. Princeton, NJ: Princeton University Press.

———. (1985). 'On the Political Consequences of Scarcity and Economic Decline.' *International Studies Quarterly*, 29(1): 51–75.

Hamilton, R. (2010). 'Young standing up for democracy in Sudan; Movement forged in run-up to April elections encourages citizens to know and demand their rights.' *The Washington Post*, 14 August: A7.

Honwana, A. (2013). *Youth and Revolution in Tunisia*. London, UK: Zed Books.

Inglehart, R. and C. Welzel. (2005). *Modernization, Cultural Change, and Democracy: The Human Development Sequence*. New York: Cambridge University Press.

Kitschelt, H. (1986). 'Political Opportunity Structures and Political Protests: Anti-Nuclear Movements in Four Democracies.' *British Journal of Political Science*, 16 (1): 57–85.

Kittilson, M. C., and C. J. Anderson (2011). 'Electoral Supply and Voter Turnout'. In R. J. Dalton and C. J. Anderson (eds.), Ch. 2, *Citizens, Context, and Choice: How Context Shapes Citizens' Electoral Choices*. Oxford, UK: Oxford University Press.

Klandermans, B. (1997). *The Social Psychology of Protest*. Cambridge: Blackwell Publishers.

Lipsky, M. (1968). 'Protest as a Political Resource.' *American Political Science Review*, 62: 1144–58.

Mattes, R. (2008). 'The material and political bases of lived poverty in Africa: insights from the Afrobarometer.' *Afrobarometer Working Paper No. 98*.

Mattes, R. and M. Bratton (2007). 'Learning about Democracy in Africa: Awareness, Performance, and Experience.' *American Journal of Political Science*, 51(1): 192–217.

———. (2009). 'Poverty Reduction, Economic Growth and Democratization in Sub-Saharan Africa.' *Afrobarometer Briefing Paper No. 68*.

McAdam, D. (1982). *Political Process and the Development of Black Insurgency, 1930–1970*. Chicago, IL: University of Chicago Press.

McCarthy, J., and M. Zald (1977). 'Resource Mobilization and Social Movements: A Partial Theory.' *American Journal of Sociology*, 82 (6): 1212–41.

Meyer, D. (2004). 'Protest and Political Opportunities.' *Annual Review of Sociology*, 30: 125–145.

National Intelligence Council (NIC). 2012. *Global Trends 2030: Alternative Worlds*. Washington, DC: NIC.

Nkinyangi, J. (1991). 'Student Protests in Sub-Saharan Africa.' *Higher Education*, 22(2): 157–173.

Norris, P. (2002). *Democratic Phoenix: Reinventing Political Activism*. Cambridge, UK: Cambridge University Press.

Philipps, J. (2013). *Ambivalent Rage: Youth Gangs and Urban Protest in Conarky, Guinea*. Paris, France: L'Harmattan.

Pinstrup-Andersen, P. (ed.). (2014). *Food Price Policy in an Era of Market Instability: A Political Economy Analysis*. Oxford, UK: Oxford University Press.

Powell, G. B. (1982). *Contemporary Democracies: Participation, Stability, and Violence*. Cambridge, MA: Harvard University Press.

Putnam, R. (1993). *Making Democracy Work: Civic Traditions in Modern Italy*. Princeton, NJ: Princeton University Press.

Rabe-Hesketh, S., A. Skrondal, and A. Pickles (2005). 'Maximum likelihood estimation of limited and discrete dependent variable models with nested random effects.' *Journal of Econometrics*, 128: 301–323.

Raleigh, C., A. Linke, and C. Dowd (2014). *ACLED Codebook 3*. University of Sussex, University of Colorado (Boulder), and International Peace Research Institute, Oslo.

Raleigh, C., A. Linke, H. Hegre and J. Karlsen (2010). 'Introducing ACLED – Armed Conflict Location and Event Data.' *Journal of Peace Research* 47(5): 1–10.

Seekings, J. (1993). *Heroes or Villians? Youth Politics in the 1980s*. Johannesburg: Ravan Press.

Stasavage, D. (2005). 'Democracy and Education Spending in Africa.' *American Journal of Political Science* 49(2): 343–358.

Tarrow, S. (1998). *Power in Movement: Social Movements and Contentious Politics*. Cambridge, UK: Cambridge University Press.

Tilly, C. (1995). *Popular Contention in Great Britain 1758–1834*. Cambridge, MA: Harvard University Press.

Tufekci, Z. and C. Wilson (2012). 'Social Media and the Decision to Participate in Political Protest: Observations from Tahrir Square.' *Journal of Communication*, 62(2): 363–379.

Valenzuela, S., A. Arriagada, and A. Scherman (2012). 'The Social Media Basis of Youth Protest Behavior: The Case of Chile.' *Journal of Communication*, 62(2): 299–314.

Verba, S., K. L. Schlozman, and H. Brady (1995). *Voice and Equality: Civic Voluntarism in American Politics*. Cambridge, MA: Harvard University Press.

van de Walle, N. (2003). 'Presidentialism and clientelism in Africa's emerging party systems.' *Journal of Modern African Studies*, 41(2): 297–321.

Villalón, L. (1999). 'Generational Changes, Political Stagnation, and the Evolving Dynamics of Religion and Politics in Senegal.' *Africa Today*, 46 (3/4): 129–47.

Walton, J. and C. Ragin (1990). 'Global and National Sources of Political Protest: Third World Responses to the Debt Crisis.' *American Sociological Review*, 55 (6): 876–890.

Weiner, M. (1967). 'Urbanization and Political Protest.' *Civilisations*, 17(1/2): 44–52.

Wonacott, P. (2012). 'Youth Protests Shake Politics across Africa – Angola's Long-Serving President, Though Seen as Secure in Re-election, is one of many Facing Pressure in Arab Spring's Wake.' *Wall Street Journal*, 30 August: A16.

Part II

Youth aspirations in urban Africa

4 Cities of youth

Post-millennial cases of mobility and sociality

Karen Tranberg Hansen

Introduction

Africa's cities are a main stage for young lives in the present and will remain so in the future. This is so for demographic reasons which include, first, the continent's fast urbanization rate and predictions of continued future high growth rates, second, the high proportion of the total population who are young, and third, average longevity that is considerably lower than in the north. This dramatic temporality creates a distinct urban youth dynamic. Drawing on recent scholarship and my own research in Lusaka, Zambia's capital, this chapter identifies some of the far-reaching ramifications of this unique temporal triangulation for youth mobility and youth engagement with urban space both in a material and an aspirational sense.

Popular media and policy makers often view youth in Africa as a problem, as a population segment experiencing crisis and prone either to violence or inactivity, although recent scholarship is beginning to cast important light on young people's constructive engagement in different realms of activity (e.g. Frederiksen 2010; Honwana 2012). This chapter demonstrates how young African urban women and men are engaged in efforts to build livelihoods and create spaces of sociality in which they establish strategic interpersonal relationships, connections, and networks of solidarity. In effect, young urban Africans are well aware of 'being in the world' and act upon it at the same time as they negotiate their everyday world through practices they craft from local resources (Hansen 2008: 5). I make three interrelated arguments that revolve around the importance of the city, the distinctiveness of the present, and the salience of sociality. My goal is to demonstrate how urban space enables social interaction beyond the home and to show that such activities in turn shape the urban environment in which young people live and move.

To demonstrate this argument, I approach African urban youth in the here and now (Bucholtz 2002). Today in Africa, youth is not so much a 'lost generation' (Cruise O'Brien 1996) as it is a population segment whom adulthood easily eludes. The term the lost generation captured the failure of the nationalist project when the adverse effects of political crisis and economic decline restricted many young people's education, work, and political participation. Today's realities differ considerably, as I discuss in more detail shortly. Briefly, young people enjoy better educational access and are in many countries exposed to the ideals of participatory democracy. Yet their formal economic options are restrained. Several scholars have argued that youth find themselves waiting (Honwana 2012; Mains 2012). Honwana captures this condition well with the title of her recent book, *The Time of Youth*, which she characterizes as 'waithood.' But given the short average longevity in much of Africa compared to the north, I suggest the term 'forever youth' as a more fitting descriptor for today's urban youth experiences in much of Africa. I do so for want of a better term and in order to provoke us to understand the youth dynamic in the present. The term captures the importance of exploring what young people in fact are doing to get on with life. That is, their future is now, and they confront their circumstances in unique and creative ways, which in turn are shaping many features of urban life in Africa in the present. Of course, there are exceptions to this characterization as in the case of the young Tanzanian miners, discussed by Bryceson (this volume), who are forced by the unique circumstances of mining camps to assume adult responsibilities.

Turn-of-the millennium politico-economic changes have unsettled the linearity of the stage-wise unfolding of the life cycle once characteristic of social science youth analysis (France 2007). Assumptions associated with the growth of industrialized society in the north viewed youth as a transitional stage between education and work in a life course with three phases: childhood, adulthood, and old age. In this view, youth is a transitional category characterized by immaturity and dependence. Yet, stages of the life course differ both historically and culturally (Mintz 2008). In the present, the notion of stages are unsettled by globally reaching politico-economically transformations that almost everywhere are changing the transition from education to school as the straightforward road to adulthood. Instead we find a variety of models for youth, many scripts, sometimes running parallel with one another, while at other times different paradigms may dominate. In short, there are several pathways for getting on with life, which young people are crafting from diverse resources available to them. Some succeed in the short term, while others experience obstacles. The scholarship on which I draw views youth as a culturally constructed, context dependent experience. Thus youth identity is agentive, flexible, and situational (Bucholtz 2002: 533). The youth experience is significantly gendered, and it defines itself and is defined by others in generational terms in relation to adults. Almost everywhere, youth are enmeshed in unequal power relationships related to age and gender. And youth counts itself, and is counted by institutions and bureaucracy, in biological age terms that differ widely.[1]

Stimulated by my own study of young people in Lusaka, Zambia's capital, at the beginning of this millennium (Hansen 2008) and continued research periods with focus on a variety of topics throughout the past decade, I draw on recent works to explore what urban youth do about their own situation by showcasing studies of socio-economic mobility and sociality. As I discuss in the pages that follow, young Africans follow a variety of pathways towards economic participation and social life. Not all are successful, but many are, demonstrating both stamina and ingenuity. Almost everywhere, young people mobilize networks of solidarity, turning space into sociality that marks the urban social and cultural fabric. Identifying trends and themes in recent works I describe interaction that bring young people together around a variety of activities, among them, music, religion, and several types of recreational encounters, including sex. My discussion draws by and large on published scholarship from eastern and southern Africa. Except for Zimbabwe, the countries within this region have experienced relatively stable political regimes for several years. Some of these regimes remain authoritative and repressive. The countries within this region sadly lie within 'the HIV/AIDS belt,' in which HIV/AIDS is affecting a high proportion of the population and constituting a leading cause of death. This raises the troubling question of how young people live 'when death abounds' (Mususa 2012).

Throughout this chapter and reflecting my professional specialization, I have relied on anthropological research first; works in geography probably rank second in my coverage. I also use some works in public health and social medicine. My discussion is not meant to be exhaustive but selective by identifying what I consider to be important trends and observations in scholarship on youth and the city in Africa. Above all, except when referring to general observations, I draw on recent scholarship, that is, works published since the turn of the millennium. Much of this scholarship approaches both youth and the city constructively with a keen eye towards understanding youth efforts to get on with their lives as well as toward the city's ever changing connections to the countryside and the world beyond. Although I have tried to include works on youth from across the socio-economic spectrum, perhaps due to the invisibility of the affluent population in urban public space and problems of accessibility, the vast majority of the published works continue to focus on the urban poor.

The city, the present, and sociality

Urban settings provide the backdrop for a distinctive youth dynamic because of their scale, size, density, and heterogeneity. To be sure, young rural Africans interact around music, church, and pursue social and sexual relations of various types. But their access pales in comparison with the diversity of urban options and the scale of the urban built environment. Africa's big cities host government institutions and a vast bureaucratic apparatus, institutions of higher learning, commercial headquarters, and international agencies and NGOs. Although rural youth may pursue the performing arts, cities are where the main action is and where the local meets the global most dramatically. Last but not least, continued rural-urban migration coupled with natural urban population increase over the last few decades is contributing to widespread economic informalization almost everywhere across urban Africa.

The recent conjuncture of unprecedented urban growth with neoliberal economic policies has profound socio-spatial consequences that are influencing the actions of urban youth and their aspirations. Young people experience a different everyday world than that so deeply restrained by the structural adjustment programmes of a bygone era.[2] Today's youth have better access to education than their parents' generation and are exposed to a democratic political rhetoric that makes them keen on participation. Although socio-economic developments in most of the countries in this region have improved since the turn of the millennium, youth unemployment is widespread and formal politics remain gerontocratic and clientelistic in many countries. As a result, young people wait.

Urban space across the region has been radically transformed in many ways since the liberalization of many economies and the involvement of foreign investment interests in anything from infrastructure, to office buildings, hotels, sports stadiums, to open air markets, requiring changes in zoning rules and prompting population shifts. In many countries open-air markets near central business districts are being demolished or upgraded to yield space for higher income activities. Everywhere, there are new shopping malls, most of them featuring South African franchises and 'China shops' (Dobler 2009). Current urban planning policies tend to prioritize high cost business developments over low cost housing. Although several countries in the region have experienced positive GNP growth during the recent economic crisis in the north, their large urban populations have not benefitted much.

Across urban Africa, the gulf between the tiny group of the very wealthy and the great mass of the very poor is increasing. Cape Town, for example, is South Africa's most racially segregated and socially unequal city (Besteman 2008). Here, as elsewhere in urban areas in the region, the very rich live in gated neighbourhoods while the poor live in settlements characterized by crowding and lack of infrastructure. Urban households tend to be large, containing immediate kin and attached relatives with children and young people frequently moving between households. Many young people cannot afford to rent rooms or houses but remain dependent members of households, subject to the authority of others; and some, who have become orphans due to disease and death of parents and guardians, at an early age become effective heads of households consisting of younger siblings and perhaps a grandparent. As I demonstrate shortly, to get on with life in the shadow of death requires not only resources and social relations but also youth drive and energy (Bajaj 2008).

Cities are not neutral backdrops to the lives of their young residents. Urban settings linked economically, socially, and culturally to countries across the African continent and worlds beyond it, providing resources and imaginaries young women and men make use of in their efforts to fulfill everyday needs and desires as they plan for, or hope about, their futures. Sociality resulting from diverse types of interaction is salient to their efforts to get on with their lives at the same time as some young people work around the cultural norms and institutions that are circumscribing their lives and activities.

Socioeconomic mobility

Employment for young people is everywhere a problem in Africa, much like in the North, but unlike the North, many countries in the South never had much of a formal employment scene to begin with. Although many countries now provide free primary school education, not all school age children go to school because of lack of school places and widespread poverty coupled with complicated household situations where parents or guardians have passed away. Paradoxically, in spite of expanding access to education, in several countries, twenty-first century socioeconomic developments in Africa's rapidly growing urban areas still reproduce illiteracy among sections of the very poor at the same time as young people from affluent backgrounds obtain post-graduate education in the world's top institutions (Bourgouin 2012). Local secondary school education that in the immediate post-independence decades assured jobs to many graduates no longer provides a direct line to employment. Likewise, university degrees in many countries do not guarantee well-paid positions. Against this depressing backdrop, it is not surprising that informality is the organizational logic that drives much urban economic activity with young women and men pressing on the informal job scene. Meanwhile those who do not make it may 'get stuck in the compound' (Hansen 2005).[3]

Recent scholarship has detailed some of the trials and tribulations of young people who do not find jobs from remarkably different perspectives. In a study entitled *Stuck: Rwandan Youth and the Struggle for Adulthood*, Sommers (2012) ranges over a wide field, both rural and urban. In Kigali, he describes young women and men who have migrated to the capital because of lack of options in their home areas. In bleak terms, the author depicts poor young men who feel isolated and without opportunities, and young women who turn to prostitution. 'Male youth with little hope of becoming men, female youth trapped in prostitution,' he notes, ' and the grinding lives that so many youth led do not inspire cautious sexual behaviour' (ibid.: 200). The pervasiveness of fatalistic behaviour described in this study and young people's awareness of doom (ibid.: 180) may have to do with the poverty focus of the work and the Rwandan background of political upheaval and authoritarian government policies.

The scenario depicted by Sommers differs considerably from that presented in the somewhat similarly entitled work undertaken in Jimma, a provincial town in Ethiopia, *Hope is Cut: Youth, Unemployment, and the Future in Urban Ethiopia* (Mains 2012) in which the author takes us into the lives of young people, revealing a diversity of possible life courses that are not encompassed by Sommers' focus on crisis, perhaps in part due to different research methodologies. Sommers' work was conducted by several interviewers in different locations whereas Mains' longitudinal research provides detailed observations based on his enduring interaction with several young people. The actors are mainly young men, secondary school graduates, who come from better-off backgrounds than the Kigali youth and tend to have access to some resources from familial or friendly networks. His focus is on the importance of employment and work within their lives. Most of these young men decline jobs they consider to be culturally degrading. As a result they wait, sometimes continuing university studies. They wait, talking with their friends while chewing khat, in the process establishing mutually beneficial relationships that facilitate exchange relationships (ibid.: 113–130). They discuss a variety of pathways to mobility, some of them including local and international migration. Because it provides access to not only material goods but also social networks, employment is critical for these young men's hopes for the future (ibid.: 89). Work, in this case, 'is not simply a means of accessing income but of situating oneself in relation to others, in both the present and the future' (ibid.: 96). And friendship, notes Mains 'without some form of economic exchange is almost inconceivable' (ibid.: 121). As I show later, a very similar observation can be made with reference to the role of economic exchange in sexual relations.

Young people in Zambia refer to waiting as 'just sitting.' But in Lusaka, sitting does not necessarily entail idleness but rather the search for opportunities. Depending on socioeconomic background, youth may pursue post-graduate education at university or business schools; there are vocational trading schools, and many NGOs offer practical training courses. Some young people combine education and training with informal work as a way of earning money for consumption. Some young women and men who establish themselves as entrepreneurs do quite well and especially enjoy being their own bosses. At the very base of Lusaka's street economy, all these options are actively pursued, some youth viewing work as an end, others as a means, like 21-year-old Ronnie who sold DVDs on the street in front of one of Lusaka's largest market complexes, copies mostly, of popular Nigerian, Ghanaian, Indian, South African, and American productions. He had spent less than one year in Lusaka, arriving straight out of school (grade 11) from the Northern Province and initially staying with an uncle. Unmarried, he shared two rented rooms with a friend in one of Lusaka's oldest and poorest settlements. When I met him in 2010, Ronnie had sold DVDs for around three month for a vendor of socks and belts in another location, receiving a small monthly wage, food, and transport money as well as a daily bonus, depending on sales. Prior to this, he walked around the market complex, selling plastic shopping bags. His uncle had provided start-up money. But Ronnie's real vocation was music. 'I am a composer,' he said, writing Zambian 'traditional' songs. He explained that he had come to Lusaka to record music with a group with whom he already had produced eight songs and one video. In short, Ronnie considered his job as a street vendor to be temporary and his desires for the future did not relate to the street economy (Hansen and Nchito 2013: 64).

Alongside the employment dynamics just depicted, new figures of success are emerging to inspire aspirations, as we have just seen. They include but are not restricted to popular musicians both male and female, and pastors, again both male and female, as well as sport stars especially football players, and various types of professionals.

Music scene

The lively popular music scene across the cities of the region not only provides jobs but also recreational space for leisure and pleasure. The music scene creates a cultural space that reaches far beyond the individual city and country, yet is also intertwined with the experiences of everyday life in ways that resonate with their time and place. Music permeates urban space transmitted from radio stations and CDs in homes, and is played in shops, markets, private cars, and busses. There is a nightclub scene ranging from taverns in the townships to sleek city bars. Around election times, NGOs recruit popular musicians for live performances to rally young people to vote. NGOs concerned with HIV/AIDS frequently hire musicians to perform at events like World AIDS Day, attracting thousands of young people.

Most of the recent works about music focus on genres/styles and the contents of lyrics rather than on the livelihoods of performers and the interaction that arises around music events and venues. In the first half of the 2000s in Lusaka, many different music styles were performed in English and local languages. You could hear rumba and zoukous from the Congo, kwaito from South Africa, Afropop from Nigeria, Zam-ragga, hip-hop, and rap. Observing the top-ten charts for two months in 2004, I found the treacherous path toward adulthood to be an important theme. The top ten lyrics depicted young people as creators of their own problems and authors of their own solutions. Some music hits admonished young people about the dangers of indulgence, including sex, and consumption (Hansen 2008: 117–19). Drawing on music mostly between 2005 and 2010 in her research on Zambia's Copperbelt, Mususa found popular lyrics to urge young people to keep on trying; and to attempt not one but different paths to explore and open up the world. In an argument resonating with Mains she concluded that 'the possibilities for what the future may bring emerge from the environment and people's engagement with it and each other' (Mususa 2012: 319).

Urban grooves music based on hip-hop emerged in Zimbabwe when the ruling party ZANU-PF demanded the arts to produce anti-Euro-American propaganda. Performing in local languages, the artists expressed resistance to Western cultural imperialism, but they also subverted the government's control of social memory. The young artists addressed uncomfortable topics of everyday survival, challenging widespread intergenerational and gender relations, including normative notions of sexuality. The urban grooves music initially created employment for aspiring artists but was banned in 2007, seven years after it first emerged, because it was considered subversive (Manase 2009; Mate 2012). Popular lyrics and individual performers and groups have been banned for political reasons in other countries, including Zambia and Senegal.

In South Africa during apartheid, rap music expressed a form of resistance. Its initial popularity offered the possibility of earning a living. The music provided young people with a voice and, argues Kunzler (2011: 31), turned rappers into agents of social change. Most rappers were male as were the production structures, as is the case with most popular music the world over. Today's popular music scene in South African urban settings also includes kwaito and house music, both of which are selling better than rap. Among the kwaito stars a material culture of success appears to be developing, where success materializes into emblematic objects as extensions of star status along with a particular body culture.

The interplay between music and urban locality is illustrated in a lively analysis of Bullet ya Kaoko, the most popular band in Opuwo (a small town in northern

Namibia), that has become noted across the country and the wider region. Using keyboards and synthesizers to rework the existing genre of praise songs, Bullet ya Kaoko fuses kwaito moves with warrior dance steps while weaving Herero polyphony into a jive-like beat. The lyrics, music, and dance address the challenges of everyday urban life and its uncertainties at the same time as they evoke a sense of belonging that challenges both the old and the new. In this way the local particularities of a small town influence the music that people in the streets are listening to, and the music, in turn, shapes their own experience (van Wolputte and Bleckmann 2012: 413–36). Achieving local and national celebrity status, this small town band represented Namibia with their deeply locally inflected music at the 2012 Football World Cup in South Africa.

Religious space

Gospel music appears to be selling especially well in South Africa (Kunzler 2011: 40), and in Zambia, gospel is listened to widely and even performed in some nightclubs (Hansen 2008: 117). Religion, as these examples demonstrate, is a pervasive force, affecting everyday lives in many ways, in religious settings as well as beyond them. In eastern and southern Africa, Christianity is widespread and Zambia, for example, was declared a 'Christian nation' in the early 1990s. While Islam is a force to be reckoned with in Tanzania and Kenya and less so in South Africa, the proportion of Islamic believers elsewhere in the region is small. Providing spiritual nodes of being and belonging, religious movements may help construct new visions of identity and community, promising young people 'a future that already exists' (Diouf 2003:7). Judging from recent scholarship, growing numbers of young people are joining religious movements, including Islamic groups, mainline churches, and increasingly, Pentecostal churches (Becker and Geisler 2007; Bochow and van Dijk 2012).

The growing popularity of Pentecostal Christianity across Africa creates space for young people to congregate for religious sociality, job openings, and potentially influences widespread gender ideologies, reshaping normative notions of male superiority and female subordination. Several recent works examine changing constructions of masculinity influenced by Pentecostal notions of companionate marriage and gender equality. Most of the works are church-based, and only rarely do scholars explore how Pentecostal believers organize their everyday lives when away from church space. It is important to explore the significance of religiosity beyond the church, argues Haynes in a study of the prosperity gospel on the Zambian Copperbelt. Believers are embedded in social relationships that include non-church members in networks of exchange that are an important dimension of urban sociality in Zambia (Haynes 2012).

Pentecostal churches are hierarchically organized. Even then, in the face of declining civil service and public sector employment, becoming a pastor constitutes an alternate career path. Quite a while ago, van Dijk (1992) noted that young born-again pastors in Malawi not only created new urban space for social mobility but also distanced themselves from their seniors. Although her recent research focuses on Kumasi in Ghana, Lauterbach's (2010: 273) observations about the intergenerational relationship between the young and senior pastors will resonate beyond the country. She noted that young pastors do not wait until they become senior by age until they build up their positions. Pastorship, she explains, 'is a life trajectory or a career that involves skillful navigation between being protected and being promoted by a senior pastor and making enough space to be able to grow' (ibid.: 274–75). Setting up their own churches, they escape the dependency on senior pastors. Drawing on diverse social networks and resources, they skillfully create space to 'become someone,' by reinventing status and power in their local setting.

The young people whose involvement with mainline and Pentecostal churches I studied in Lusaka in 2003 came to church for many reasons. Churches have extensive social involvements, including educational programmes and clinics, HIV/AIDS prevention programmes, lay activity, programmes for couples, women, children, and increasingly a variety of youth activities. Many churches offer skills training of various kinds and programmes for orphans and street children (Hansen 2008: 113–17). Some of the Pentecostal churches that are supported by large churches in the United States, Nigeria, and Brazil, have IT facilities and instrument rooms for practice at the church site that attract youth, enhancing the significance of religious sociality.

Pentecostal faith, for one, appears to offer a strategy for urban living that may have special appeal to young people in their formative age. The churches encourage morality, responsibility, discipline, and hard work. The blueprint for family living stresses monogamy, marriage as a precursor to child bearing and puts the husband in charge of households as the chief provider. I found in Lusaka that Pentecostal faith helped young men fashion, at least temporarily, a construction of masculinity that differed from the aggressive, sexually active version so prevalent in urban Zambia. They subordinated this dominant version to a notion of manhood as disciplined, careful, hardworking, and not 'indulging,' that is, not drinking, smoking, taking drugs, and pursuing casual sex (Hansen 2008: 115). Van Klinken (2012) made similar observations among young men attending a long-established Pentecostal church in Lusaka with a largely middle-class following. On being born again, they renounced their prior life as 'bad boys,' giving up the 'manly norms' of drinking and womanizing. In the process, these men considered themselves better men than they were before their conversion and better than their former peers. Their male identity, the author claims, is not damaged but rather reshaped and reaffirmed (ibid.: 220–21).

While Pentecostalism remains hierarchical and male dominated, within it here is room for some redefinition of patriarchy and gender roles. As there are new notions of manhood available, likewise there are new images of what it means to be a woman. In a study of young single professional women with tertiary education and management careers in the Gauteng area (greater Johannesburg), Frahm-Arp (2012) engages with the dilemma these Pentecostal women encounter. They dream about the social ideal and symbol of social and economic success, consisting of a nuclear family of husband, wife, and two-to-three children. But the social and religious worlds in which they live exert a set of contradictory pressures they find difficult to balance. One is that men want sex and children; the second is that women want to marry first. The pressures make them struggle to find suitable husbands to marry (ibid.: 370). Pentecostal churches provide social space in which singleness is an accepted state. And church interaction encourages the women to keep alive their dream of marriage, nuclear family, and fulfilling normative gender roles while pursuing their personal economic plans.

Tensions around gender and sexuality are marked in Pentecostal settings. In Cape Town's low-income areas, Pentecostal youth struggle to reconcile the call for sexual abstinence with other notions of intimate life. In such settings, religious teachings about sexuality 'sit uneasily with the social and cultural realities that structure the lives of most urban youth' (Burchardt 2011:669). Young people negotiate Pentecostal sexual morality by shifting dating practices and sexual intercourse across different spaces and times, alternating between Sunday services, workshop settings, and township streets (2011:674). Importantly, the author stresses a point that rarely is mentioned in other works on Pentecostalism carried out exclusively in church settings. At issue is church membership, which fluctuates considerably, in the Cape Town context probably reflecting the insecure economic situation, frequent changes of young people's residence as well as their on and off interest in church community life (2012:674).

There is a widespread moral double standard across the gender divide. In spite of discourses about abstinence, having multiple partners demonstrates the virility of men in the eyes of their peers (Burchardt 2010:65). On Makerere University's campus Pentecostal promotion of sexual abstinence clashes with sexual practices among women students who experience pressure from peers to pursue a lifestyle of tangible and visible means. When young campus men cannot deliver the mobile phones, shopping trips, clothes, dinner, and nightlife, young women turn their attention to older, financially stable, successful, and often, married men. Some young women who declare their born-again conversion use Pentecostalism's insistence on abstinence as a strategy to avoid sex, promising sex in the future by extracting money in a practice referred to as 'de-toothing.' The strategy creates a risky sexual dynamic because of the implicit understanding of reciprocity connected with gift-giving (Sadgrove 2007:123–26).

Sexual practices

In popular and religious discourse, sexual activity is often conflated with adulthood. But on the ground in Africa today, sexuality reaches the core of constructions of both youth and gender identities. Young Africans' ideal of sexual relations combines notions of romantic love with emotional attachments and sexual exclusivity. Both young women and young men engage in casual sex but on different terms (Burchardt 2011: 678). Because nearly half of all new cases of HIV/AIDS worldwide occur among young people between the ages of 15–25 years, young people's intimate lives demand our attention. The gendered nature of the disease and women's particular vulnerabilities make young women in the

15–25 year age range infected at much higher rates that young men of the same age group (McIlwaine and Datta 2004: 483). For this, we blame unequal gender relations combined with socio-economic pressures to make a living. The result is sex for money and/or a variety of material goods.

Intimate relationships are often accompanied by gifts and exchange, and the transactional nature of sexual behaviour has prompted an extensive literature. As Sadgrove (2007:121) cautiously comments: 'it is difficult for the outside observer to quantify the proportion of sexual relationships that exist as a series of transactions, and those which sexual intimacy is motivated by a broader set of emotional, physical, social and relational concerns.' A constructive approach to exploring this entangled topic is to suggest, as I did earlier, that money and love do not inevitably exclude one another. Hunter (2002; 2009) has made this argument forcefully for South Africa.

Ideals of love are bound up with desires for material goods. Among like-age young people in a study in Durban, gift-giving was important in shaping sexual relationships. Young people associated money with prostitution but did not view gifts in that way. They rather saw gifts as a regular part of dating experiences, a natural part of a relationship that did or did not involve sexual coercion (Kaufman and Stavrou 2004:378). In Johannesburg, young women hoped for relationships of financial independence and freedom to make decisions about sexuality, yet a study found that most of them were in relationships marked by partner violence, infidelity, and lack of condom use. The women also acknowledged the importance of financial support when they enter intimate relationships although their desire is for emotional intimacy and love (Pellitor et al. 2012: 487). The disconnection between expectations and lived reality is striking and young women's economic insecurity makes them vulnerable.

Observations about transactional sex among low-income youth in Dar es Salaam parallel these findings. Sex was exchanged for money or material goods in all types of relationships, including from committed partners. Rather than seeing themselves as exploited victims, the young women talked about extracting material support from partners as an active strategy to initiate, maintain, and terminate relationships, labeling it 'skinning the goat' (Maganja et al. 2007). On a South African university campus in the Western Cape, sugar daddies and 'ministers of finance' were a common presence involving richer male students, sugar daddies, and employed men from off campus. Although economic motivations were uppermost, women considered a range of other resources to be important in transactional sexual relations, which they did not necessarily view as exploitative, but occasionally as equitable. Such transactional sexual encounters were not only about money but also involved other exchanges, benefitting both men and women (Shefer et al. 2012: 442).

Among young urban professionals attitudes toward sex are more relaxed, perhaps because they are fairly securely positioned economically. Among them we may see shifts in attitudes to gender and sexuality that lessen the hold of existing gerontocratic and patriarchal power structures. Such a shift is beginning to be noted in South Africa where the 1996 Constitution and Bill of Rights are destabilizing long-held expressions of sexuality. Even then, as I discuss shortly, this does not represent a complete break with the past, and violent masculinities have according to one observer become more violent than in the past (Walker 2005: 226–27). Young professionals born and raised in Nairobi and working as IT specialists, accountants, and junior NGO staff were financially independent from relatives with the freedom to enjoy their own life. They preferred to delay marriage until they reached their 30s, because they wanted to work on their careers, or did not want the responsibility of married life. Discussing how these young professionals used media as tools to envision new types of intimate relations, Spronk explores how Western romantic films, locally produced magazines, and church counseling classes exposed these young professionals to a variety of love scripts (Spronk 2009a). Their careers were important markers of their self-identification as were 'fashionable dressing, going out and progressive attitudes' (Spronk 2009b: 504). Although they represent a minority group, these young professionals are easily recognizable in the urban landscape. They are cosmopolitans, argues the author, but with a Kenyan flavour of which they are proud.

Space, place, and social relations

How do young urban African women and men experience their situation? The secondary school students in Lusaka who in the early part of this millennium wrote essays for me on what it meant to be a young person in Zambia's capital explained that being in the city was where life was happening, in real terms as well as in their imagination. Everywhere in their narratives were the icons of modern life: shopping malls, institutions of learning, electricity, television, cars, and discos, along with the architecture of government, its institutions, international agencies, and commercial firms. They also took note of the big, urban markets and the crowded, low-income residential areas where they would rather not live, if they had a choice. The young women were more cautious in their urban enthusiasm than the young men, expressing concerns about their freedom to move in urban public space (Hansen 2008).

Where do young people socialize? The vast majority who reside in crowded quarters in low-income residential areas get together away from home in streets, neighbourhood markets, pool halls, and local drinking venues. Such areas frequently are located at some distance from the central business districts. When they have the means to travel into the city, they may go to shopping malls to meet friends, hang out in the food courts, and window shop. The big public markets in most African cities also attract youth both for business and social activity. Because of the overall lack of places for peer sociality in the low-income residential areas, streets are central to young people's dating landscape. Cramped living conditions at home limit places for sexual play, and young lovers seek recourse to backyard shacks, paths between buildings, and open areas between the townships. In the late 1980s, when I consulted court records from one of Lusaka's low-income townships about claims for compensation ('damages') in cases of premarital pregnancy, I commonly found pregnant young women explaining that they had met their partner in the street (Hansen 1997: 147–156).

Place and personhood are intimately interconnected and influence experiences of place attachment. Young people's experience of 'where they are' and 'how they live' in Lusaka; that is, in the low-income areas, mediates their understanding of what they might become, and what it takes to move beyond their present circumstances (Hansen 2005:12; 2008:107–09). The dynamic interconnections between conditions of place, relationships, and personhood have been explored in a variety of other urban settings, focusing for example on the tensions in inter-generational relationships between young peri-urban women in Zimbabwe and their mothers due to socioeconomic transformations during the first decades after independence in 1980 (Adams 2009).

Specific parts of cities characterized by precarious livelihoods readily acquire negative place associations. For example, young men in South Africa's urban areas are frequently depicted as violent, if not criminals, and gangsters. Yet growing up on the Cape Flats in Cape Town, not all young men fit these images. Studying young male high school students at close range, Lindegaard (2009: 19; 230) demonstrates that they managed to lead normal lives not characterized by crime and violence in spite of the miserable conditions in which they frequently grew up. Some of these young men developed routes that took them away from criminal pathways and were able to make plans for the future even in the face of changes in society around them.

Although not all young men in the Cape Flats end up in gangs, many consider joining a group because of its importance in navigating the streets of the township. Such groups provide their members with protection in a dangerous environment. Jensen (2006) analysed the reconfiguration of backstreet urban space on the Cape Flats where young coloured men congregate to navigate the terrains of violence. The confinement resulting from their activities produced as sense of territoriality specific to the young men's everyday life worlds and their relations to state institutions. In such groups, place and personhood came together in producing a particular violent masculine identity and criminal livelihood. In the popular discourse of space and social relations, such spaces are equated with and treated as gang territory (Jensen 2006: 288–89).

Trans-local spaces

Sociality is not always or necessarily space-and place-associated but rather global in scope. This is evident from the emergence of sites of interaction around popular culture, such as music and media use. The case of sport provides an excellent example. The power of sport to bring people together, including youth, has been well-documented in terms of playing but less so in terms of viewing. Throughout the cities of the region in recent years, venues for electronic viewership of sport have proliferated, extending from the townships, to video clubs, upscale bars, and special theatre showings. Collective viewing occurs in private households in the townships as well and in video parlours in township markets that charge a small fee for viewers of sport, blue movies, and Indian and Nigerian films, among others.[4]

A recent study of collective football viewing describes such venues as trans-local 'stadiums' (Akindes 2011). Football, the most popular sport in Africa by far, provides a recreational outlet for young men and increasingly, young women (Hansen 2014). The international migration it has fuelled has landed African players on football teams across the world. It is not surprising that football playing is part of many young men's imaginary. What is more, football viewing on television is generating a new form of fandom that is primarily urban, creating a palpable experience in African urban space. During important games, the streets are empty. Urban residents are glued to the television set at home, with neighbours and friends, or at a bar or special venue. 'The collective convergence,' observes Akindes (2011:2180), 'of a whole city or nation is visual and audible.' When in February 2012 the Zambian 'chipolopolo boys' won the Africa Cup of Nations over the Ivory Coast, they were met on their return in the international airport by a thunderous welcome, song, and dance by jubilant fans, who lined up alongside the streets into the city. The fans were dressed in creative costumes and their faces painted in the national colours while vuvuzelas and car horns were sounding loudly as the open vehicle with the winning team, proudly displaying the Africa Cup trophy, wound its way into the city.

Trans-local stadiums and their accompanying fandom enable the temporary creation of a localized collective sociality, which is neither unique to Africa nor specific to youth. Still, such a localized collective sociality matters importantly to African urban youth, permitting them an embedded platform for participation that is both local and global, giving them the experience of being-in-the-world rather than confined, for example, to a generator operated TV in a low-income settlement without electricity.

Because of its collective aspect, this kind of trans-national sociality differs from the interaction created through mobile telephony, which is connecting Africans at faster rates than anywhere else (Hansen 2014). The active mobile phone users include young entrepreneurs, accessing social networks for resources, and young lovers making dates. There is also Internet dating, which in Ghana is enabling urban youth to meet, chat, and form distance relationships with people from across the world, crafting desired lifestyles, and forming identities (Fair et al. 2009). The Internet no doubt is involving urban youth across the continent who have the skills and means to engage in trans-local identity and relationship quests, the ramifications of which invite our attention as scholars. Taken together, the relations young people craft in the process of pursuing their ambitions contribute to the creation of a virtual space that is simultaneously local and global.

Conclusion

As this chapter has demonstrated from eastern and southern Africa, cities are where the action is for young people. This is so because of the unique temporal triangulation (high urbanization rates, marked youth bulge, and low life expectancy) that make African urban youth is a high profile issue and because of the size, scale, density, and heterogeneity of urban areas. The recent regional scholarship I have drawn on reveals several crucial observations that may contribute to qualify some of the conventional wisdom about urban youth. Importantly, young people are not idling, passively waiting for things to happen, even if they describe themselves, as in Zambia, as 'just sitting.' While waiting, they craft interpersonal relationships that are important to their everyday existence and to their future. When addressing the urban youth dynamic, scholars and policy makers must take into account the new experiences of young people that the last two decades of political and economic transformations, with their changes in markets, employment, and household arrangements, have helped set into motion.

Taken together, these studies demonstrate that the time of urban youth is now, which is why it may make sense to characterize them, provocatively as I suggested at the outset, as 'forever youth.' In effect, their future has already begun. The term 'forever youth' reckons with the simultaneity of different youth scripts and trajectories, some operating alongside each other while others are in conflict with dominant notions of gender and personhood or contest them. Above all in this chapter , the term 'forever youth' has helped me showcase youth interaction in the here and now related to efforts at creating livelihoods as well as to spaces of sociality where young women and men establish interpersonal relationships, connections, and networks of solidarity.

Such observations have consequences in many domains of urban life from sexual and gender relations that introduce new ideas of love and family structure in an expanding engagement with religion and media to self-identification as a born-again, a designer who is the boss of a small enterprise, to an identity as a young IT professional with global exposure. Such youth identities are agentive and situational. Alongside new ideas remain difficulties many young men experience in establishing independent households and women in finding the right marriage partners, which in turn encourage intermittent sexual relations, and the prolongation of youth is likely to affect the age and rate of marriage as well as the birth rate. Meanwhile, some young women find new options to pursue single lives, at least for a while.

Overall, the scholarship on which I have drawn opens windows onto ongoing shifts in the cultural norms and practices that guided an older generation, even though hierarchically structured gender relations continue to shape male to female interaction among young people and between them and their seniors within the home, in the streets, and in public settings. Social and economic resources play in here as young urbanites in well-paid positions find more freedom to pursue their individual desires; the very poor, on the other hand, may be propelled into risky activities by economic and household adversity. Above all, the recent works demonstrate the significance of social relations and sociality for young people's trajectories. Young people's efforts at crafting sociality are not confined by the boundaries of households and residential areas but also take place within the city and beyond, connecting them, as in life-style and consumption pursuits, and in electronic sport viewing, with people and worlds far away from home.

Recent worldwide politico-economic changes have significantly changed the urban life options of today's youth compared to their parents' generation. New success figures give evidence of how changes in economy, functioning of markets, and social fabric are converging to produce emerging opportunity structures (Banegas and Warnier 2001). This chapter has introduced the young Pentecostal pastor who becomes someone of importance in his local setting by establishing himself as head of a new church, away from the demands of senior pastors. Then there are the musicians, including aspiring ones as Ronnie is Lusaka whose desire is to compose, rather than to work as a street vendor. And although most are likely to remain where they are, many young people practice sports as an important part of their recreation, which has opened up avenues to local stardom and international celebrity status and plays an important role in activating young people's imagination about lives in the future. Meanwhile, young successful business professionals from affluent backgrounds across the continent in middle and senior management positions pursue cosmopolitan lifestyles within new emerging social hierarchies with global reach. There is no doubt that new opportunity structures will emerge over the short and longer term as young urban people in Africa with drive and energy bring their skills and resources to bear on getting on with their lives.

Notes

1 There are differences, for example, between youth definitions used by the UN, the African Union, and the ILO. This volume has adopted the broad age span from the African Union, which defines youth as ranging from 15–35 years of age.
2 The 1980s and 1990s were characterized by neo-liberal structural adjustment programmes aimed at fiscal restraint while encouraging foreign investment and private enterprise under the aegis of market forces. The increased poverty rates these programmes helped to generate in many countries have been addressed in the most recent World Bank development approach in so-called Poverty Reduction Strategy Programmes (PRSP) that seek to improve education and health and create economic growth in selected sectors with investment potential. The PRSP approach is tied up with political and economic decentralization.
3 The colloquial term compound refers in Zambia to informal urban settlement.
4 I have seen such parlours in markets in Lusaka but have not come across any scholarship analysing the significance neither of their operation as an income source nor of their consumption.

References

Adams, M. (2009). 'Playful Places, Serious Times: Young Women Migrants from a Peri-urban Settlement, Zimbabwe.' *Journal of the Royal Anthropological Institute*, 15: 797–814.
Akindes, G. A. (2011). 'Football Bars: Urban Sub-Saharan Africa's Trans-local 'Stadiums.'' *The International Journal of the History of Sport*, 28(15): 2176–90.
Bajaj, M. (2008). 'Schooling in the Shadow of Death: Youth Agency and HIV/AIDS in Lusaka.' *Journal of Asian and African Studies*, 43(3): 307–29.

Banegas, R., and J. P. Warnier (2001). 'Nouvelles Figures de la Reussite et du Pouvoir.' *Politique Africaine*, 85: 5–21.

Becker, J., and P. W. Geisler (2007). 'Introduction: Searching for Pathways in a Landscape of Death.' Special Issue on Religion and AIDS in East Africa. *Journal of Religion in Africa*, 37(1): 1–15.

Besteman, C. (2008). *Transforming Cape Town*. Berkeley: University of California Press.

Bochow, A., and R. van Dijk (2012). 'Christian Creations of New Spaces of Sexuality, Reproduction, and Relationships in Africa: Exploring Faith and Religious Heterotopia.' Special Issue, *Journal of Religion in Africa*, 42(4): 325–344.

Bourgouin, F. (2012). 'On Being Cosmopolitan: Lifestyle and Identity of African Finance Professionals in Johannesburg.' *Ethnos*, 77(1): 50–71.

Bucholtz, M. (2002). 'Youth and Cultural Practices.' *Annual Review of Anthropology*, 31: 525–52.

Burchardt, M. (2010). 'Ironies of Subordination: Ambivalences of Gender and Religious AIDS Interventions in South Africa.' *Oxford Development Studies*, 38(1): 63–82.

———. (2011). 'Challenging Pentecostal Moralism: Erotic Geographies, Religion and Sexual Practices among Township Youth in Cape Town.' *Culture, Health & Sexuality*, 13(6): 669–83.

Cruise O'Brien, D. B. (1996). 'A Lost Generation? Youth Identity and State Decay in West Africa.' In R. Werbner and T. Ranger (eds.), *Postcolonial Identities in Africa*. London: Zed Books.

Diouf, M. (2003). 'Engaging Postcolonial Culture: African Youth and Public Space.' *African Studies Review*, 46(2): 1–12.

Dobler, G. (2009). 'Chinese Shops and the Formation of a Chinese Expatriate Community in Namibia.' In J. Strauss and M. Saavedra (eds.), *China and Africa: Emerging Patterns in Globalization and Development*. Cambridge: Cambridge University Press.

Fair, J. E., M. Tully, B. Ekdale, and R.K.B. Asante (2009). 'Crafting Lifestyles in Urban Africa: Young Ghanaians in the World of Online Friendships.' *Africa Today*, 55(4): 29–49.

France, A. (2007). *Understanding Youth in Late Modernity*. Berkshire: Open University Press.

Frederiksen, B. F. (ed.) (2010). Special Issue on 'Young Men and Women in Africa: Conflicts, Enterprise and Aspiration.' *Young: Nordic Journal of Youth Research*, 18(3).

Frahm-Arp, M. (2012). 'Singleness, Sexuality, and the Dream of Marriage.' *Journal of Religion in Africa*, 42: 369–83.

Hansen, K. T. (1997). *Keeping House in Lusaka*. New York: Columbia University Press.

———. (2005). 'Getting Stuck in the Compound: Some Odds against Social Adulthood in Lusaka, Zambia.' *Africa Today*, 51(4): 3–18.

———. (2008). 'Introduction: Youth and the City,' and 'Localities and Sites of Youth Agency in Lusaka.' In K. T. Hansen et al. *Youth and the City in the Global South*. Bloomington: Indiana University Press.

———. (2014). 'Urban Africa: Lives and Projects.' In M. Grosz-Ngate, J. Hanson, and P. O'Meara, (eds.), *Africa*. Third Edition. Bloomington: Indiana University Press.

Hansen, K. T., and W. N. Nchito (2013). 'Where have all the Vendors Gone? Redrawing Boundaries in Lusaka's Street Economy.' In Hansen, K. T., W. Little, and B. L. Milgram (eds.), *Street Economies in the Global Urban South*. Santa Fee: SAR Press.

Haynes, N. (2012). 'Pentecostalism and the Morality of Money: Prosperity, Inequality, and Religious Sociality on the Zambian Copperbelt.' *Journal of the Royal Anthropological Institute*, 18:123–39.

Honwana, A. (2012). *The Time of Youth: Work, Social Change, and Politics in Africa*. Stirling, VA: Kumarian Press.

Hunter, M. (2002). 'The Materiality of Everyday Sex: Thinking beyond Prostitution.' *African Studies*, 61: 99–120.

———. (2009). 'Providing Love: Sex and Exchange in Twentieth Century South Africa.' In J. Cole and L. Thomas (eds.), *Love in Africa*. Chicago: University of Chicago Press.

Jensen, S. (2006). 'Capetonian Back Streets: Territorializing Young Men.' *Ethnography*, 7(3): 275–301.

Kaufman, C. E, and S. E. Stavrou (2004). '"Bus Fare Please": The Economics of Sex and Gifts among Young people in Urban South Africa.' *Culture, Health & Sexuality*, 6(5): 377–91.

Kunzler, D. (2011). 'South African Rap Music, Counter Discourses, Identity, and Commodification Beyond the Prophets of Da City.' *Journal of Southern African Studies*, 37(1): 27–43.

Lindegaard, M. R. (2009). 'Navigating Terrains of Violence: How South African Male Youngsters Negotiate Social Change.' *Social Dynamics*, 35(1): 19–35.

Lauterbach, K. (2010). 'Becoming a Pastor: Youth and Social Aspirations in Ghana.' *Young*, 18(3): 259–78.

Maganja, R. K., S. Maman, A. Groves, and J. K. Mbwambo (2007). 'Skinning the Goat and Pulling the Load: Transactional Sex among Youth in Dar es Salaam, Tanzania.' *AIDS Care*, 19(8): 974–81.

Mains, D. (2012). *Hope is Cut: Youth, Unemployment and the Future in Urban Ethiopia*. Philadelphia: Temple University Press.

Manase, I. (2009). 'Zimbabwean Urban Grooves and their Subversive Performance Practices.' *Social Dynamics*, 35(1): 56–67.

Mate, R. (2012). 'Youth Lyrics, Street Language and the Politics of Age: Contextualizing the Youth Question in the Third Chimurenga Campaign in Zimbabwe.' *Journal of Southern African Studies*, 38(1): 107–27.

McIlwaine, C., and K. Datta (2004). 'Endangered Youth? Youth, Gender and Sexualities in Urban Botswana.' *Gender, Place and Culture*, 11(4): 483–512.

Mintz, S. (2008). 'Reflections on Age as a Category of Historical Analysis.' *Journal of the History of Childhood and Youth*, 1(1): 91–94.

Mususa, P. (2012). 'Topping Up: Life amidst Hardship and Death on the Copperbelt.' *African Studies*, 71(2): 304–22.

Pellitor, A., MacPhail, A. D. Anderson, and S. Maman (2012). '"If I Buy the Kellog's then He Should [Buy] the Mill." Young Women's Perspectives on Relationship Dynamics, Gender Power and HIV Risk in Johannesburg.' *Culture, Health & Sexuality*, 14(5): 477–90.

Sadgrove, J. (2007). '"Keeping up Appearances": Sex and Religion amongst University Students in Uganda.' *Journal of Religion in Africa*, (37(1): 116–44.

Shefer, T., L. Clowes, and T. Vergnani (2012). 'Narratives of Transactional Sex on a University Campus.' *Culture, Health & Sexuality*, 14(4): 435–47.

Sommers, M. (2012). *Stuck: Rwandan Youth and the Struggle for Adulthood*. Athens: University of Georgia Press.

Spronk, R. (2009a). Media and the Therapeutic Ethos of Romantic Love in Middle-Class Nairobi.' In J. Cole and L. Thomas (eds.), *Love in Africa*. Chicago: University of Chicago Press.

———. (2009b). 'Sex, Sexuality and Negotiating Africanness in Nairobi.' *Africa*, 79(4): 500–19.

Van Dijk, R. (1992). 'Young Puritan Preachers in Post-independence Malawi.' *Africa*, 62(2): 159–81.

Van Klinken, A. S. (2012). 'Men in the Remaking: Conversion Narratives and Born-Again Masculinity in Zambia.' *Journal of Religion in Africa*, 42: 215–39.

van Wolputte, S., and L. E. Bleckmann (2012). 'The Ironies of Pop: Local Music Production and Citizenship in a Small Namibian Town.' *Africa*, 82(3): 413–36.

Walker, L. (2005). 'Men Behaving Differently: South African Men since 1994.' *Culture, Health & Sexuality*, 7(3): 225–38.

5   Youth in Tanzania's urbanizing mining settlements

Prospecting a mineralized future

Deborah Fahy Bryceson

Introduction

Over the past decade, a clutch of studies of African youth has focused on urban male youth's role in national and local political economies (Abbink and van Kessel 2005; Burgess and Burton 2010; Honwana and De Boeck 2005; Trudell et al. 2002). Cast against a backdrop of unemployment and economic cutbacks, they tend to be portrayed as dissident urbanites disillusioned with the post-colonial state (Burgess and Burton 2010). Male youth, earning a bare economic survival in the informal sector, are seen to be prone to incipient violence, including vigilantism under the sway of one or another 'big men' or political parties, with destabilizing influences on the political and social order of the nation-state and city as exemplified in Kenya and West Africa (Anderson 2002; Jua 2010; Meagher 2007).

This chapter questions the behavioural characterizations of African youth as either overly materialistic, alienated, and nihilistic in reaction to their diminished economic prospects relative to that of their parents' generation; or alternatively forced or willingly in the pay of self-serving big men needing youthful strong-arm militias to back their policies or challenge rivals during elections or other decisive moments of power politics. In either case, the agency of youth is seen as thwarted or controlled by an older commanding generation.

Honwana (2012) has developed a notion of African youth's 'waithood,' a period between childhood and adulthood in which young people are in a state of suspension before gaining adult responsibilities and rights, while nonetheless acquiring political awareness and forming a critique of the context in which they live. Many feel their generation has been marginalized by corrupt, clientelist political elites and voice resentment against nepotistic practices. Most youth shun formal politics and are hesitant to become politically vocal for fear of being penalized by their elders and persons of authority.

After decades of economic stagnation, the 21st century has witnessed changing fortunes for sub-Saharan Africa's economies, particularly those with mineral wealth. The existence of widespread poverty in a continent abundantly rich in mineral resources is paradoxical. Apart from a long history of mineral extraction in Southern Africa, the Democratic Republic of Congo and Ghana, it is thought that the rest of sub-Saharan Africa has barely scratched the surface of its mineral wealth. At the turn of the century, a rapid rise in demand for mineral resources – prompted primarily by industrializing countries – led to a surge in foreign corporate investment in African mining.[1] Over a third of the major metallic mineral-producing countries in the world are currently African (ICMM 2012). According to the World Bank (2012: 11), 21 African countries are already pegged as 'middle-income countries' with another ten in line to achieve that status by 2025. These are encouraging economic projections, but will they translate into improved work prospects and living standards for today's youth? In the following, I probe this question via consideration of the attitudes, expectations, and agency of youth revealed in recent survey findings from Tanzanian artisanal gold mining sites.

Tanzania has an impressive mineral endowment including gold, diamonds, several types of precious stones, and recently discovered off-shore natural gas reserves. Most attention is focused on the expansion of large-scale mining investments, which involves employment of thousands of mostly well-educated and skilled personnel. On the other hand, the artisanal mining sector is highly labour-absorptive, with hundreds of thousands actively engaged as miners or raw material processors of minerals, in response to a proliferation of mineral rushes over the last couple of decades (Bryceson et al. 2012).

Economic and social relational ties associated with mineral production differ profoundly from those prevailing in Tanzania's agrarian countryside. The country's village settlements were and continue to be structured by a division of labour and decision-making that privileges the power of male elders. In contrast, mining areas are populated primarily by men and women in their peak economically active years between 15 and 45 years of age, who take an active part in decision-making, distanced from gerontocracy. Economic life of the mining settlement is premised heavily on muscular strength and youthful vigour. Mineralizing economies are inclined toward urban agglomeration, which is attractive to youth stimulating their creative energies as cultural trendsetters (Bryceson et al. 2012).

This chapter addresses how the rise of artisanal mining is altering youth's social relations and economic expectations and, it seems, providing an avenue for greater autonomy. Nonetheless youth mining or living in mining settlements confront constraints and trade-offs in their quest for decision-making autonomy and a new lifestyle. Despite the meteoric rise of mining over the last two decades, very little research on local economic and cultural change in mining communities has been undertaken. The attitudes and agency of mining settlement residents, and especially youth, remain largely undocumented. With this empirical gap in mind, this chapter begins with a discussion of traditional occupational ascription and youth's historical role in work migration to plantations, urban areas and now mines, before turning to brief background history on Tanzania's mineralization, followed by consideration of data findings from the 2012 Urbanization and Poverty in Mining Africa (UPIMA) household survey of three Tanzanian artisanal and large-scale mining settlements and a 2007 survey of miners' migration and career development at two artisanal settlements in Tanzania. Youth's demographic presence in mining settlements is analysed alongside their educational and occupational activities. Through a content assessment of themes found in essays, poems, songs, and plays created by youth for a 'Life in the Mines' (*Maisha Machimboni*) cultural festival hosted by the UPIMA research programme in July and August

2012, youth's perspectives on daily life in their communities and the trade-offs they face in gaining autonomy and occupational choice are analyzed. The conclusion summarizes the broad trends and youth's future trajectory in artisanal mining.

Youth, autonomy, and occupational change in Tanzania

Tanzanian history over a century and a half ago testifies to male youth's frontal role in economic sectoral change, as warriors, porters, and labourers strategically positioned over the country's sparsely populated terrain during pre-colonial slave raiding[2] and ivory porterage, associated with the Zanzibar sultanate's commercial empire. Traditionally male youth served as warriors in tribal confrontations. With the rise of the ivory and slave trade, youth derived considerable freedom from gerontocratic authority in the course of their work. Ivory porterage was preponderantly based on paid labour and constituted the early beginnings of a territorial wage labour force (Iliffe 1979: 45; Rockel 2000).[3]

Arab ivory traders relied heavily on a youthful cadre of specialized Nyamwezi ivory porters. Historical accounts including that of Tippu Tip (Brode 2000), a renowned Zanzibari ivory trader, suggested that ivory porters were often undisciplined and unreliable, displaying a will of their own and large numbers to back the exercise of that will. While they earned wages and travelled enormous distances away from their home areas, nonetheless, it bears noting that one of the primary motivations for becoming a porter was a rite of passage: 'Not one of them was allowed to marry before he had carried a load of ivory to the coast, and brought back either calico or brass wire. It was the tribal stamp of true manhood, at once making him a citizen and warrior' (Swann 1910 quoted in Rockel 2000: 179).

During the 1890s, the imposition of German colonial rule quelled the up-country violence and insecurity associated with slave raiding but engendered the widespread Maji Maji rebellion against German tax collection and colonial autocracy, involving thousands of young men in military activities. This was followed by military encounters between British and German-trained African troops on German East African soil during the First World War (Iliffe 1979). Reid (2010: 43) observes that the period witnessed 'the emergence of youth as potentially more strident, militarized (in the loosest sense of the word) socio-political group, more willing than even in the 19th century to challenge older generations and engage in new patterns of intergenerational conflict.'

After the defeat of the Germans in the First World War, German East Africa became Tanganyika Territory, a League of Nations-mandated territory under British rule. Its economy combined European-owned plantations employing African wage labour, and peasant agrarian subsistence and export crop production of cotton, coffee, tea, and cashews. Approximately 50 percent of the territorial wage labour force was deployed in European sisal production on the basis of the *kipande* system in which male migrant labourers were contracted to labour a year and a half to two years away from their home areas (Bryceson 1990). Although the colonial migrant labour system was diverting youthful male labour from peasant smallholder farming, colonial officials and African male elders saw it as an interlude in the life of young men facilitating home-focused income earning for bridewealth payment. Heavy Native Authority sanctions against young women's migration away from their home areas constituted the foundations for this labour management system (Mbilinyi 1989). Youthful male wage-earning migrant labourers were afforded some degree of individual autonomy, but within the context of the demographic renewal of farming households in which rural patriarchs retained direct control over young women and indirect influence over young men. Not surprisingly, marriage and the setting up of autonomous households formed the dividing line between youth and adults.

Defining adulthood through new family formation

In Tanzanian agrarian society, spinsterhood was unthinkable for both women and men. Girls were traditionally considered marriageable soon after puberty. Older polygamous male patriarchs, who had accumulated wealth and were in a position to make large bridewealth payments, were in an advantageous position to marry young women (Wilson 1977; Bryceson 1995). Thus girls were likely to marry in their teens whereas boys, who had to gain sufficient means to pay bridewealth, married later.

Youth comprised an indefinite period beginning roughly at the age of 15. In Sukumaland, where the mining settlement case studies cited in this chapter were conducted, Varkevisser (1973) documents that the young had traditionally been obliged to join the *kisumba*, a neighbourhood organization of young men and unmarried young women. The *kisumba* hired themselves out as a group for a collective wage of cash and beer. Girls left the *kisumba* at the time of their marriage, usually by the age of 16, whereas boys were likely to marry some five to ten years later. Nonetheless, the achievement of full adulthood tended to be transitional for young married people who were obliged to spend the first years of their married life doing labour service for their in-laws, first the wife's family and later the groom's, in accordance with the terms of the negotiated bridewealth. Bridewealth obligations could last in perpetuity, however, there came a point when the married couple was considered ready to set up their own household, joining the 'old people' and gaining full autonomy (Varkevisser 1973).

A major theme of youth studies and indeed a dynamic for change in Tanzania economic history has been male youth's struggle for autonomy from the older generation related to bridewealth transfers and labour service demands (Giblin 2010; Iliffe 1979; Wilson 1977). Young men's earnings from migrant labour are likely to have eased the generational struggle over bridewealth. The transition from cattle and in-kind payments to a stronger cash component of bridewealth assisted young men to marry earlier in their life cycle and reduce the age imbalance between couples (Iliffe 1979: 531).

Attaining educational credentials for occupational flexibility

The off-farm avenues of work that youth had access to in the 19th century required heavy manual labour. The colonial labour market was structured by a racial three-tier system in which Africans were primarily agriculturalists, Asians were traders, service providers, and clerks and Europeans were government administrators and professionals. There was very little scope for other work aspirations for African youth. Over the long term, their residence in tribal villages and work in peasant agriculture under the control of rural patriarchs was ascribed. But in this restricted context, male youth came to value literacy and educational attainment as a means of gaining labour autonomy from their elders. Christian missionary activity during the German colonial period first made inroads amongst ex-slaves and other marginalized categories, but over time youth gravitated to Christianity as an alternative world view and catapult to non-agrarian occupational pursuits (Iliffe 1979). The numbers who gained literacy and some form of technical training, like carpentry or medical auxiliary, etc., were few but noticeable. They generally practiced their trade alongside farming in their home areas throughout adulthood.

While many Christian missionaries clustered in the cooler highland areas of the country provided educational opportunities for youth in the immediate vicinity, the overall level of education provisioning in Tanganyika was abysmally low. Colonial government investment was restricted such that on the eve of independence in 1961 the country had only 12 African university graduates and a mere 16 percent of the population were literate (Pratt 1978; Iliffe 1979). Table 5.1 presents the slow, uneven development of educational attainment in Tanganyika cum

Table 5.1 Educational enrolments, selected years 1931–2010

Year	Primary		Secondary	
	Number	% male	Number	% male
1931	167,523	66	0	
1946	115,179	74	1,446	98
1956	368,924	70	2,409	91
1961	506,260	65	6,031	86
1966	740,991		27,628	
1976	1,954,442		57,143	
1981	3,538,183		67,602	
1985	3,169,759		83,077	
1989	3,258,601		139,586	
		% School age pop. enrolled		
1995		55		
2000		59		
2004	4,875,764		379,534	
2005		95		
2006	8,166,608			
2009		96	1,466,402	55
2010		95		

Source: 1931–89: compiled by Buchert (1994) (includes government, Native Authority, mission, and private schools); 1995–2010: United Republic of Tanzania (2009); United Republic of Tanzania (2010a); Wedgwood (2005).

Tanzania, evidencing three notable spurts in primary school enrolments: (i) during the 1950s and 1960s, prompted by the spur of national independence; (ii) the implementation of Universal Primary Education (UPE) beginning in 1976, which progressed into the early 1980s before being reversed by IMF-enforced structural adjustment cutbacks by the mid-1980s; and (iii) the re-introduction of UPE in 2004 with a massive expansion of primary school education thereafter.

Until independence, roughly two-thirds of all students were male. At secondary level, the imbalance rose to 86 percent. Since independence measures to address the male bias have reduced the gender gap at both levels.

During the Nyerere period, priority was on expanding primary schools and in the process the rate of growth of secondary schools lagged behind to create a severe educational bottleneck. In 1985, the number of secondary school students was a mere 2.6 percent of the numbers in primary education, creating an educational elite of mostly urban-born secondary school students eligible to take up the government-supported university places. During the late 1980s, the number of private secondary schools expanded. By 2004, the percentage of primary school leavers going on to secondary school had improved to 7.8 percent. During the 2010s secondary educational prospects became even more promising for youth, being especially important as the agrarian economy gave way to mining and service sector expansion.

Mineralization of Tanzania

Mining has been a part of colonial and post-colonial 20th-century Tanzania history, but it is only in the last couple of decades that the sector's growth has gained increasing momentum, impacting on youth in many localities. Having been a primarily agrarian-dominated country, Tanzania is undergoing a process of 'mineralization,' defined as 'alteration in both the form and content of the African continent's social, political, and cultural foundations arising from the rising importance of mining in national, local, and household economies' (Bryceson and Jønsson 2014). This section traces the entwined development of large-scale and artisanal mining.

Evolution of the mining sector

During the 1980s and 1990s, in response to the contraction of peasant agriculture under structural adjustment policies, a rising tide of artisanal miners, living in mineral-rich parts of the country, started discovering minerals in their local areas (Bryceson 1999; 2002). At the same time, world gold prices were steadily rising following the removal of the international gold standard. Tanzania's post-independence government, like its colonial predecessor, did not sanction private artisanal mining, but in view of the economic crisis gripping the country, government officials tended to turn a blind eye to coalescing artisanal mining activity.

The Mining Act of 1979 accorded small-scale artisanal miners legal recognition, ending the Tanzanian government's insistence on mining being exclusively controlled by the state (Kulindwa et al. 2003). Citizens were afforded the possibility of posting mining claims in designated areas for prospecting and mining that did not require large expenditure or specialized equipment. By the mid-1990s, there were estimates of over a half million artisanal miners operating in Tanzania (Tan Discovery 1996).

Under pressure from the World Bank, the Tanzanian government promulgated a raft of legislation aimed at attracting foreign direct investment (FDI) at the end of the 1990s.[4] Over the next decade, annual FDI trebled, amounting to US$5.6 billion between 1999–2009, most of which was invested in the Tanzanian mining sector, notably that of gold (United Republic of Tanzania 2009). In 2010, 97 percent of Tanzania's mineral exports were gold valued at US$1.56 billion (United Republic of Tanzania 2010b). Nonetheless, the corporate mining sector employed very few people. Roe and Essex (2009) estimated employment at between 6,000–12,000 from 2003–2009, most of whom were skilled or highly educated. In contrast, a recent World Bank-funded study conducted in 2011 estimates that there were 685,000 artisanal miners in Tanzania.[5]

Estimates of the artisanal mining sector's productive output are not available. However, extraction of gold, diamonds, and an array of precious minerals has clearly boosted Tanzania's export earnings, ushering in a new era of optimism about the future of the country and its citizenry, not least its youth. Artisanal gold makes it way primarily through informal market channels into the global gold market (Jønsson and Fold 2011). Increasingly, the Tanzanian government has favoured large-scale mining interests over that of artisanal miners, leading to contestation between the large-scale mines and artisanal miners' over their mining rights in specific areas (Bourgouin 2014).

Demographic growth, urbanization, and cultural lifestyle experimentation

Most of the known gold deposits are located in a 'ring of gold' south of Lake Victoria along the bifurcated contours of the East African Rift Valley (Bryceson et al. 2012). News of a gold strike travels fast with the near ubiquitous ownership of mobile phones in Tanzania. Particularly promising sites have been known to amass ten thousand or more people in the space of a few months (Jønsson and Bryceson 2009).

The spread of artisanal mining and the influence of mineral rushes are reflected in small town growth (Bryceson et al. 2012) in the mining regions. While the precise size and composition of the migration stream is not known, Jønsson and Bryceson's (2009) 2007 survey of 108 migrant miners at two locations in the ring of gold revealed a diverse ethnic mix.[6] Many of Tanzania's mining sites were originally remote rural locations, but the economic promise of a mineral rush attracts a youthful, cosmopolitan population. Although the majority of surveyed migrants came from rural birthplaces (77 percent), the settlements had a strong urban character. The miners arrive first, but businessmen and women follow soon thereafter. Both the men and women are intent on material success (Bryceson, Jønsson, and Verbrugge 2013).

The miners, and especially the young ones, are generally known to 'work hard and play hard.' There are often tensions between the mining settlement and the neighbouring villagers who view the migrant population with consternation. While eager to sell food, goods, and services to the migrants, they fear that their way of life will set a bad example for their youth (Bryceson and Jønsson 2010).

Youth at the mining frontier

Studying a mining frontier with a continuous sequence of rush sites involved selection of study sites (described below in Table 5.2) on the basis of large-scale versus artisanal mining and time duration of the settlement's existence. The UPIMA research team's fieldwork at three gold settlements in Geita region between May 2011 and March 2012 consisted of qualitative interviews with key informants and a random sample household survey of 108 household heads.[7]

Tanzania's current mineralization has to be understood as a continually dynamic frontier of artisanal mining sites being discovered, prospected, exploited and gradually diminishing in activity, alongside bigger sites of corporate capital investment. Youthful miners are well-represented at gold mining sites; but it is necessary to distinguish between those who dedicate most of their time to mining as opposed to those who attend school and mine part time on the side.

Table 5.2 UPIMA 2012 Tanzania study sites

Site type	Gold sites
Artisanal rush	Ikuzi, Geita region – estimated pop. 5,500. Originally a small agro-pastoralist village numbering only 3600. In July 2010, gold was discovered in a forested area approximately 2 km from the village centre bringing an influx of between 9,000–13,000 people into a crowded, deforested settlement without sanitary facilities. The post-peak gold rush population at the time of the study in 2012 numbered between 5,000–6,000 people.
Artisanal mature	Nyarugusu, Geita region – estimated pop. 11,000. Its gold mining activities date back to the colonial period, when an industrial gold mine operated in the vicinity of the village until the 1960s. In the 1980s, artisanal mining activities revealed multiple gold discoveries attracting in-migration of miners. Since then Nyarugusu was divided into two villages in 2000. In 2009 the new Nyarugusu village, with a population of around 27,000 people, was again divided into three new villages with the newly designated Nyarugusu village having a population of around 11,000.
Large-scale	Geita, Geita region – estimated pop. 100,000. Geita town is the headquarters of the new Geita region, and one of the fastest growing towns in East Africa. It is the location of Geita Gold Mine (GGM), Tanzania's largest gold mining operation. The Germans discovered gold close to Geita in 1898. Large-scale production commenced in the 1930s and continued to 1966 followed by population decline. GGM operated by Anglo-Gold Ashanti commenced production in 2000. Geita is now a major commercial town in northwest Tanzania.

Source: 2012 UPIMA survey (Bryceson and Jønsson forthcoming).

Profiling young miners

Artisanal gold miners are generally men in their peak economically active years. Jønsson and Bryceson's (2009) random sample survey of miners at two sites in Tanzania's ring of gold cited above provides a localized indication of the structure of the artisanal mine labour force. Twenty-eight percent of the miners were under 30 years of age, the overall average age was 36 years with a mean gold mining entry age of 24 years (Jønsson and Bryceson 2009). Some youth had been attracted to artisanal mining in their teens, with a minority (seven percent) of pre-teens (10–12-year-olds). The exceptionally young miners tended to be living in mining settlements as children and acquired their first experience of mining as assistants for family members or neighbours. For others, independent migration to mining sites began in their teens (Jønsson and Bryceson 2009; Terres des Hommes Schweiz 2012). The majority (77 percent) of the surveyed miners were from rural backgrounds (Bryceson and Jønsson 2010). Only 23 percent of the sampled miners had less than five years of schooling, suggesting that the majority of artisanal miners have basic literacy and numeracy.

Tracing the careers and income differentials between the 108 sampled miners, Bryceson and Jønsson (2010) found that miners who were 'early starters' with an average mining entry age of 17 years had higher mean monthly earnings than 'average starters' with an entry age of 22 years, while 'late starters' entering at an average age of 40 received the lowest earnings (see Table 5.3). The early starters had the advantage of having not only longer but broader mining experience, having worked at more sites. The survey evidence suggests that success in mining was a cumulative process of career progression associated with increasing experience, skill, and mobility, which expanded know-how and social networks for information exchange and pit access. It should be noted that 'early starter' miners tended to marry at an earlier age than other miners, presumably because they could afford to do so. Marriage and having children did not necessarily interfere with mine work. Married men readily moved to new mine sites leaving their wives and children behind (Bryceson, Jønsson, and Verbrugge 2014).

Table 5.3 Entry age of miners into artisanal mining

Age range	Percentage	Cumulative percentage
10–19 years	45.4	45.4
20–29 years	31.5	76.0
30–39 years	14.8	91.7
40–49 years	7.4	99.1
50–59 years	0.9	100.0

Source: 2007 artisanal miners' survey data (Jønsson and Bryceson 2009).

Youth's presence in the mining settlements

Tanzanian mining settlements have a hybrid character. While Geita has a population of over 100,000, the rest of the survey sites are located in rural settings but nonetheless, due to their migrant influx, they are demographically complex and represent extremely cosmopolitan concentrations of population with diverse occupational pursuits in mining and the service sector. It is generally assumed that mining sites will be male-dominated. In Tanzania, this is true only in the very early days of a mineral rush. Women service sector migrants quickly follow male mining migrants. There are a small number of children below 10 years and a preponderance of people in peak economically active age groups, as indicated by the age/sex pyramid in Figure 5.1.

In mining sites, it cannot be assumed that all houses accommodate 'households' in the conventional sense. There are at least three types of housing with distinct household compositions, namely: (i) dwellings comprising a reproductive couple and children, (ii) bachelor housing in the form of single room rental, room clusters, or dormitories for men, notably miners living individually; and (iii) houses that accommodate some combination of family households as well as paying lodgers. The UPIMA sample survey of 2012 was biased towards categories: (i) and (iii) given that the survey took place during working hours when single and dormitory-housed miners and others were at work.

Thus the age/sex pyramids of the surveyed settlements are likely to reflect the more stable family-based population of the settlements who live in housing units where there are occupants on the premises during daylight hours.[8] However, unlike Tanzanian agrarian settlements characterized by high dependency ratios consistent with a broad-based age/sex population pyramid, households in the surveyed mining sites have a lower number of child dependents and erratic differences between age groups and their respective sex ratios due to selective migration (Figures 5.1 and Table 5.4).

Table 5.4 infers the marked differences in household formation between the three types of gold settlements. Ikuzi, the active gold rush site has an exceptionally small household size, a high incidence of non-family members lodging in the household and a heavily male biased sex ratio. The numbers of sons and daughters within the Ikuzi households is under one with double the number of sons relative to daughters. Ikuzi is essentially a mining camp populated primarily by male miners. Also it is apparent that schooling is not a priority with roughly half of sons and only a quarter of daughters studying.

The mature artisanal site has above average household sizes and substantial numbers of sons and daughters attending school. Nonetheless the sex ratio is still tipped towards males and there is greater investment in the education of sons. The bulge in the female 10–14 years category in Nyarugusu (Figure 5.1) may relate to the common practice of relying on the labour of young migrant girls from their extended family to assist with childcare and domestic labour. In this case this would facilitate mothers' involvement in service sector and mineral processing work outside the home. Parents in mining settlements tend to work long hours and lack time to devote to their children.

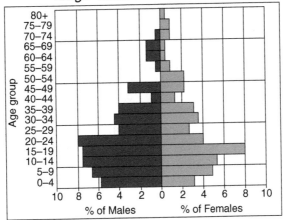

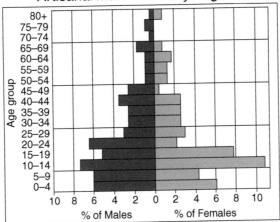

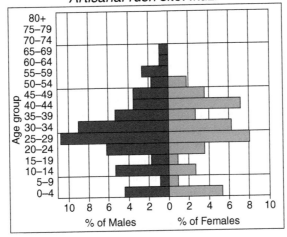

Figure 5.1 Age/sex pyramids for Tanzanian gold mining sites

Table 5.4 Tanzanian mining settlements' household membership, gender composition, and student offspring

Mean averages	All settlements	Geita large-scale	Nyarugusu mature artisanal	Ikuzi rush artisanal
Household members	5.26	6.25	6.42	3.11
No. of non-family	0.15	0.03	0.08	0.44
No. of males	2.78	3.44	3.28	1.75
No. of females	2.48	2.78	3.14	1.36
Sex ratio	112	123	104	129
No. of sons	1.24	1.36	1.89	.42
No. of daughters	1.07	1.11	1.58	.25
No. of students	1.68	2.17	2.04	.28
Male students	0.96	1.33	1.17	0.22
Female students	0.72	0.83	1.03	0.06
Male/Female education ratio	133	160	114	367
% Sons studying	77%	98%	62%	52%
% Daughters studying	67%	75%	65%	27%

Source: 2012 UPIMA mining settlement survey.

The households in the large-scale mining settlements are quite different. Geita is a town experiencing rapid growth through in-migration. It is class-stratified with a wealthy educated elite working at the Geita Gold Mine (GGM) and, at the opposite end of the spectrum, there are many people working in the informal service sector and artisanal mining. The high sex ratio is likely to reflect the presence of male artisanal miners and male contract workers for GGM. School attendance is high with a considerable male bias. There is a noticeable bulge in young women in the 15–19 age bracket (see Figure 5.1). They are likely to be helping with childcare and working in the service sector.

Bearing in mind that our UPIMA household survey data is biased towards the more settled households in the community, we must distinguish between 'working' youth and 'schooling' youth. There is clearly a trade-off between youth who decide to specialize in mining after primary school as opposed to those who attend secondary school. In Tanzania, primary schools involve seven years of education (Standards 1–7), followed by secondary schools of six years split into Forms 1–4, and students showing academic promise are encouraged to move on to Forms 5–6. Generally, primary school children are aged 7–15 years old and, as in the case of the surveyed Form 4 secondary school students, they ranged in age from 16 to 22. Many Tanzanian children start school well after their seventh birthday, which delays the completion of both their primary and secondary education. School attendance in our surveyed households differs quite markedly across the three sites, with almost all sons (98 percent) and three-quarters of daughters studying in Geita town, falling to 62 and 65 percent in Nyarugusu, down to only half of sons and roughly a quarter of daughters at the Ikuzi gold rush site. Having a chance to attend school is heavily conditioned by family circumstances as documented in the following section.

Youth mining narratives: The good, the bad, and the ugly

Seeking to gain insight into youth's views on artisanal mining life, the *Maisha Machimboni* (Life in the Mines) arts festival was held under the auspices of the UPIMA project at government secondary schools in the combined large-scale and mature artisanal site and at the rush site's primary school, given that there was no secondary school. There was generally a fairly even representation of male and female students at the festivals. After close consultation and collaboration with their teachers, the students were asked to express what it is like to live in a mining settlement in an artistic medium of their choice: poem, short story, essay, song, dance, sculpture, drawings, or plays.[9]

I will focus on the work of the secondary school students who wrote essays analysing the impact of mining generally enumerating an array of both pros and cons with a heavy weighting to the latter. The students were in their late teens or older with a mature appreciation of the complexities of social and political processes taking place in Tanzanian mining at local, regional, and national levels. They were acutely aware of living in pioneering settlements whose boom and bust economies made for a great deal of opportunities and excitement as well as poverty and pathos, many felt that they were the 'lucky ones' residing in a place where they were availed both a secondary school education and opportunities to earn cash. Uppermost in their minds was a sense of relativity and awareness about the inequalities associated with large-scale and artisanal mining.

In their daily lives, Honwana (2012) sees youth gravitating towards associational ties with like-minded youth, spending time in leisure-time pursuits that may have political undertones such as rap music that forcefully expresses disenchantment with the status quo. Composing rap songs as an outlet for expressing their feelings of exclusion and neglect, youth share a sub-culture of muted protest that instills a sense of solidarity and empowerment. At the same time, many youth, from a position of marginality and need, have to engage in economic activities on the border between legality and illegality. As daily survival practices, such activities are generally tolerated by the elites, but if threatened, youth are capable of rising up in mass protest and fighting for their rights to subsistence, not unlike peasants' protests insisting on a moral economy when they encounter barriers to the pursuit of adequate household food production (Bryceson 2010).

The poems, stories, and plays written by Form 4 students combined youthful political indignation with a pragmatism moulded by the economic realities and opportunities of their mining settlements, affirming Howana's (2012) argument. Attitudes are conditioned by the location and unfolding nature of the specific mining sites. In Geita, students weighed the expansion of business opportunities, the availability of employment and more social services against the impact of mining's deforestation, environmental pollution and weak government administration in matters related to ownership, control and contestation of mining areas and mineral rights sometimes leading to serious and occasionally deadly conflicts. While critical of the Geita Gold Mine and miners generally, the students stressed that the allure and sometimes corrupting influence of mining affected most of the settlements' residents, including themselves. This was evident in the repeated theme of being torn between pursuing one's studies as opposed to male youth becoming miners, and female youth becoming 'good time' girls engaged in a search for love, fun, and economic security with miners. The following story is illustrative of the moral dilemmas that students-cum-miners face, as well as the resort to illegal activities in the contentious divide between large-scale and artisanal mining.

Box 5.1 Geita town short story: 'Wealth without trace'

Omary arrived in Geita at half past nine in the morning and without wasting time, he boarded a bus that was going to the mines. After arrival, he headed to a *genge* (small restaurant) to order some food. While eating he heard three young people roughly his age talking nearby.

'I have put everything in order. After we arrive it is about collecting the waste rock fast and getting out quickly. If we succeed, then we are out of poverty' he said.

'OK when?' one of them asked. 'We'll go at night-time so that we are not visible. You know we are entering without permission.'

Omary thought: Aha..! They are going to the mines, I should go with them. He approached them and asked: 'How are you?' They answered: 'Fine, how about you?'

There was a silent hesitation then he continued, 'My name is Omary. I'm going to the mine. Can I join you as I am new to the mines?'

'Where are you from, and what makes you come here? I am a Form 4 student, but I failed to pay for my examination fees, so I decided to leave school and come to look for money, so that I can pay the fees as I like to study very much.'

'Who gave you the idea of coming here?' they queried.

'One day I heard some people talking about mining, and how successful they were, so I became interested and here I am.'

'Where are you staying?'

'I have just arrived.'

'OK, no problem. We have a room just nearby and we will stay together. We will prepare to go to the mine tomorrow night and everybody will take his share if we are successful'

'Thank you very much for your kindness.'

'Don't worry.'

The next day, at ten in the evening they started their journey to the mine. They used shortcut paths and went straight to the area where the company kept its waste rock (*magwangala*). They collected the rocks and filled their bags. Without wasting time they left quickly using the same paths that they had passed earlier. They were moving carefully but at high speed. After managing to get out they went to the wash and ball mill to process the minerals. To their delight the extracted gold was considerable and it was worth a good price. They divided the money between themselves.

Omary was very happy, congratulating himself that indeed he had escaped poverty. He thought to himself: 'There's no need to go back to school. I am going to rent a room in Geita town and start a business.' He announced to his friends 'I'm not returning to school.' His new friends seemed to be totally in agreement with his thinking.

He went to Geita and rented a room and opened up a small shop selling hardware equipment. He started drinking alcohol and enjoying the ladies. He became well known in the various dance clubs in Geita. One day he met a girl called Tina, who he fell in love with. She started living with him and he entrusted all his belongings to her. One night he didn't make it home. Angry, Tina promptly sold all his goods and disappeared. The following morning Omary arrived at home still drunk and opened the door to find the house empty. He could not do anything because of his drunken state and slept on the floor.

When he woke up in the afternoon, he tried calling Tina but she was unreachable. As he sat feeling sorry for himself, he heard somebody knocking at the door. It was the landlord demanding the rent. Unable to pay, Omary was instructed to surrender his room. Thinking about his options as he vacated the house, he decided he had to get back to the mines to look for money.., 'and if I succeed I will shun women and shun luxury . . .'

He started the journey of going back to the mines, this time he was alone, he followed the same short cut paths. He managed to enter the mine and collect the *magwangala*, filling his bags and moving quickly to get off the mine premises. But alas he heard a big sound 'puuu' followed by a bullet penetrating his chest. He cried out 'Aaaahh I am dying.' He collapsed on the spot and became still like water in a pot, already his soul had left his body.

Source: UPIMA Maisha Machimboni festival, written by Zainabu Rashid, Form 4 female student, Geita Secondary School, 1 August 2012, translated by Elard Mawala.

Unlike Geita, where large and artisanal mining exist side by side, Nyarugusu was an artisanal settlement experiencing booms and lulls in gold mining for over 30 years. Some mining families had witnessed the entire period, and had 'mining in their blood.' Artisanal mining is a quick option for getting cash and, during boom times it can be a route out of poverty. The Form 4 secondary students were both lured towards mining and wary of its consequences, as evidenced in the following essay as illustrated in extracts from an essay by a 'mining-student':

> Mining is my livelihood. I am the oldest one in our family and our parents died when we were very young. I am now the father and mother of the family. So minerals help to meet our needs . . . I sell the gold that I dig to get income to use for buying food and other necessities for myself and my young brother and sisters. Mining has helped me to gain income that assists me in paying my school fees . . . However, mining activities have interfered with my education. When I need money I mine and find myself missing classes. I failed to perform well in my exams last term.
>
> (Form 4 male student, 19 years, Nyarugusu
> Secondary School, 30 July 2012)

While boys are drawn to working in the pits, girls are distracted by the prospects of enjoying the good life as girlfriends of miners. There are many bars in and around Nyarugusu where young girls can find employment as barmaids and meet men, often several years older than themselves (Bryceson, Jønsson, and Verbrugge 2014). The tensions that young women face are reflected in the following poem written by three female students.

Box 5.2 Nyarugusu poem: 'Life in the mines is entering our minds'

We attend school, but it takes time and doesn't pay,
We don't value studying, we think about minerals,
When we go to the mines, we find temptations,
Life in the mines is entering our minds.

Our academic studies are falling, the mines are ruling,
Teachers instruct, but students don't listen,
We miss classes, gold is ruling us,
Life in the mines is entering our minds.

When we leave school, to go home,
Our parents are at work, we end up cooking
The food is poor, at school and at home
Life in the mines is entering our minds.

The mines are disturbing us, especially us girls,
We surrender to temptations, failing to avoid them,
And we see our studies suffer,
Life in the mines is entering our minds.

Girls are getting pregnancies and HIV/AIDS,
We are confronted with the mines' effects,
Problems we can never erase,
Life in the mines is entering our minds.

There are also deaths, people are buried in the pits,
We see orphans, roaming the streets,
We lack someone to take care of us,
Life in the mines is entering our minds.

We are now at the end, but not our end,
It is true that we face temptations and threats,
We live here, we need to fight against,
Life in the mines entering our minds.

Source: UPIMA Maisha Machimboni festival, by Justina Tano, Pili Juma, and Diana Shinde, Form 4 female students, all 17 years old, Nyarugusu Secondary School, 30 July 2012, translated by Elard Mawala.

This poem alludes to the frequent absence of parents from the home. Some students extended their critique of the status quo beyond the government and mining companies to their parents. Either the parents were seen to be too engrossed in their mining and other cash-earning activities, prone to separation or divorce related to the migratory movements of miners, or absent due to death connected with mining accidents or HIV/AIDS. Children and youth may be orphaned without extended family support given that they have been members of mining households, which are distanced from the natal homes of the parents.

Such complaints mark a radical twist in generational tensions. Preceding cohorts of youth were characterized by attempts to gain autonomy from parental control and elders' bridewealth impositions, whereas now, in the case of youth from families living *in situ* in mining settlements, there is regret that their parents are not on hand to give them care and concern. It should be added that the traditional generational contract has been broken with most people in mining settlements no longer marrying formally or paying bridewealth. Sexual relationships veer heavily toward casualization, a tendency found elsewhere in urban Tanzania, but not to the extent found in mining communities (Bryceson, Jønsson, and Verbrugge 2013; 2014; Rwebangira and Liljeström 1998).

Paradoxical expectations for youth's future careers

Despite the pre-occupation with mining on the part of youth and their parents, the 2012 UPIMA survey revealed that occupations requiring a high level of education were preferred by heads of household when they were asked about what aspirations they had for their children's future work lives. Curiously, mining was barely mentioned. Most hoped that their children would gain high status professional jobs. Interview findings from a total of 108 heads of households who commented on the career expectations of their children overwhelmingly revealed preferences for their pursuit of professional careers (68 percent) requiring educational qualifications, followed by work in defense (9 percent), semi-skilled, skilled, or natural talent fields (11 percent), politics (4 percent) with one budding president predicted, religious leadership (4 percent), business (1 percent), and farmers, housewives, waitresses, or miners (4 percent) (see Appendix 5.1).

Only one percent of the children were projected to become future miners. While parents worldwide are prone to wishful thinking in regard to their children's future, it is telling that such a minute percentage of children were expected to become miners, service sector workers, and business people, occupational categories that overwhelmingly prevail in the mining settlements. This, however, accords with the fact that economically well-off parents in the mining settlement, who had money to invest in their children's futures, endeavoured to send their children to secondary schools in the regional towns away from the distracting influences of the gold-mining settlement (Bryceson, Jønsson, and Verbrugge 2013). People avidly worked in mining but most did not see it as a lifetime career from which they could gain personal fulfillment and social status.

Conclusion

Tanzania's mineralization, notably the expansion of the artisanal mining sector over the last 20 years, has provided enhanced employment prospects for youth. Migration from the countryside to the country's urbanizing mine settlements has been pronounced on the part of men. Young men have sought mining as well as tertiary service sector work in the booming mining settlements, while young women have concentrated primarily on service provisioning. This chapter has distinguished youth who pursue mining as a full-time activity as opposed to those who mine part time in combination with their studies.

Regarding the latter, raising children in mining settlements is posing several developmental dilemmas. First, there is a high incidence of family instability in which one or both parents may be absent; and second, youth face the dilemma of allocating their time between school and mining. Although they are not mutually exclusive, it is difficult to excel in both. There is a striking contrast between the immediate attraction of mining and its dismissal as a desirable occupational pursuit over the longer term. For many, artisanal mining is an interlude in their life and indeed an interlude in Tanzanian history that they know will pass. However, it offers an economic opportunity that they are eager to grab while they can, hoping to later move on to work with fewer physical risks and social costs. This bears some resemblance to youth's participation in new sectors of the Tanzanian economy that arose in the past, notably the ivory and slave trade during the 19th century and migration and work in colonial plantations during the first half of the 20th century. In each of these cases, youth were target workers who left the work once they had accumulated enough earnings.

Honwana's (2012) and Jua's (2010) stress on youth's disenchantment with the status quo is readily observable in Tanzanian mining settlements. Youth's censure of corrupt politicians extends to foreign mining corporations. Both are viewed as actors in an unholy alliance for mutual enrichment. In many cases, youth are also critical of their parents for insufficient care and attention to their upbringing and welfare. But they also engage in brutally honest self-criticism about the lure of mining for themselves in the here and now. For a number of reasons, Honwana's concept of 'waithood' bears reconsideration in the Tanzanian mining context.

Artisanal mining has opened a window of economic opportunity for youth. In artisanal mining areas, young people are likely to be experiencing greater economic empowerment than youth in rural and urban settings elsewhere in Africa. However there are serious trade-offs between: (i) pursuing education with long-term benefits versus mining with short-term benefits; (ii) gaining autonomy from parents and elders versus a lack of parental oversight; and (iii) traditional family coherence reinforced by bridewealth and strong ties to rural kin versus physical mobility, casual relationships, and urban lifestyles.

By taking on economic responsibility in a risk-filled occupation, and/or living in families where parents employed in the mining sector and associated service sector are so heavily pre-occupied, it is likely that youth, rather than postponing full adult maturity are being catapulted into premature adulthood. Is the loss of a relatively carefree and innocent adolescence worth the gain in economic autonomy? Most young Tanzanian miners would defiantly answer yes (Terres des Hommes Schweiz 2012).

The issue of youth employment in mining settlement is both delicate and complex. Young people who are full-time miners are likely to be identified as 'miners' rather than as 'youth.' They would be wary of being distinguished from other miners because of their young age since the vast majority are there by their own independent volition and are intent on being accepted as full-fledged miners and striking gold. Secondary school students, on the other hand, lured into part-time mining are responding to the need for cash, but they are clearly torn between that immediate goal and their desire to study to secure a professional job in the future. At present, they have little support when facing this dilemma. In contrast to the policy measures directed at HIV/AIDS awareness in mining communities and youth, identification of policy measures to help students cope with the school fee dilemma as well as other educational constraints they encounter rarely exists. The formulation of effective policies to address this problem would need to be grounded in in-depth dialogue with students and educational personnel about possible solutions. Above all, at this point, there is need for expanding general awareness about the on-going economic, social, and cultural transformation in mining settlements in which youth are playing a central role.

In conclusion, as in previous eras, youth are playing an active role in the emergence of new economic sectors and are currently engaging in and shaping the artisanal mining sector. Nonetheless, there is a discontinuity with the past in terms on the part of full-time, youthful miners, intent on improving their lives and gaining autonomy, who tend to be completely removed from elder or parental control and are rarely planning to return to their home areas. They are no longer endeavouring to earn bridewealth payments and return to their home areas to farm, which marks a distinct break in the inter-generational contract between older and younger generations. So too, secondary school students' criticisms of their parents' absence from the home and their lack of parental care, can be interpreted as a new tension between the young and older generation.

Artisanal mining, particularly that related to mineral rushes, places high demands on male mobility and has an erosive effect on family life. There are several other drawbacks: artisanal mining is physically dangerous, its excavation depth is technically limited and as large-scale mining expands, it is bound to contract spatially as government-granted large-scale mineral rights increasingly gain precedence over those of artisanal miners, displacing artisanal miners and fuelling their conflictual incursions on large-scale mining. Most miners and mining settlement residents see artisanal mining as an opportunity of the moment, not one that can be counted on far into the future. Thus Tanzanian youth, whether they are full-time or part-time miners, think of artisanal mining as a temporary fix or more optimistically a stepping stone to gaining capital to invest in another occupation elsewhere. In other words, for most youth, despite all its pitfalls, mining can be a means to a better future, but not their chosen future.

Acknowledgements

Data findings from the Urban Growth and Poverty in Mining Africa (UPIMA) study funded by the United Kingdom's Department for International Development (DfID) and the Economic and Social Research Council (RES 167–25–0488) empirically support this research. I am grateful to the Tanzania UPIMA survey team: Dr. Jesper Bosse Jønsson (field coordinator), Dr. Crispin Kinabo, Mike Shand, Elard Mawala, as well as the Urban Foundation sponsoring my Senior Research Fellowship at the University of Glasgow. Thanks go to Mike Shand for his data processing and mapping work.

Notes

1 Existing mining companies from South Africa, Australia, Canada, and the United Kingdom were joined by China, India, and Brazil as new entrants in African mining.
2 Iliffe (1979: 62–63) quotes the remark of Mirambo, the 19th-century warlord and chief who terrorized the countryside with his extensive slave raiding: 'We never take middle aged men or old men to our wars, always youth not yet troubled with wives and children. They have keener eyes and lither limbs.'
3 It was a period of exceptionally widespread political insecurity and economic upheaval due to predatory slave raiding taking place alongside the environmentally depleting pursuit of ivory. Many agricultural tribes retreated into palisaded settlements and young women and children lived in fear of being seized by slave raiders (Wright 1993).
4 The 1997 Mineral Policy, the 1997 Investment Act, the 1998 Mining Act, and the 1999 Mining Regulations.
5 According to Dr. Crispin Kinabo, Geology Department, University of Dar es Salaam, member of the investigating committee. The report has yet to be published.

6 Twenty-seven of Tanzania's approximately 125 tribal groups were represented in our random sample survey, the dominant group (22 percent) being the agro-pastoral Sukuma whose home area is in the Lake Victoria region where the gold mines are concentrated.

7 Our survey research questions encompassed: migration patterns; family formation; livelihood and income; land access and food production; housing accommodation and living conditions; content and level of consumption; attitudes towards home and settlement; investment; and leisure activities. We conducted 97 semi-structured qualitative interviews with key informants, and six focus group discussions, five with students from primary and secondary schools located in the sites and one with small-scale miners at one site location. The qualitative interviewing focused primarily on settlement history, infrastructure and institutional development, but also touched upon specific topics related to the work and livelihood of the interviewees.

8 Achieving even coverage in sampling mining populations poses logistical difficulties, given the array of residential housing units and the variation of occupants' occupational composition and temporal presence in the dwellings. Surveying miners at their place of work can be trying for the enumerators and intrusive for the households. The problem can be offset by interviewing miners during their leisure time, generally at bars and recreational centres, like pool halls, during evening hours.

9 At Geita and Nyarugusu secondary schools the performances of students' plays, poems, and short stories were accompanied by written scripts; this was not the case at Ikuzi primary school, so analysis of the students' narratives was restricted to Geita and Nyarugusu.

References

Abbink, J., and I. van Kessel (eds.) (2005). *Vanguard or Vandals: Youth, Politics and Conflict in Africa*. Leiden: Brill.

Anderson, D. (2002). 'Vigilantes, Violence, and the Politics of Public Order in Kenya.' *African Affairs*, 101: 531–55.

Bourgouin, F. (2014). 'The Politics of Mining: Foreign Direct Investment, the State and Artisanal Mining in Tanzania.' In D. F. Bryceson, J. B. Jønsson, E. Fisher, and R. Mwaipopo (eds.), *Mining and Social Transformation in Africa*. London: Routledge, 148–60.

Brode, H. (2000). *Tippu Tip: The Story of His Career in Zanzibar and Central Africa Narrated from His Accounts* (trans. H. Havelock). Zanzibar: The Gallery Publications.

Bryceson, D. F. (1990). *Food Insecurity and the Social Division of Labour in Tanzania, 1919–85*. London: Macmillan.

Bryceson, D. F. (1995). 'Gender Relations in Tanzania: Cultural Consensus or Power Politics?' In C. Creighton and C. K. Omari (eds.), *Family, Household and Gender in Tanzania*. Aldershot UK: Avebury, 37–69.

Bryceson, D. F. (1999). 'African Rural Labour, Income Diversification and Livelihood Approaches.' *Review of African Political Economy*, 80: 171–89.

Bryceson, D. F. (2002). 'Multiplex Livelihoods in Rural Africa: Recasting the Terms and Conditions of Gainful Employment.' *Journal of Modern African Studies*, 40(1): 1–28.

Bryceson, D. F. (2010). 'Between Moral Economy and Civil Society: Durkheim Revisited.' In D.F. Bryceson (ed.), *How Africa Works: Occupationality, Identity and Morality*. Rugby: Practical Action Publishing.

Bryceson, D. F., and J. B. Jønsson (2010). 'Gold Digging Careers in Rural East Africa: Small-Scale Miners' Livelihood Choices.' *World Development*, 38(3): 379–92.

Bryceson, D. F., and J. B. Jønsson (forthcoming). 'Getting Grounded: Migrants' Household and Occupational Formation in Tanzanian Gold and Diamond Mining Settlements.' *Urban Mining Settlements in Africa: Towards Urban Prosperity and Precarity*.

Bryceson, D. F., and J. B. Jønsson (2014). 'Mineralizing Africa and Artisanal Mining's Democratizing Influence.' In D. F. Bryceson et al. (eds.), *Mining and Social Transformation in Africa: Mineralizing and Democratizing Trends in Artisanal Production*. London: Routledge, 1–22.

Bryceson, D. F., J. B. Jønsson, C. Kinabo, and M. Shand (2012). 'Unearthing Treasure and Trouble: Mining as an Impetus to Urbanisation in Tanzania.' *Journal of Contemporary African Studies*, 30(4): 631–49.

Bryceson, D. F., J. B. Jønsson, and H. Verbrugge (2013). 'Prostitution or Partnership? Wife-styles in Tanzanian Artisanal Gold-mining Settlements.' *Journal of Modern African Studies*, 51(1): 33–56.

Bryceson, D. F., J. B. Jønsson, and H. Verbrugge (2014). 'For Richer, for Poorer: Marriage and Casualized Sex in East African Artisanal Mining Settlements.' *Development and Change*, 45(1): 1–26.

Buchert, L. (1994). *Education in the Development of Tanzania 1919–1990*. London: James Currey.

Burgess, G. T., and A. Burton (2010). 'Introduction.' In A. Burton and H. Charton-Bigot (eds.), *Generations Past: Youth in East African History*. Athens, OH: Ohio University Press, 1–24.

Giblin, J. L. (2010). 'Setting a Moral Economy in Motion: Youth in Tanzania's Age of Improvement.' In A. Burton and H. Charton-Bigot (eds.), *Generations Past: Youth in East African History*. Athens, OH: Ohio University Press, 68–83.

Honwana, A. (2012). *The Time of Youth: Work, Social Change and Politics*. Herndon, VA: Kumarian Press.

Honwana, A., and F. De Boeck (2005). *Makers and Breakers: Children and Youth in Postcolonial Africa*. Oxford: James Currey.

Iliffe, J. (1979). *A Modern History of Tanganyika*. Cambridge: Cambridge University Press.

International Council of Mining and Metals (ICMM) (2012). *The Role of Mining in National Economies*. London: ICMM.

Jønsson, J. B., and D. F. Bryceson (2009). 'Rushing for Gold: Mobility and Small-Scale Mining in East Africa.' *Development and Change*, 40(2): 249–79.

Jønsson, J. B., and N. Fold (2011). 'Mining "from Below": Taking Africa's Artisanal Miners Seriously.' *Geography Compass*, 5(7): 479–93.

Jua, N. (2010). 'Body and Soul: Economic Space, Public Morality and Social Integration of Youth in Cameroon'. In D. F. Bryceson (ed.), *How Africa Works: Occupational Change, Identity and Morality*. Rugby: Practical Action Publishing, 129–48.

Kulindwa, K., O. Mashindano, F. Shechambo, and H. Sosovele (2003). *Mining for Sustainable Development in Tanzania*. Dar es Salaam: Dar es Salaam University Press.

Mbilinyi, M. (1989). 'Women's Resistance in "Customary" Marriage: Tanzania's Runaway Wives.' In A. Zegeye, and S. Ishemo (eds.), *Forced Labour and Migration: Patterns of Movement within Africa*. London: Hans Zell, 211–54.

Meagher, K. (2007). 'Hijacking Civil Society: The Inside Story of the Bakassi Boys Vigilante Group of South-eastern Nigeria.' *Journal of Modern African Studies*, 45(1): 89–115.

Pratt, C. (1978). *The Critical Phase in Tanzania 1945–1968*. Nairobi: Oxford University Press.

Reid, R. (2010). 'Arms and Adolescence: Male Youth, Warfare, and Statehood in Nineteenth-century Eastern Africa.' In A. Burton and H. Charton-Bigot (eds.), *Generations Past: Youth in East African History*. Athens, OH: Ohio University Press, 25–46.

Rockel, S. J. (2000). '"A Nation of Porters": The Nywamwezi and the Labour Market in Nineteenth-century Tanzania.' *Journal of African History*, 41: 173–95.

Roe, A. R., and M. Essex (2009). 'Mining in Tanzania – What Future can we Expect?' Paper presented at the ICMM Workshop on 'Mining in Tanzania,' Dar es Salaam, 18 May 2009 (revised 28 June 2009).

Rwebangira, M. K., and R. Liljeström (eds.) (1998). *Haraka, Haraka: Youth at the Crossroad of Custom and Modernity.* Uppsala: Nordiska Afrikainstitute.

Swann, A. J. (1910). *Fighting the Slave Hunters in Central Africa.* New York: J. B. Lippincott Company.

Tan Discovery (1996). 'Final Report on Baseline Survey and Preparation of Development Strategy for Small Scale and Artisanal Mining Program.' Dar es Salaam: Ministry of Energy and Minerals/World Bank.

Terres des Hommes Schweiz (2012). 'Study of Migration of Youth in Mining Areas in Tanzania: Geita Gold Mines, Shinyanga Diamond Mines, Kahama Gold Mines.' Dar es Salaam: AMCA Inter-Consult Ltd.

Trudell, B., K. King, S. McGrath, and P. Nugent (2002). 'Africa's Young Majority.' Paper. University of Edinburgh: Centre for African Studies.

United Republic of Tanzania (2009). 'The Economic Survey.' Dar es Salaam: Ministry of Finance and Economic Affairs.

United Republic of Tanzania (2010a), 'Basic Education Statistics in Tanzania: National Data, 2006–2010,' Dar es Salaam: Ministry of Education and Vocational Training.

United Republic of Tanzania (2010b). 'The Economic Survey.' Dar es Salaam: Ministry of Finance and Economic Affairs.

Varkevisser, C. M. (1973). *Socialization in a Changing Society: Sukuma Childhood in Rural and Urban Mwanza, Tanzania.* Den Haag: Nuffic.

Wedgwood, R. (2005). 'Post Basic Education and Poverty in Tanzania.' Post-Basic Education and Training Working Paper Series No. 1. Edinburgh: University of Edinburgh.

Wilson, M. (1977). *For Men and Elders: Changes in the Relations of Generations and of Men and Women among the Nyakyusa-Ngonde People 1875–1971.* London: International African Institute.

World Bank (2012). 'Africa's Pulse: An Analysis of Issues Shaping Africa's Economic Future.' Washington DC: World Bank.

Wright, M. (1993). *Strategies of Slaves and Women: Life-Stories from East/Central Africa.* London: James Currey.

Appendix

Table 5.A1 Parents' expectations for children's future careers (213 children)

Anticipated occupation of offspring	% of total	Educated, professional	Defence	Semi-skilled, skilled, talented	Business	Politics	Religion	De facto work
Doctor	15.5	15.5						
Nurse	17.4	17.4						
Teacher	18.0	18.0						
Police, soldier	8.7		8.7					
Lawyer, judge	5.0	5.0						
Engineer, scientist	3.7	3.7						
Semi-skilled*	5.0			5.0				
Journalist, broadcaster	3.7	3.7						
Pilot	2.5	2.5						
Religious leader: pastor, sheik	3.7						3.7	
Banker, accountant	0.6				0.6			
Skilled**	3.1			3.1				
Regional politics***	3.1					3.1		
Public service****	1.9	1.9						
National politics: President	0.6					0.6		
Business administration & management	0.6				0.6			
Talent: artist, footballer	2.5			2.5				
Farmer	1.2							1.2
Housewife, waitress	1.9							1.9
Miner	1.2							1.2
TOTAL	100.0	67.7	8.7	10.6	1.2	3.7	3.7	4.3

Source: 2012 UPIMA survey.

Notes: *Semi-skilled: mechanic, tailor, secretary, mason, driver; **Skilled: technician, computer programmer, electrician, plant operator, communications, artisan, ***Regional politics: Member of Parliament, Councillor, District Commissioner; ****Public service: civil servant, agronomist, land surveyor

Part III

Assessing extant policy options for improving youth employment

6 Young people, agriculture, and employment in rural Africa

James Sumberg, Nana Akua Anyidoho, Michael Chasukwa, Blessings Chinsinga, Jennifer Leavy, Getnet Tadele, Stephen Whitfield, and Joseph Yaro

Introduction

Despite long-term processes of migration and urbanization, it is estimated that more than 60 percent of Africans continue to live in rural areas (World Bank 2011a), and many are engaged to some degree with agriculture. At the same time, poverty in Africa continues to be concentrated in rural areas (Baulch 2011). There are well-established arguments about the ability of agriculture to act as an engine of economic growth, and evidence of strong poverty reduction effects associated with growth in the smallholder sector (Christiaensen et al. 2011; Dercon 2009; Dorward et al. 2004). And, after decades of neglect, there is now significant policy, development agency and private sector investment interest in and around agriculture in Africa, which can be linked to rising food prices, the rush to biofuels and fears of climate change effects on food production and availability, as well as the influence of new actors including some private foundations.

Despite a decade in which some African economies have experienced relatively high rates of economic growth, and the fact that the 2008 global economic crisis had only muted effects on most African economies, in many parts of the sub-continent unemployment and under-employment among young people are increasingly seen as the hard core of the development challenge (World Bank 2006, 2009). While often hidden by official statistics, many young people find themselves stuck in informal sector jobs with few prospects. This is the (youthful) human face of the phenomenon of 'jobless growth,' and undermines any possibility of realizing the much heralded 'demographic dividend' (Eastwood and Lipton 2011; USAID 2012). Unemployment and under-employment among young people sits in tension with the increased investment in education through the Millennium Development Goals and the heightened expectations among young people associated with access to education.

The persistence of rural poverty, the renewed interest in agriculture and a sense of urgency in relation to employment for young people have coalesced in the minds of policy makers and development professionals, to the point where the agricultural sector has become one (if not *the*) obvious place to look for solutions to the crisis in youth employment (e.g. Bernard and Taffesse 2012). Policy and programmes typically seek to realize this apparent potential through group farming schemes, training in entrepreneurship, and improved access to markets, micro-credit and other productive assets. These interventions are informed by two contrasting views. The first is that bright, educated, and ambitious young people do not find small-scale farming an attractive employment or career option, and therefore the challenge is to make them aware of the opportunities available and provide them with entrepreneurial attitudes, skills, and the resources needed to move into 'farming as a business.' The second is that rather than a lack of interest, the problem is with agrarian institutions and dynamics – e.g., around land – that stop young people from getting a start in agriculture (e.g. Amanor 2010).

The question that underpins this chapter is: what role can policy and associated programmes and projects play in re-aligning rural young people's engagement with agriculture and thus drive social and economic mobility? Our contribution is to provide a conceptual framework with which to address this question, and we use this framework to guide a preliminary exploration of a selection of programmes from three countries. We argue that these programmes are never likely to provide the promotive and transformative employment opportunities that will attract large numbers of young people to farming. We further argue that this goal is itself flawed. On the other hand, through a longer-term process of structural change there is scope to make the broader agrifood sector a source of employment that can help deliver increased social and economic mobility to rural young people. The remainder of this chapter is organized as follows. The next section sets out the background, theory, and concepts, with a focus on transitions (youth and poverty) and mobility (aspirational, economic, social, and spatial). Following this we propose a conceptual framework that focuses on difference and diversity among work opportunities, rural areas and young people. The notion of opportunity space is at the heart of this framework. We then use this framework to briefly explore programmes from Ethiopia, Malawi, and Ghana. The final section concludes.

Background and concepts

The African rural youth employment challenge

In response to global recognition of the problem of youth unemployment and under-employment,[1] and talk of a 'lost generation,' academic inquiry into its causes, consequences and potential policy solutions has increased greatly since the mid-2000s. Contributions from across the social sciences have added new insights to a field traditionally dominated by labour market studies. Within this broad literature, the causes of unemployment and underemployment are usually seen from one of two perspectives. The first focuses on those mechanisms through which young people become prepared for employment with a focus on the effectiveness of the education system and the rates of attainment of secondary and tertiary education (Bennell 1996; Glick and Sahn 1997; Kingdon and Knight 2004). The second perspective highlights characteristics of the labour markets that young people are attempting to enter. Here the spotlight is on the availability and accessibility of opportunities and the factors that result in an employment supply shortfall including reductions in public sector jobs (Calves and Schoumaker 2004; Floro and Schaefer 1998) and limited private investment (Anyanwu 2013; Oviasuyi et al. 2012). Inequality of opportunity associated with institutional bias or ineffective (or non-existent) legal protections is also increasingly recognized (Deranty and MacMillan 2012; OECD 2012), particularly, but not exclusively, associated with gender.

From both perspectives, addressing the employment problem is usually understood as a matter for national policy, whether in terms of restructuring public education systems (Pauw et al. 2008); the creation of public sector employment (Thwala 2011); the creation of a more attractive environment for private sector investment (Oviasuyi et al. 2012); or the protection of equal worker's rights (Deranty and MacMillan 2012). Much of the consequent policy and development intervention is grounded in the International Labour Organization's 'Decent Work Agenda,' which highlights the responsibility of governments to prioritize job creation and the protection of workers' rights and freedoms with the objective of reducing unemployment and promoting a more productive and sustainable high-employment economy (ILO 2007).

In recognition of the complexity and structural origins of youth unemployment and underemployment, and governments' limited abilities to simply create jobs, both academic and policy attention has turned to the potential for young people to essentially create their own employment. 'Entrepreneurship' has become a critical pathway for creating employment to simultaneously drive productivity and economic growth (e.g. the FAO-ILO-NEPAD Partnership on Decent Employment for Rural Transformation) (Jeffrey and Dyson 2013).

Rural young people

All too often in African policy discourse young people are lumped into the category 'youth.' Trapped in the void between children and adults, 'the youth' are at once 'the future of the nation,' vulnerable, at risk, and in need of close supervision. If their agency is acknowledged, it is often associated with anti-social or politically disruptive behaviour. Labeled as 'the youth,' it should perhaps not be surprising that policy most often frames young people simplistically and instrumentally – as a homogeneous group whose primary role is to build the economy and the nation (Anyidoho et al. 2012a; te Lintelo 2012). However, it should go without saying that rural young people are socially and spatially embedded, and differences in gender, age, religion, ethnicity, education and family position, and the strength and breadth of social networks, social norms – and personality – all bear on their ambitions and aspirations, and their engagement with the world of work. It follows that for research, policy analysis, and formulation, the category 'youth' is every bit as problematic as 'the poor,' 'women,' 'rural people,' and 'small-scale farmers' which deny the nuanced, complex reality within which people make their way.

Agricultural policy and employment

The basic logic of agriculture sector development policy in Africa as it relates to employment creation is shown in Figure 6.1. On the right hand side there are three different employment outcomes: the first relating to the self-employed farmer or producer, the second to farm labour and the third to agriculture-related off-farm

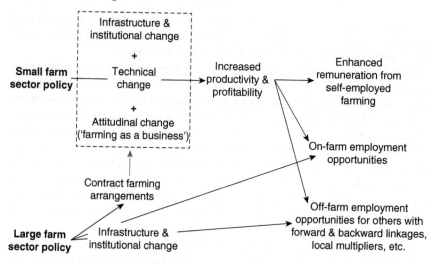

Figure 6.1 Agricultural policy and employment
Source: Authors' compilation.

jobs. The small farm channel in the top half of the figure continues to dominate agricultural policy and programmes in much of Africa, although there has
recently been a resurgence of interest in and argument for the large farm channel
(e.g. Collier 2008). The problem with this figure is that it gives no recognition to
the interplay between larger economic and social processes (and their associated
politics) and local factors and processes (and their politics). This interplay mediates the dynamics of change in the agricultural sector and how it is experienced
in particular settings and by different groups of people, including young people.

Two transitions and three mobilities

In this section we begin to build the foundation for a conceptual framework by
introducing two overarching concepts: transition and mobility. Both of these concepts are integral to contemporary understandings of young people, livelihoods,
and poverty. Critically, both concepts suggest movement, action, and dynamics.
Specifically we will focus on two transitions: youth transitions and poverty transitions, and three mobilities: aspirational, economic, social, and spatial mobility.
The suggestion is that both youth and poverty transitions are to a significant degree
underpinned by – and are part and parcel of – these mobilities and their interactions. Notions of structure, agency, and networks are central to this understanding.

Two transitions

Poverty transitions refer to the dynamic poverty status of a household or individual: 'movements into poverty, escapes from poverty and the inability to escape
from poverty' (Lawson et al. 2006: 1226). Research on chronic poverty highlights

multiple and intersecting determinants, from the personal to the social, political, and structural. Literature on poverty transitions and their drivers and dynamics is closely linked to the broader understanding of social mobility (Baulch 2011; Bird 2007; Dercon and Shapiro 2007; Harper et al. 2003; Narayan and Petesch 2007; Smith and Moore 2006). Economic and livelihoods approaches to poverty transitions focus at both individual and household levels and highlight factors such as access and returns to various assets, and how these are mediated by markets, social norms, gender relations, macroeconomic policies, and shocks.

'Youth transitions' theories conceptualize the processes, drivers, and determinants of the changes experienced by young people as their dependence relationships evolve (Locke and te Lintelo 2012; MacDonald 2011; Worth 2009). Whilst changing dependency relationships are perhaps most commonly associated with a transition to economic independence marked by the life changing event of moving from education to employment (Ansell 2004), it has been recognized that adulthood can be identified by a whole set of social and cultural markers (Lloyd 2006; MacDonald et al. 2001); that trajectories of transition are plural, diverse, and often partial, constituting a range of possible life events (Locke and te Lintelo 2012); and that these trajectories and their end points might be determined by a combination of individual choices, initial and changing social capital, and structural barriers (Worth 2009). In rural and developing country contexts, the negotiation of structural constraints – including location, social expectations, quality of education, economic resources, employment opportunities – is a critical part of any transition (Crivello 2011; Locke and te Lintelo 2012). In many cases, internal and international migration is important both as a strategy and a marker of transition, and changing geographies of opportunity represent an important driver of the transitions of rural young people (Crivello 2011). Bynner (2005) suggests it is not helpful to try to standardize an experience that is so diverse (also see Crivello 2011; Hall et al. 2009; te Riele 2004); nevertheless more linear and deterministic models of transition out of economic dependence (or poverty) based on a progression from educational achievement to employment, still informs the policy of some international agencies (USAID 2012; World Bank 2009).

Three mobilities

In this section we draw attention to three interacting mobilities – aspirational, economic and social, and spatial – as they relate to young people, livelihoods, and poverty dynamics. Aspirations – what someone hopes will happen in the future – are thought to play an important role in influencing life choices and life outcomes (Schaefer and Meece 2009); they are therefore an important component of poverty dynamics. Aspirations tend to be formed in early childhood and are shaped and modified over time into expectations (what someone believes is likely to happen) and ultimately outcomes (see review by Leavy and Smith 2010). The interplay of different forces in the contemporary context, spanning globalization, urbanization and migration, engagement in diverse labour markets, and the connectivity offered by new media and communications technology, means young people increasingly construct their aspirations and identities by drawing inspiration from outside their local, historical, and socio-political contexts (Langevang and Gough 2012). A strong policy focus on education, embodied in the second Millennium Development Goal on universal primary education, as well as efforts to encourage and support young people to complete secondary schooling, has seen increasing average education levels in developing countries (UNESCO 2012; World Bank 2011b), fostering rising aspirations and expectations of what these higher education levels might bring. Factors that have an 'inflationary' effect on aspirations, however, may also serve to widen the gap between aspirations and attainment, and can result in vulnerability to impacts of negative external events such as an economic downturn. However, poor quality schooling and other features inherent in rural areas (e.g. isolated communities with limited social networks, a narrower range of experiences and limited role models, and fewer clear and effective transmission mechanisms for poor rural populations to benefit from economic growth) act as a constraint on aspirational mobility (see Lieten et al. 2007; Mulkeen 2005). Social norms and social pressures in rural areas – including gender prescribed roles and responsibilities – reinforce 'traditional' ways of living and doing, further constraining (or channeling) aspirations.

In the research literature there is a longstanding interest in the link between education and aspirations, with some work highlighting 'aspiration gaps' in relation to education (e.g. Del Franco 2010 on adolescent girls in Bangladesh), employment (Kritzinger 2002), and social norms, well-being and poverty (Camfield et al. 2012; Copestake and Camfield 2010). However, based on work from the United Kingdom, St Clair and Benjamin (2011) warn against a deficit approach to aspirations that 'can lead to people being blamed for being poor and at the bottom of the social hierarchy on the grounds that this simply reflects their own aspirational deficits' (St Clair and Benjamin 2011: 503). Suggesting that there is an important 'performative' element to aspirations, they argue that 'there are no 'true' aspirations, simply responses that young people find effective to utter in particular situations' (St Clair and Benjamin 2011: 504). It follows that an isolated focus on young people's aspirations is unlikely to be of much value, but shifting aspirations must certainly be considered in analysing young people's engagement with the world of work.

Social mobility is the movement over time from one social class or socioeconomic status to another. Sociology tends to consider social mobility in terms of movement across occupational groups, while economics focuses more on income (Bowles and Gintis 2002; Erikson and Goldthorpe 2002; Heath 1981). The social mobility literature makes the distinction between *intra-generational* (over the course of a life-time: specifically a change in class and/or income over a single life-time) and *inter-generational* (change in socio-economic status between parents and their children) social mobility. Key drivers of social mobility include: income; education; human capital; social capital and social networks; physical capital; and choice of occupation and other markers of status or prestige (so-called 'symbolic' capital). Two commonly used measures of social mobility are: the index of educational opportunity (defined as the effect of family background on student performance (see Crawford et al. 2011)); and intergenerational income elasticity (i.e. the extent to which parents' income predicts their children's income (Solon 1992; Zimmerman 1992). The latter has a strong correlation with income inequality, and in some studies social mobility has been measured as increased consumption expenditure (e.g. Bezu et al. 2012 on rural non-farm incomes in Ethiopia).

While social mobility is well established in northern scholarship and political discourse, it is less prominent in relation to international development in general and Africa in particular (although in the 1960s and 1970s there was some considerable research interest in social mobility in Africa, particularly in relation to education, migration, and urban populations (Hurd and Johnson 1967; Kelley and Perlman 1971). More recent studies focus on occupational mobility, especially in South Africa, e.g. Woolard and Klasen (2005), on household income mobility dynamics in Kwa-zulu; Ziervogel and Crankshaw (2009) on inter-generational occupational mobility amongst blacks in Cape Town; and Finn et al. (2012) on income mobility. Education and skills training has been central to thinking about both social and economic mobility (see Buchmann and Hannum 2001 for a review), although Bowles and Gintis (2002) question the significance of this link. Of course, education-social mobility linkages are mediated by labour market mechanisms, and where the rate of expansion of employment opportunities fails to keep pace with expansion in education there can be 'education devaluation' with higher levels of education needed to achieve the same positions over time (Hurd and Johnson 1967).

Our third mobility, spatial mobility, includes daily movements within a local space, occasional travel, and long-term migrations and resettlements (Kaufmann 2002); it may be within rural or urban locations or between them (De Bruijn et al. 2001); and involve crossing local spaces or international boundaries. The motivations for movement are varied: to access resources; in pursuit of opportunities; for building human and social capital (Ansell et al. 2012; Langevang and Gough 2009; Porter et al. 2011); or forceful displacement in response to natural disasters, conflict or land acquisition. A growing body of literature considers spatial mobility in relation to employment and economic independence (Ansell et al. 2012; Porter et al. 2011; van Ham et al. 2001). The ability to access employment and market opportunities that are outside a person's local geography is an important determinant of economic success and career status, and this understanding underpins the concept of 'mobility as capital' (Kaufmann et al. 2004). However, the relationship between spatial mobility and social and economic mobility is not simple (Gough 2008; Savage 1988). Scholars interested in the 'geographies of children and youth' recognized spatial mobility as a component of independence, and central to the shaping of identity: mobility helps define both growing up and adulthood (Holdsworth 2009; Holt and Costello 2011; Valentine et al. 2009). Movement involves direct and indirect costs, including transport costs and foregone earnings whilst travelling, but also personal and social sacrifices (Ansell et al. 2012; Gough 2008). An individual's 'mobility capital' – in essence their ability to meet these costs – might depend on economic resources, status, social networks (Ansell et al. 2012; Gough 2008; White and Green 2011), and access to transport (Bryceson et al. 2002), amongst a host of other factors (Gough 2008; Porter et al. 2012).

With some notable exceptions there has been relatively little research on spatial mobility of African young people, and particularly those living in rural areas. Ansell et al. (2012) identified four particular spatial strategies adopted by young people in rural South Africa in the pursuit of productive livelihoods: (1) travel for access to better education; (2) migration for work; (3) using dispersed social networks (e.g. to join an extended family business); and (4) travel to distant markets for selling produce. The mobility of African populations, particularly in rural areas, has been recognized (Adepoju 1995), despite constraints such as underdeveloped infrastructure (Porter 2010), on-farm and at-home income generating responsibilities (Ansell et al. 2012; Porter et al. 2010) and social and cultural expectations (Ansell et al. 2012).

The 'transformative work' and 'opportunity space' framework

With these two transitions and three mobilities firmly in mind, in this section we introduce a conceptual framework, which we argue can provide a useful lens for the analysis of policies, programmes and projects touching on young people and agriculture in Africa. First, we explore the diversity of rural areas. Then we introduce the transformative work element of the framework before linking these together through the concept of opportunity space.

Economic geographers have long recognized that in order to take advantage of labour and economies of scale, economic activity from the secondary and tertiary sectors locates in and around urban centres (Fujita and Krugman 1995; Krugman 1993). Whilst diversification of some economic activity in rural areas is observed (Barrett et al. 2001; Bryceson 2002; Ellis 2011), it is inevitably limited compared to more urban areas (Wiggins and Proctor 2001). It is only in regards to 'immobile natural resources' (Wiggins and Proctor 2001), such as farm land, forests, water bodies, landscapes, and minerals that rural areas have a competitive advantage. Wiggins and Proctor (2001) have argued that there are two key dimensions of rural areas that determine economic opportunities: proximity to urban centres (markets) and quality of natural resources. As illustrated in Table 6.1, a matrix of three stylized zones (peri-urban, 'middle' countryside and remote rural) and a stylized assessment of the quality of natural resources (good or poor) helps to characterize potential development and employment opportunities. The value of this simple disaggregation is that it highlights the diversity of rural areas, and consequent impacts on the labour market. It is of course important to remember that for any particular area such analysis is contingent: urban centres expand and new ones materialize; the market value of natural resources change, as population grows (or shrinks); and, as new infrastructure and communications technology reduce the 'distance' between spaces (Wiggins and Proctor 2001).

Table 6.1 Rural diversity – a characterization, with most likely activities

Quality of natural resources	Location characteristics		
	Peri-urban zones	'Middle' countryside	Remote rural areas
Good	Market gardening & dairying Daily commuting to the city Weekend recreation activities Manufacturing industry may 'deconcentrate' from city properinto this space	Arable farming & livestock production, specialized, with capital investment, producing surpluses for the market Tourism & recreation Some crafts By-employment in rural industry Migration	Subsistence farming, with only the production of surpluses of high value items that can bear transport costs Crafts & services for local markets Tourism & recreation Migration
Poor	As above: *i.e. Market gardening & dairying* NB: Quality of natural resources not so important since capital can be used to augment poor land – e.g. by irrigation, fertiliser – when needed for intensive farming	Extensive farming, probably livestock. Probably lightly settled *Few jobs* Tourism & recreation Some crafts Migration	Subsistence farming, low productivity. *Surpluses very small or negligible* Crafts & services for local markets Tourism & recreation Migration

Source: Adapted from Wiggins and Proctor (2001) emphasis added.

If there is a diversity of rural areas, the same is true of work opportunities. It is widely appreciated that work opportunities, whether in the formal or informal sector, vary in respect to the skills required, the level of remuneration, risks to personal safety, social status, social identity, and so on. While these differences are obviously important, from a development perspective that places poverty reduction, social justice, and social transformation at centre stage, they are not sufficient. Here we borrow from the literature on social protection (Devereux and Sabates-Wheeler 2007) to suggest that work opportunities can usefully be placed into four categories:

- **Protective** work, such as food-for-work and labour-intensive public works schemes, provides relief from the immediate effects of deprivation. These opportunities are directly dependent on government or other relief programmes, and often form part of a broad system of benefits designed to act as a social safety net.
- **Preventative** work is also defined relative to deprivation, but in this case, it is a matter of forestalling rather than directly relieving deprivation. Examples in rural areas include low productivity, small-scale farming, and low-paying, insecure, informal sector work.

- **Promotive** work allows real incomes and capabilities to be enhanced, and for capital to be accumulated. Some types of farming (e.g. the rapid accumulation of capital – 'quick money' – by young tomato producers in Brong Ahafo, Ghana described by Okali and Sumberg (2012)) and trading could be considered promotive, as could some formal sector work.
- **Transformative** work allows real incomes and capabilities to be enhanced, *and* addresses social equity and exclusion issues. In the case of women, transformative work might be regarded as that which increases their social status and contributes to the achievement of gender equity (Kantor et al. 2006). Labour laws that regulate worker rights are the most common means of addressing equity and exclusion in the workplace, and it is therefore logical that transformative work opportunities will be associated essentially with the formal sector (e.g. Barrientos et al. 2003).

This spectrum of work is not specific to young people, and at the same time it maps to Dorward's (2009) three rural livelihood strategies: 'hanging in' ('concerned to maintain and protect current levels of wealth and welfare in the face of threats of stresses and shocks' (Dorward 2009: 136) which maps to protective and/or preventative work opportunities); 'stepping up' ('investments in assets to expand the scale or productivity of existing assets and activities' (Dorward 2009: 136) which maps to promotive work opportunities); and 'stepping out' ('accumulation of assets to allow investments or switches into new activities and assets' (Dorward 2009: 136) which maps in part to the notion of transformative work).

We argue that policy and programmes addressing unemployment among rural young people must focus on the promotive-transformative end of the continuum. This brings us back to agriculture. While in rural Africa it is certainly possible to identify some examples of promotive work, much of today's smallholder farming, and particularly in remote areas, or where plots are small, natural resources poor and/or productivity low, would have to be considered preventative at best, (i.e. while employment in farming under these conditions averts deprivation it provides little opportunity for the processes of capital or asset accumulation that might drive social or economic mobility and/or satisfy aspirational mobility). This is not to say that protective and preventative employment opportunities within agriculture are not valuable. Indeed they are likely to be particularly so for the most disadvantaged. In a way these kinds of employment opportunities might even act as drivers of social and economic mobility for the most disadvantaged groups. However, we hypothesize that protective and preventative employment opportunities are unlikely to be (1) sufficient to attract increasingly educated young people with rising aspirations to agriculture or (2) an adequate basis on which to envisage the transition to a more modern agricultural sector.

We now build on the notion of opportunity space to being together the differences in rural areas and work opportunities highlighted above. Sumberg et al. (2012: 5) defined opportunity space as 'the spatial and temporal distribution of the universe of more or less viable [work] options that a young person may exploit as she/he attempts to establish an independent life.' In terms of the spatial dimension, and in the light of well-established patterns of both short- and long-term migration among young people, it is useful to distinguish between 'near' and 'distant' opportunity space.

The near opportunity space available to rural young people is to a significant degree structured by two sets of factors. We have already referred to the characteristics of the particular rural location, and specifically the quality of natural resources and proximity to or accessibility of markets, which go a long way in determining the kinds of economic activities that are likely to be viable in a particular location. The second set of factors is both social and relational. Social difference (including gender, age, class, ethnicity, level of education, and marital status), norms and expectations, and social relations and networks frame accepted ways of being and doing, and the kinds of activities and engagements that are considered appropriate and those that are not. In many societies, for example, women are expected to focus on household food security and welfare, which may have implications – at least during the early years of married life or when they have children – for their interest and/or ability to engage in entrepreneurial activity, especially when these activities involve working away from home. Social difference and social relations are critical in determining how easily and under what conditions key resources (like land, labour, credit, and information) can be accessed; family relations, be they supportive or constraining, can be particularly important for young people in the early stages of livelihood- building. Our basic argument is that characteristics of the rural location on the one hand, and social difference, norms, and relations on the other, structure the opportunity space for members of particular social groups in particular contexts. The resulting opportunity space can be analysed in terms of its depth (referring to number/extent of particular types of opportunities), diversity (of opportunities both within the agricultural sector and across other sectors), and dynamism (referring to the rapidity and extent of change).

These characteristics of the near opportunity space will be associated with the distribution of work opportunities across the categories from preventative to transformative. Some opportunity spaces might, for example, offer little potential for promotive or transformative work, while others might be far richer in such opportunities. It is within such a structured opportunity space that an individual young person gravitates toward some available work opportunities and away from others. In addition to everything else, this process that reflects personal (individual) aspirations, interests, aptitudes, and attitudes (i.e. toward risk, travel, etc.), as well as an element of chance.

There is also a distant opportunity space, the characteristics of which are independent of local spatial and natural resource conditions. The distant opportunity space might include other rural areas and/or urban areas, and not uncommonly has an international dimension. The exploitation of the distant opportunity space requires spatial mobility, through for example, short- or long-term migration. A willingness and ability to travel and live away from home are necessary in order to exploit the distant opportunity space. Many rural young people – both men and women – will at some point exploit part of their distant opportunity space; however, rather than a once and for all cutting of links with the rural world and with agriculture, a decision to explore the distant opportunity space can result in new capital, skills, information, and networks being incorporated into the rural economy. A longer-term view of the dynamics between the near and distant opportunity space, and between rural and urban areas, is therefore essential.

We believe that the transformative work and opportunity space framework as laid out above can be useful in the analysis of policies, programmes, or projects that seek to link young people, agriculture, and employment in rural areas of Africa. As illustrated in the next section, many of these seek to provide or facilitate access to skills (e.g. through technical, entrepreneurial, and/or management training, often framed as 'farming as a business' or the 'professionalization of agriculture'), productive resources (e.g. land and capital), markets and/or increase scale, efficiency, and/or market power through group-based strategies. The contribution of this framework is to insist that in relation to these kinds of initiatives, analysis of 'what works, where and for whom?' must take account of the diversity of employment types (from protective to transformative), the diversity of rural areas and the diversity of young people.

Case material

Five types of interventions that are relevant to the discussion of rural young people, employment and agriculture can be identified:

1   Government agriculture sector programmes that while not specifically targeting young people, may benefit some of them.
2   Government initiatives that specifically target young people in order to provide them with additional or enhanced employment opportunities in agriculture.
3   Government initiatives focused on young people's employment, and which have an agriculture component.
4   NGO projects that specifically target young people in order to provide them with additional or enhanced employment opportunities in agriculture.
5   Private sector agribusiness initiatives that while not specifically targeting young people may provide some of them with additional or enhanced employment opportunities.

In this section we use the framework developed above to begin an initial exploration of four examples of government initiatives that seek to provide employment opportunities to young people (the section draws on Anyidoho and Yaro 2013; Chinsinga and Chasukwa 2013; Tadele 2013). The example are from Ghana, Malawi, and Ethiopia, countries within which the Young People and Agrifood research theme of the Future Agriculture Consortium is active (see e.g. Anyidoho et al. 2012a; Anyidoho et al. 2012b; Chinsinga and Chasukwa 2012; Okali and Sumberg 2012; Tadele and Gella 2012). Only one of the cases is focused solely on agriculture, while the other three include agriculture. We believe these are representative of the range of government programmes in this area.

Ghana: National Youth Employment Programme (NYEP) (2006-present) and Youth In Agriculture Programme (YIAP) (2009-present)

The NYEP aims is to bridge the gap between education and formal employment and, in doing so, to 'empower the youth to contribute meaningfully to the socio-economic and sustainable development of the nation' (MMYE 2006). It operates through an internship model: selected applicants are placed within various government and quasi-government agencies. Participating young people are given a small allowance throughout the internship. In rural areas the specific objectives of the NYEP is 'to create employment opportunities for the youth through self-employment' (MMYE 2006). NYEP was established in 2006 and is implemented by the Ministry of Youth and Sport. The main indicator of success is the number of young people placed in jobs. In addition, the programme identifies other broad changes that it seeks to support including the creation of employment opportunities for the youth, for example, through self-employment; ensuring that the drift of youth from rural to urban communities is checked; the empowerment of young people to contribute to national development; and the reduction of deviance (MMYE 2006).

The internship model at the heart of NYEP limits the number of participants and does not provide a basis for a serious attack on the problem unemployment among young people. The programme does not address the extensive education and training required to make many young people employable. Further, it downplays the myriad challenges that young people face when trying to establish a business.

Does the programme address the dimensions of diversity highlighted in the conceptual framework? Young people are recruited and placed into modules based on the need and assets of their district of residence: the 'agri-business module' is meant to be particularly appropriate to rural areas. While it purports to cater to all young people, the programme appears to be geared towards those with more formal education. Recently an attempt has been made to be more inclusive of persons with disabilities.

YIAP seeks to increase youth employment and employability within agriculture and to bolster national economic development and slow down rural-urban migration. To do this it provides young people with access to land and equipment, or assistance to acquire these, and also training and some supervision. The focus is on 'block farms' (state land or land acquired from chiefs or private individuals is ploughed and shared in blocks among young farmer under supervision of Ministry of Food and Agriculture staff), livestock and poultry, fisheries and aquaculture, and agri-business. YIAP was initiated in 2010 as part of a reorganization and revamping of the NYEP. The main indicators of success are the number of jobs created, the number of hectares cultivated and that young people 'accept and appreciate farming/food production as a commercial venture, thereby taking up farming as a life time vocation.'[2]

A review of the block farm programme by Benin et al. (2013) concluded that on average only 25 percent of participants could be considered 'youth,' and suggested that one reason for their apparent lack of interest was that the potential income was not sufficiently high. There was also some indication that extension agents may have introduced an element of negative selection against young people because their results are often less impressive than those of older participants (thus reflecting badly on the agent).

While the crop production and other activities undertaken under YIAP are in principle matched to the district context, there is little indication that diversity among potential or actual participants is taken into account, or that the activities themselves have much promotive or transformative potential.

Malawi: Youth Enterprise Development Fund (YEDF) (2010–present)

The objective of YEDF is to help young people earn independent livelihoods and create employment for other youth particularly in rural areas. Specifically it provides loans to young entrepreneurs for capital equipment and working capital. Loan recipients must be organized in groups with at least 10 members (although in some rare cases loans have gone to individuals after appraisal by the YEDF district committee and the Malawi Rural Development Fund (MARDEF) secretariat). When it was introduced in 2010, YEDF targeted young people between 18–30 years of age, but eligibility was then extended to 35. According to its guidelines, the fund caters for out-of-school youth, both skilled and unskilled who are expected to engage in various trades such as agricultural production, construction, carpentry and joinery, panel beating, welding, metal fabrication, and woodwork. The fund is implemented by MARDEF, the Ministry of Youth and Sports (MYS) and district YEDF committees and is characterized as 'a key development agenda for young people in Malawi in as far as the current government policy portfolio is concerned' (Interview with the Regional Manager for MARDEF, Ntcheu, 2 February 2013).

YEDF is open to criticism on three fronts. First, in terms of the link between the credit and the training that is supposed to help build recipients' entrepreneurial attitudes and skills. According to one informant the training in business management and entrepreneurship is rarely offered and even then is not adequate 'to transform youth into competitive entrepreneurs' (Interview with the Principal Youth Officer, MYS, Lilongwe, 28 January 2013). Second, YEDF can do little to help young people gain access to key markets that are jealously guarded by elites with close links to government. Finally, there is a perception that YEDF is more or less of a handout to young people who are well-connected politically as there is reported to be pressure from politicians to disburse loans to groups with which they are associated. As one informant puts it, this is 'a way of saying thank you to the youth who supported them in their campaign for office in the May 2009 elections [. . .] and to mortgage their support for the forthcoming May 2014 elections' (Interview with the Programme Officer at the National Youth Council, Lilongwe, 26 January 2013).

Does YEDF address the dimensions of diversity highlighted in the conceptual framework? Neither the official documentation nor the interviews gave any indication that diversity among either rural areas or work opportunities were taken into account. However, the fund makes a point of saying that it caters for both skilled and unskilled and youths from various social backgrounds.

Ethiopia: The UNICEF-assisted youth development program (2007–11)

This programme provided credit to young people to start small businesses or expand existing ones, but more broadly focused on life skills, behaviour change, peer education, youth dialogue, participation in policy advocacy, local level development planning, and implementation and livelihood development. The programme was designed and implemented under the auspices of the former MYS to address the problems of unemployment, poverty, and vulnerability among young people. Financial and technical assistance were provided by UNICEF.

The main indicators of success were growth of self-employment and formal/informal employment opportunities and increased participation of young people in the economic, social, and political transformation of the country. An evaluation of the programme revealed that the number of young people who benefited from the different components was generally small (Zeleke 2012). While many targets were achieved, the programme suffered from poor management, and the lack of a regular budget. Neither the available literature nor interviews provided any insights into how the programme addressed diversity amongst rural areas, work opportunities, or young people.

What can we learn from these four government initiatives? First, while they use the language of entrepreneurship, they are essentially about creating opportunities for self-employment. A more encompassing notion of entrepreneurship, including innovation, risk-taking and employment creation is by and large absent. Second, they are built around a simplistic view of what is required in order to establish and grow a successful enterprise: there is, for example, no reference to the relatively high number of 'failures' that experience says should be expected. Third, they tend toward an 'individual uplift' rather than a structural change approach (except perhaps the YIAP in Ghana where the normal structures governing access to land are bypassed). The implication of this is that opportunities for creating promotive (to say nothing about transformative) work opportunities are likely to be constrained. Finally, these programmes do not appear to recognize or take into account the implications of different kinds of work opportunities or the diversity of rural areas and young people; rather, they tend toward blueprint or 'one size fits all' approaches.

It is also important to note that in some of these programmes, employment is one of several objectives. For example, in Ghana, both programmes also seek to slow rural to urban drift, while NYEP seeks to reduce 'deviance'; in Ethiopia, the Youth Development Programme also sought to strengthen life skills and political participation. The link between rural young people, employment creation in agriculture and reduced rural to urban movement is striking in that it highlights the tension between greater awareness of the world, rising aspirations, and the use of spatial mobility on the one hand, and on the other, the longstanding official view of the risks and dangers – both personal and political – associated with young people in the urban environment.

None of this is to say that these programmes or others like them may not be delivering some useful benefits to some young people. Rather, we are suggesting that their potential to deliver benefits efficiently and effectively – and 'at scale' – would appear to be quite limited.

Conclusions and implications for policy

The new policy and development interest that has coalesced around young people, agriculture, and work in rural Africa is clearly to be welcomed. However, policy advocates and development agencies face this particular policy moment from a relatively weak position. Specifically, the lack of a research and evidence base, ideology (e.g. concerning the potential of market-based empowerment through entrepreneurship) and entrenched (and outdated) framings and narratives concerning the nature of the problem and potential solutions, hamper both policy development and programme implementation and impact.

If agriculture or the agrifood sector more broadly is to be an attractive source of employment for rural young people it will be necessary that promotive work becomes the norm.[3] This implies real structural change which is unlikely to be an overnight (or painless) process. In any case, there is little evidence to suggest that modernization of the production side of African agriculture is likely to result in large numbers of promotive or transformative employment opportunities for young people in rural areas, so the whole notion of 'impact at scale' needs to be critically re-examined. It is important to note that as agriculture has modernized in other contexts and regions, the creation of large numbers of promotive jobs has not generally been observed. This picture changes somewhat if the focus shifts from agriculture to the agrifood system more broadly, where urbanization, changing patterns of labour force participation, and rising incomes result in increasing numbers of formal sector and potentially promotive jobs in areas such as transport, processing and manufacture, food retail, and catering.[4]

If policy and programmes are to be successful in promoting social and economic mobility they will need to be based on context-specific social and economic analysis that acknowledges and takes account of difference and diversity in relation to both rural locations and young people as encompassed in the transformative work and opportunity space framework. There was little evidence of this kind of analysis in the government-led programmes in Ghana, Malawi, and Ethiopia that we examined. There is a specific need for life course analysis and an appreciation of the various ways that young rural men and women use agriculture to serve their needs and interests. Critically this analysis must also privilege the social and relational aspects of young people's lives and worlds. More nuanced analysis along these lines should result in policies and programmes that are better grounded in the realities of both young people and place. It is also important to begin to trim what we believe are the unrealistic expectations associated with the rhetoric of market-based empowerment through entrepreneurship. There is at present little evidence about how, in what situations or for whom these programmes deliver promotive or transformative work opportunities. To confuse self-employment and petty enterprise in the informal sector with entrepreneurship is not particularly helpful.

While it is tempting to conclude that agriculture can and should be a central part of the solution to the employment problems faced by the present generation of African rural young people, this may not be realistic simply because, as argued above, both transformation of the agricultural sector and the changes required to position young people to take advantage of the resulting job opportunities will only happen over the medium to long term. Thus, we suggest that the real development challenge is in relation to future generations, and the critical questions over the next 5–10 years will be: How many and what kinds of agrifood-related jobs will be created? Where will they be located? What knowledge and skills will be required? What kinds of education and training programmes will be needed? Now is the time to address these questions systematically. While entrepreneurship will certainly have a place, the young people who engage with the agrifood sector will increasingly do so as employees of formal sector businesses.

Notes

In addition to UNU-WIDER, we would like to also acknowledge support for this research from the Future Agricultures Consortium (FAC).

1 It is important to note that in Africa. official unemployment rates for rural young people are generally low. However, they mask high levels of underemployment and engagement in the informal sector jobs that are by-and-large insecure and low paying.
2 YIAP webpage on the Ministry of Food and Agriculture website from www.mofa.gov.gh (accessed 9 March 2013).
3 We use the term 'agrifood sector' to refer to the broad range of activities related to the production, processing, manufacture, distribution, retail, preparation, and serving of food, including the provision of agricultural inputs.
4 For example, in the United Kingdom, the agrifood sector broadly conceived is a major source of work; however, many of these jobs are not located in rural areas, and the sector is characterized by low-skill and low-paid jobs (Lloyd et al. 2008).

References

Adepoju, A. (1995). 'Migration in Africa: An Overview.' In, Baker, J., Aina, T. A. (eds.), *The Migration Experience in Africa*. Uppsala: Nordiska Afrikainstitutet.

Amanor, K. S. (2010). 'Family Values, Land Sales, and Agricultural Commodification in South-eastern Ghana.' *Africa*, 80: 104–125.

Ansell, N. (2004). 'Secondary Schooling and Rural Youth Transitions in Lesotho and Zimbabwe.' *Youth & Society*, 36: 183–202.

Ansell, N., van Blerk, L., Robson, E., and Hajdu, F. (2012). 'The Spatial Construction of Young People's Livelihoods in Rural Southern Africa.' *Geography*, 97: 135–140.

Anyanwu, J. C. (2013). 'Characteristics and Macroeconomic Determinants of Youth Employment in Africa.' *African Development Review*, 25: 107–129.

Anyidoho, A. N., and Yaro, J. (2013). Agricultural Policy, Employment Opportunities and Social Mobility of Africa's Rural Youth: Ghana Country Case Study. Unpublished Report.

Anyidoho, N. A., Kayuni, H., Ndungu, J., Leavy, J., Sall, M., Tadele, G., and Sumberg, J. (2012a). Young People and Policy Narratives in sub-Saharan Africa. FAC Working Paper 32. Brighton@ Future Agricultures Consortium.

Anyidoho, N. A., Leavy, J., and Asenso-Okyere, K. (2012b). 'Perceptions and Aspirations: A Case Study of Young People in Ghana's Cocoa Sector.' *IDS Bulletin*, 43: 20–32.

Barrett, C. B., Reardon, T., and Webb, P. (2001). 'Nonfarm Income Diversification and Household Livelihood Strategies in Rural Africa: Concepts, Dynamics, and Policy Implications.' *Food Policy*, 26: 315–331.

Barrientos, S., Dolan, C., and Tallontire, A. (2003). 'A Gendered Value Chain Approach to Codes of Conduct in African Horticulture.' *World Development*, 31: 1511–1526.

Baulch, B. (2011). *Why Poverty Persists: Poverty Dynamics in Asia and Africa.* Cheltenham: Edward Elgar.

Benin, S., Johnson, M., Abokyi, E., Ahorbo, G., Jimah, K., Nasser, G., Owusu, V., Taabazuing, J., and Tenga, A. (2013). Revisiting Agricultural Input and Farm Support Subsidies in Africa The Case of Ghana's Mechanization, Fertilizer, Block Farms, and Marketing Programs. IFPRI Discussion Paper 01300. Washington, DC: IFPRI.

Bennell, P. (1996). 'Rates of Return to Education: Does the Conventional Pattern Prevail in sub-Saharan Africa?' *World Development*, 24: 183–199.

Bernard, T., and Taffesse, A.S. (2012). Measuring Aspirations: Discussion and Example from Ethiopia, IFPRI Discussion Paper 01190. Washington, DC: Interntaional Food Policy Research Institute.

Bezu, S., Barrett, C., and Holden, S.T. (2012). 'Does the Nonfarm Economy Offer Pathways for Upward Mobility? Evidence From A Panel Data Study in Ethiopia.' *World Development*, 40: 1634–1646.

Bird, K. (2007). The Intergenerational Transmission of Poverty: An Overview. CPRC Background Paper. London and Manchester: Chronic Poverty Research Centre.

Bowles, S., and Gintis, H. (2002). 'The Inheritance of Inequality.' *Journal of Economic Perspectives*, 16: 3–30.

Bryceson, D. F. (2002). 'The Scramble in Africa: Reorienting Rural Livelihoods.' *World Development*, 30: 725–739.

Bryceson, D. F., Mbara, T. C., and Maunder, D. (2002). 'Livelihoods, Daily Mobility and Poverty in sub-Saharan Africa.' *Transport Reviews*, 23: 1–20.

Buchmann, C., and Hannum, E. (2001). 'Education and Stratification in Developing Countries: A Review of Theories and Research.' *Annual Review of Sociology*, 27: 77–102.

Bynner, J. (2005). 'Rethinking the Youth Phase of the Life-Course: The Case for Emerging Adulthood?' *Journal of Youth Studies*, 8: 367–384.

Calves, A. E., and Schoumaker, B. (2004). 'Deteriorating Economic Context and Changing Patterns of Youth Employment in Urban Burkina Faso: 1980–2000.' *World Development*, 32: 1341–1354.

Camfield, l., Masae, A., McGregor, A., and Promphaking, B. (2012). 'Cultures of Aspiration and Poverty? Aspirational Inequalities in Northeast and Southern Thailand.' *Social Indicators Research*, 114, 3: 1049–1072.

Chinsinga, B., and Chasukwa, M. (2012). 'Youth, Agriculture and Land Grabs in Malawi.' *IDS Bulletin*, 43: 67–77.

Chinsinga, B., and Chasukwa, M. (2013). 'Agricultural Policy, Employment Opportunities and Social Mobility in Rural Malawi.' Unpublished Report.

Christiaensen, L., Demery, L., and Kuhl, J. (2011). 'The (Evolving) Role of Agriculture in Poverty Reduction-An Empirical Perspective.' *Journal of Development Economics*, 96: 239–254.

Collier, P. (2008). 'The Politics of Hunger: How Illusion and Greed Fan the Food Crisis.' *Foreign Affairs*. 87(6), 67–79.

Copestake, J., and Camfield, L. (2010). 'Measuring Multidimensional Aspiration Gaps: A Means to Understanding Cultural Aspects of Poverty.' *Development Policy Review*, 28: 617–633.

Crawford, C., Johnson, P., Machin, S., and Vignoles, A. (2011). *Social Mobility: A Literature Review*. London: UK Government Department for Business, Innovation, and Skills.

Crivello, G. (2011). '"Becoming Somebody": Youth Transitions Through Education and Migration in Peru.' *Journal of Youth Studies*, 14: 395–411.

De Bruijn, M., Van Dijk, R., and Foeken, D. (2001). 'Mobile Africa: An Introduction.' In *Mobile Africa: Changing Patterns of Movement in Africa and Beyond*. Leiden: Brill.

Del Franco, N. (2010). 'Aspirations and Self-Hood: Exploring the Meaning of Higher Education for Girl College Students in Rural Bangladesh.' *Compare: A Journal of Comparative and International Education*, 40: 147–165.

Deranty, J. P., and MacMillan, C. (2012). 'The ILO's Decent Work Initiative: Suggestions for an Extension of the Notion of "Decent Work."' *Journal of Social Philosophy*, 43: 386–405.

Dercon, S. (2009). 'Rural Poverty: Old Challenges in New Contexts.' *World Bank Research Observer*, 24: 1–28.

Dercon, S., and Shapiro, J. (2007). 'Moving On, Staying Behind, Getting Lost: Lessons on Poverty Mobility from Longitudinal Data.' Global Poverty Research Group Working Paper 75. Oxford: Global Poverty Research Group.

Devereux, S., and Sabates-Wheeler, R. (2007). 'Social Protection for Transformation.' *IDS Bulletin*, 38: 23–28.

Dorward, A. (2009). 'Integrating Contested Aspirations, Processes and Policy: Development as Hanging In, Stepping Up and Stepping Out.' *Development Policy Review*, 27: 131–146.

Dorward, A., Kydd, J., Morrison, J., and Urey, I. (2004). 'A Policy Agenda for Pro-Poor Agricultural Growth.' *World Development*, 32: 73–89.

Eastwood, R., and Lipton, M. (2011). 'Demographic Transition in Sub-Saharan Africa: How Big Will the Economic Dividend Be?' *Popul. Stud.-J. Demogr.* 65: 9–35.

Ellis, F. (2011). *Rural Livelihoods and Diversity in Developing Countries*. Oxford: Oxford University Press.

Erikson, R., and Goldthorpe, J. (2002). 'Intergenerational Inequality: A Sociological Perspective.' *Journal of Economic Perspectives*, 16: 31–44.

Finn, A., Leibbrandt, M., and Levinsohn, J. (2012). 'Income Mobility in South Africa: Evidence From the First Two Waves of the National Income Dynamics Study.' NIDS Discission Paper 2012/5. Cape Town: SALDRU, University of Cape Town.

Floro, M. S., and Schaefer, K. (1998). 'Restructuring of Labor Markets in the Philippines and Zambia: The Gender Dimension.' *The Journal of Developing Areas*, 33: 73–98.

Fujita, M., and Krugman, P. (1995). 'When is the Economy Monocentric?: von Thünen and Chamberlin Unified.' *Regional Science and Urban Economics*, 25: 505–528.

Glick, P., and Sahn, D. E. (1997). 'Gender and Education Impacts on Employment and Earnings in West Africa: Evidence from Guinea.' *Economic Development and Cultural Change*, 45: 793–823.

Gough, K. V. (2008). '"Moving Around": The Social and Spatial Mobility of Youth in Lusaka.' *Geografiska Annaler: Series B, Human Geography*, 90: 243–255.

Hall, T., Coffey, A., and Lashua, B. (2009). 'Steps and Stages: Rethinking Transitions in Youth and Place.' *Journal of Youth Studies*, 12: 547–561.

Harper, C., Marcus, R., and Moore, K. (2003). 'Enduring Poverty and the Conditions of Childhood: Lifecourse and Intergenerational Poverty Transmissions.' *World Development*, 31: 535–554.

Heath, A. (1981). *Social Mobility*. Glasgow: Fontana.

Holdsworth, C. (2009). '"Going Away to Uni": Mobility, Modernity and Independence of English Higher Education.' *Environment and Planning A*, 41: 1849–1864.

Holt, L., and Costello, L. (2011). 'Beyond Otherness: Exploring Diverse Spatialities and Mobilities of Childhood and Youth Populations.' *Population Space and Place*, 17: 299–303.

Hurd, G. E., and Johnson, T. J. (1967). 'Education and Social Mobility in Ghana.' *Sociology of Education*, 40: 55–79.

ILO. (2007). The Decent Work Agenda in Africa 2007–2015, Eleventh African Regional Meeting. Addis Ababa: International Labour Organization.

Jeffrey, C., and Dyson, J. (2013). 'Zigzag Capitalism: Youth Entrepreneurship in the Contemporary Global South.' *Geoforum*, 49: R1-R3.

Kantor, P., Rani, U., and Unni, J. (2006). 'Decent Work Deficits in the Informal Economy: Case of Surat.' *Economic and Political Weekly*, 41: 2089–2097.

Kaufmann, V. (2002). *Rethinking Mobility: Contemporary Sociology*. Aldershot: Ashgate.

Kaufmann, V., Bergman, M. M., and Joye, D. (2004). 'Motility: Mobility as Capital.' *International Journal of Urban and Regional Research*, 28: 745–756.

Kelley, J., and Perlman, M. L. (1971). 'Social Mobility in Toro: Some Preliminary Results from Western Uganda.' *Economic Development and Cultural Change*, 19: 204–221.

Kingdon, G. G., and Knight, J. (2004). 'Race and the Incidence of Unemployment in South Africa.' *Review of Development Economics*, 8: 198–222.

Kritzinger, A. (2002). 'Rural Youth and Risk Society – Future Perceptions and Life Chances of Teenage Girls on South African Farms.' *Youth & Society*, 33: 545–572.

Krugman, P. (1993). 'First Nature, Second Nature, and Metropolitan Location.' *Journal of Regional Science*, 33: 129–144.

Langevang, T., and Gough, K. V. (2009). 'Surviving Through Movement: The Mobility of Urban Youth in Ghana.' *Social and Cultural Geography*, 10: 741–756.

Langevang, T., and Gough, K.V. (2012). 'Diverging Pathways: Young Female Employment and Entrepreneurship in sub-Saharan Africa.' *Geographical Journal*, 178: 242–252.

Lawson, D., Mckay, A., and Okidi, J. (2006). 'Poverty Persistence and Transitions in Uganda: A Combined Qualitative and Quantitative Analysis.' *Journal of Development Studies*, 42: 1225–1251.

Leavy, J., and Smith, S. (2010). 'Future Farmers: Youth Aspirations, Expectations and Life Choices.' FAC Discussion Paper 013. Brighton: Future Agricultures Consortium.

Lieten, K., de Groot, A., and van Wiesen, R. (2007). 'Education in Rural Areas: Obstacles and Relevance.' Amsterdam: Foundation for International Research on Working Children.

Lloyd, C., Mason, G., and Mayhew, K. (2008). *Low-wage Work in the United Kingdom: Case Studies of Job Quality in Advanced Economies*. New York: Russell Sage Foundation.

Lloyd, C. B. (2006). *Growing Up Global: The Changing Transitions to Adulthood in Developing Countries*. Washington, DC: National Research Council and Institute of Medicine of the National Academies.

Locke, C., and te Lintelo, D.J.H. (2012). 'Young Zambians "Waiting" for Opportunities and "Working Towards" Living Well: Lifecourse and Aspirations in Youth Transitions.' *Journal of International Development*, 24: 777–794.

MacDonald, R. (2011). 'Youth Transitions, Unemployment and Underemployment.' *Journal of Sociology*, 47: 427–444.

MacDonald, R., Mason, P., Shildrick, T., Webster, C., Johnston, L., and Ridley, L. (2001). 'Snakes and Ladders: In Defence of Studies of Youth Transition.' *Sociological Research Online*, 5: 4.

Ministry of Manpower, Youth and Employment (MMYE). (2006). 'Youth Employment Implementation Guidelines.' Accra: Government of Ghana, MMYE.

Mulkeen, A. (2005). *Teachers for Rural Schools: A Challenge for Africa*. Rome: FAO.

Narayan, D., and Petesch, P. (2007). 'Moving Out of Poverty.' From Cross-Disciplinary Perspectives on Mobility, vol 1. Washington, DC: World Bank.

OECD. (2012). *Gender Equality in Education, Employment and Paris*. Organisation for Economic Co-operation and Development.

Okali, C., and Sumberg, J. (2012). 'Quick Money and Power: Tomatoes and Livelihood Building in Brong Ahafo, Ghana.' *IDS Bulletin* 43, 44–57.

Oviasuyi, P. O., Arowoshegbe, A. O., and Isiraoje, L. (2012). 'Graduates/Youths Unemployment Question in Nigeria: A Case Study of Edo State.' *Anthropologist*, 14: 177–184.

Pauw, K., Oosthuizen, M., and Van Der Westhuizen, C. (2008). 'Graduate Unemployment in the Face of Skills Shortages: A Labour Market Paradox.' *South African Journal of Economics*, 76: 45–57.

Porter, G. (2010). 'Transport Planning in Sub-Saharan Africa III: The Challenges of Meeting Children and Young People's Mobility and Transport Needs.' *Progress in Development Studies*, 10: 169–180.

Porter, G., Hampshire, K., Abane, A., Munthali, A., Robson, E., Mashiri, M., and Tanle, A. (2012). 'Youth, Mobility and Mobile Phones in Africa: Findings From a Three-Country Study.' *Information Technology for Development*, 18: 145–162.

Porter, G., Hampshire, K., Abane, A., Robson, E., Munthali, A., Mashiri, M., and Tanle, A. (2010). 'Moving Young Lives: Mobility, Immobility and Inter-Generational Tensions in Urban Africa.' *Geoforum*, 41: 796–804.

Porter, G., Hampshire, K., Abane, A., Tanle, A., Esia-Donkoh, K., Amoako-Sakyi, R. O., Agblorti, S., and Owusu, S. A. (2011). 'Mobility, Education and Livelihood Trajectories for Young People in Rural Ghana: A Gender Perspective.' *Childrens Geographies*, 9: 395–410.

Savage, M. (1988). 'The Missing Link? The Relationship between Spatial Mobility and Social Mobility.' *The British Journal of Sociology*, 39: 554–577.

Schaefer, V. A., and Meece, J. L. (2009). 'Facing an Uncertain Future: Aspirations and Achievement of Rural Youth.' Paper presented at the Annual Meeting of the American Educational Research Association. San Diego, CA, April 12–17, 2009.

Smith, B., and Moore, K. (2006). 'Intergenerational Transmission of Poverty in Sub-Saharan Africa.' CRPC Working Paper 59. Manchester and London: Chronic Poverty Research Centre.

Solon, G. (1992). 'Intergenerational Income Mobility in the United States.' *American Economic Review*, 82: 393–408.

St Clair, R., and Benjamin, A. (2011). 'Performing Desires: The Dilemma of Aspirations and Educational Attainment.' *British Educational Research Journal*, 37: 501–517.

Sumberg, J., Anyidoho, N. A., Leavy, J., te Lintelo, D.J.H., and Wellard, K. (2012). 'Introduction: The Young People and Agriculture "Problem" in Africa.' *IDS Bulletin*, 43: 1–8.

Tadele, G. (2013). 'Development Policies and Programmes: Implications for Rural Youth Employment Opportunities and Social Mobility in Ethiopia.' Unpublished Report.

Tadele, G., and Gella, A. A. (2012). 'A Last Resort and Often Not an Option at All: Farming and Young People in Ethiopia.' *IDS Bulletin*, 43: 33–43.

te Lintelo, D.J.H. (2012). 'Young People in African (Agricultural) Policy Processes? What National Youth Policies Can Tell Us.' *IDS Bulletin*, 43: 90–103.

te Riele, K. (2004). 'Youth Transition in Australia: Challenging Assumptions of Linearity and Choice.' *Journal of Youth Studies*, 7: 243–257.

Thwala, W. D. (2011). 'Public Works Programmes as a Tool to Address Unemployment and Skills Shortages Among the Youth in South Africa.' *African Journal of Business Management*, 5: 6011–6020.

UNESCO. (2012). 'Education for All Global Monitoring Report 2012.' *Youth and Skills: Putting Education to Work*. Paris: UNESCO.

USAID. (2012). *Youth in Development: Realizing the Demographic Opportunity*. Washington, DC: USAID.

Valentine, G., Sporton, D., Bang, and Nielsen, K. (2009). 'Identities and Belonging: A Study of Somali Refugee and Asylum Seekers Living in the UK and Denmark.' *Environment and Planning D: Society and Space*, 27: 234–250.

van Ham, M., Mulder, C. H., and Hooimeijer, P. (2001). 'Spatial Flexibility in Job Mobility: Macrolevel Opportunities and Microlevel Restrictions.' *Environment and Planning A*, 33: 921–940.

White, R. J., and Green, A. E. (2011). 'Opening Up or Closing Down Opportunities?: The Role of Social Networks and Attachment to Place in Informing Young Peoples' Attitudes and Access to Training and Employment.' *Urban Studies*, 48: 41–60.

Wiggins, S., and Proctor, S. (2001). 'How Special are Rural Areas? The Economic Implications of Location for Rural Development.' *Development Policy Review*, 19: 427–436.

Woolard, I., and Klasen, S. (2005). 'Determinants of Income Mobility and Household Poverty Dynamics in South Africa.' *Journal of Development Studies*, 41: 865–897.

World Bank. (2006). 'World Development Report 2007: Development and the Next Generation.' Washington, DC: World Bank.

World Bank. (2009). 'Africa Development Indicators 2008–9: Youth and Employment in Africa – The Potential, The Problem, The Promise.' Washington, DC: World Bank.

World Bank. (2011a). 'African Development Indicators 2011.' Washington, DC: World Bank.

World Bank. (2011b). 'World Development Report 2012: Gender Equality and Development.' Washington, DC: The World Bank.

Worth, N. (2009). 'Understanding Youth Transition as "Becoming": Identity, Time and Futurity.' *Geoforum*, 40: 1050–1060.

Zeleke, S. (2012). 'Evaluation of The UNICEF/MOWCYA Adolescent/Youth Development Programme In Ethiopia (2007–2011).' Addis Ababa: UNICEF.

Ziervogel, C., and Crankshaw, O. (2009). 'Intergenerational Occupational Mobility among Coloureds and Africans in the Mitchell's Plain Magisterial District, Cape Town.' *Urban Forum*, 20: 235–251.

Zimmerman, D. J. (1992). 'Regression Toward Mediocrity in Economic Stature.' *American Economic Review*, 82: 409–429.

7 Education policy, vocational training, and the youth in sub-Saharan Africa

Moses Oketch

Introduction

Although the incidence of youth unemployment in sub-Saharan Africa (SSA) is lower than several other regions of the world, it is still high at 20 percent (African Economic Outlook 2013; ILO 2012). Youth unemployment is therefore a major concern to governments in the region and is seen as undermining Africa's demographic dividend (ILO 2012). To address youth unemployment, too often technical, vocational education, and training (TVET) is seen both by donor organizations and national governments as the panacea. Consequently, policy prescriptions have, over the years, promoted expansion of TVET in schools (Middleton, Ziderman, and Adams 1993; Oketch 2007).

Based on a survey carried out in 2004, Oketch (2007) noted that TVET is defined to include a range of learning experiences which are relevant to the world of work and which may occur in a variety of learning contexts, including educational and workplace-related. It is important to note that TVET is desperately varied in terms of patterns of emphasis and provision across the countries of SSA (Oketch 2007). Provision of TVET involves lower and upper secondary levels, post-secondary but non-tertiary provisions, and provision at first stage tertiary level (Oketch 2007). The second kind of provision is one that is outside the formal education systems. These tend to be in the informal sector through apprenticeships or traditional forms of training offered via artisan workshops owned by master craftsmen and women. The latter leads to preparation and trades in carpentry, masonry, auto-mechanics, welding, foundry, photography, tailoring, dress-making, cosmetics, and so on (Atchoarena and Delluc 2001). They can be provided as commercial entities where students pay some fees, or through family ties. Often one of the characteristics of these informal training provision is the lack of technical skills although there is great evidence of creativity amongst the master craftsmen/women (Atchoerena and Delluc 2001). The focus of this discussion will be on TVET offered within the formal public education systems.

The work of Philip Foster in the 1960s was the first to challenge the notion that vocational education is what African countries needed to address youth unemployment (Foster 1965). Foster's work was considered to be at the heart of the debate about whether schools and what was taught can influence society through changing students' attitudes toward jobs and work, or whether schools and their pupils are themselves influenced by the existing economic structure and reward systems around them. Foster warned about the limitations of schooling to change a society based on his in-depth study in Ghana (King and Martin 2002). As noted by Oketch (2007), he exploded the vocational school myth in Africa. Forster argued and cautioned against full-scale TVET policy and promotion and advocated for small-scale TVET that was more aligned to the actual ongoing development and one that was not within the formal education system (Foster 1965: 154). To operationalize his proposal, he went further to recommend that 'the burdens of vocational training should be shifted to those groups who are demanding skilled labour of various types' (Foster 1965: 158).

There has been much response to Foster proposals, some in support and others offering differing perspectives. Supporters included Blaug (1973), who questioned the prevailing notion that vocational education can offer the best solution to youth skills and employment. However, to date, as noted by Oketch (2007: 220), 'many of the arguments over TVET continue to rest on the assumption that vocational training is more specific to job entry than general education.' Much time has passed and today, vocational education is no longer simply training to facilitate job entry, but instead a way to facilitate vocational-specific skills over lifetime. The content has changed in the rest of the world, but the question is whether this change has also occurred in SSA in a manner that can harness the youth bulge. To assess this, this chapter discusses the effectiveness of formal TVET education systems in Africa, especially in terms of preparing the youth for job markets. The chapter elaborates on the strengths and weaknesses of placing greater emphasis on vocational training by reviewing the cases of two countries, Kenya and Ghana, as countries that introduced comprehensive vocationalization policies at the same time, but which failed to address youth unemployment. This was in contrast to Botswana, which cautiously introduced vocational subjects, but had a successful vocationalization approach that was similar to what Foster (1965) had recommended. It reflects on the African youth dividend and the growing interest in TVET as the solution to Africa's youth unemployment.

TVET potential and conundrum

The theoretical debate promoting TVET in general is that it produces 'specific human capital,' which provides specific job-relevant skills that can make the worker more readily suitable for a given job, thereby making him/her more productive, in contrast to general education, which creates 'general human capital' with attitudes and aspirations associated with limited white collar jobs (Tilak 2002). The promotion of TVET is thus based on the notion that it can improve youth attitude toward work so that they embrace skilled manual work as opposed to limited white collar jobs (Middletone, Ziderman and Adams 1993).

Some of the arguments used to advance policies in favour of TVET are as follows: (1) TVET can cure youth unemployment; (2) TVET leads to technological know-how, which is associated with innovation and technical change development; (3) for those youth who are not very academically capable, TVET offers hope as an alternative to the competitive general education; (4) TVET trains mid-level personnel who are much needed for the full functionality of the labour force system; (5) TVET can reduce poverty as it offers skills leading to employment and to income – a simple theory of change and the power of TVET; and (6) global interconnectedness means that TVET needs to be regarded as a means of promoting global technical skills (Psacharopoulos 1997).

The theoretical debate and arguments in support of TVET have been seriously questioned, leaving TVET an explosive education topic. TVET has presented inconsistent arguments over the years. On the one hand, it is seen as the panacea to addressing youth unemployment, and on the other hand, vocationalization has proven never to be a straightforward solution or remedy to youth unemployment because it has not been able to address the mismatch between education and the labour market, and it has equally failed to prepare youth adequately for the specific occupations associated with it (Blaug 1973; Oketch 2007). Over the years, the reality for individuals has been that general education has the promise of better career mobility and higher wages than vocational streams. TVET thus acquired the tag of being 'useless' education and only useful for those with less aspiration for better paying jobs (Oketch 2007). Yet, as noted by Oketch (2007) 'such strong arguments against full acceptance of vocational education and training have to date not deterred many countries from continuing vocational education and training programmes in public education systems' (Oketch 2007: 222). Consequently TVET continues to maintain its inherently powerful but also paradoxical appeal in education systems (Oketch 2007). Indeed Middleton, Ziderman, and Adams (1993) argued that TVET had fallen 'under the cloud in the minds of some analysts and policy makers, while it continued to hold a place in the sun for others' (Middleton, Ziderman, and Adams 1993: 69).

SSA's experience with TVET has not been all positive, and the arguments in favour of TVET and the notion that it is a cure to youth unemployment have been contradictory in themselves in the region in the sense that they relegate TVET to a second class type of education, which is primarily occupational and undesirable for those with higher aspirations (Oketch 2007). In practice, those who have followed the TVET path often take longer to find jobs, and when they find employment, the jobs are perceived to be of dead-end in nature career-wise. TVET has also retained its colonial tag as it was what the colonial education policy recommended and provided to a majority of Africans who had a chance of training. It is not surprising that the initial educational policy in SSA emphasized the expansion of access, the elimination of illiteracy, and the elimination of ignorance, but did not lay any particular emphasis on the role of TVET in addressing these challenges. The educated African was meant to take over the jobs that were performed by the colonial government, and TVET was not considered the means to attain such skills (Oketch 2007).

However, soon after independence, many governments in SSA realized that they needed to embrace TVET, but this was done within the traditional assumptions without much thinking on how to cast TVET to be complementary to general education and vice versa. Instead, what was ensued was a system of education that placed TVET against general education, but relegating it to an education training that did not have prominence and did not attract those with higher aspirations. It was more or less creating a two tier education system – general track for those with higher ability, often also associated with their socio-economic status and/or prior education of their parents, against TVET, for those of lower ability and always from low socio-economic status and/or low or zero prior education of their parents. Emphasis of TVET by these newly independent nations was bolstered by massive support from international agencies, notably the World Bank, which provided educational loans for the establishment and expansion of public TVET and thus legitimizing pre-employment training as an important component of public education (Middleton, Ziderman, and Adams 1993). Between 1963 and 1976 over half of the Bank's investment in education in developing countries was directed towards TVET. Even as the focus changed within the Bank to embrace and broadened investing towards general education (basic education) after much initial resistance in the 1970s, investing in TVET still held a special central place in the expanded lending (Middleton, Ziderman, and Adams 1993: 4). As noted earlier, there was already a wave of research, led by Foster's work, which showed that massive investment in TVET was not yielding the promises that were associated with it, in terms of employment, and not meeting the aspirations of the youth. Simply put, the evidence that was gathered by research did not match the benefits that were associated with TVET. Foster questioned this massive assumption that TVET could change the attitudes of the youth to employment, and highlighted the limitation of schools to change society independent of the surrounding environment (Foster 1965).

Overview of TVET trends in SSA

Oketch (2007) provides a comprehensive review and discussion of TVET in SSA and notes that school systems in nearly all the countries have maintained two paths: a general education path, which enables pupils who gain access to them to continue in their schooling to higher levels, and a vocational path, which focuses on immediate entry into the labour market and addresses limited access opportunities that crowd out the majority of youth from the general education pathway at the post-primary level. Some countries have tinkered with policies that create integration between general and vocational and to minimize these two running as parallel systems, but there is no evidence of much success. This is mainly because TVET still retains its traditional mould and is perceived as a low status strand of education that has got no proper equivalency and transferability of credits and skills to the general education and vice versa.

By contrast, the general education track graduates enjoy a career pathway that has career progression and often they are also able to continue with their education to the higher levels of the educational ladder. Moreover, general education track has been the emphasis of the Education for All (EFA) framework which operationalizes the Millennium Development Goal (MDG) commitment to universal access to basic education. The general track is also homogenous and well-organized. Its link to the MDGs has made governments pay greater attention to it and devote more resources toward expanding access.

In the most part, it is training meant for direct entry into the world of work. TVET acting as a foundation for entry into higher levels of education has remained problematic and in his review, Oketch (2007) notes that there is no evidence of this among the countries studied. It is noted that 'much of TVET is initial vocational training (IVT) undertaken by young people prior to entering the labour market and in preparation for self-employment in both the rural and agricultural sector and the urban informal sector.' The study concluded that 'there was lack of massive evidence of any schemes aimed at re-skilling and up-skilling demanded by the knowledge-driven economic set up that has been associated with globalization (Oketch 2007: 224).'

The review also noted that most TVET for which there is data is that which is provided publicly within the school systems. Informal learning that forms part of TVET is mainly not represented in the available data.

Another element reviewed by Oketch (2007) is the level of TVET provision within the formal education systems; there are varied practices. In some cases, TVET is completely parallel to general education with its own separate institutions. In others, which is a majority of cases, TVET is offered alongside general education in an integrated school system forming a dual track system. Much of TVET starts at secondary level in several countries but there is variation with some having TVET starting at what is referred to as junior secondary whereas for others, it starts at senior secondary. Still for others, what is referred to as full TVET starts at post-secondary level, often with their own institutions parallel to the general education strand. Table 7.1 summarizes some of the features of TVET in SSA countries that were selected on the basis of availability of data.

So, there are potentially two policy issues to be addressed here. The first is to seek ways to integrate TVET with general education and vice versa so that TVET is not perceived as second rate education. This integration should make it possible for those with TVET to move through the educational ladder. The second issue is to develop and implement policies that encourage greater investment in TVET. In fact, Lauglo (2010), in his overview of TVET in secondary education, notes that Botswana has succeeded because it has been able to invest good levels of resources into TVET. Oketch (2008), however, questions whether it is only resources that will make TVET in SSA to function. Clearly, resources are one aspect; integration and content specificity levels are others. Ambivalence remains in its status and supporting policies that do not relegate it into a lower type of education compared with the general track.

Oketch (2007) notes that governments have in fact failed to provide functional and quality TVET. Instead they should leave it to the private sector and retain a supervisory and/or financing role. Private providers of TVET are growing more than was the case in the 1970s and 1980s, or earlier years of independence around 1960s. Atchoarena and Esquieu (2002) are among the last to conduct extensive research on private TVET provision. From their research, they concluded the

Table 7.1 Some indicators on TVET provision in SSA

	When does TVET start	*TVET offered in parallel with general education*	*TVET integrated or follows specific curriculum*	*TVET share of secondary enrolment, in %*
Botswana	Senior secondary school	–	Integrated	5
Ghana	Lower secondary	–	Follows specific curriculum	–
Senegal	Senior secondary	Not clear	Not clear	–
Seychelles	Post–secondary level	–	–	–
Zimbabwe	Post–secondary	–	12 of curriculum is integrated	–
Eritrea	Secondary level (no distinction as in lower/ junior secondary and senior/upper secondary)	–	Specific curriculum	2
Ethiopia	Secondary level (no distinction as in lower/ junior secondary and senior/upper secondary)	–	Specific curriculum	2
Malawi	Secondary level (no distinction as in lower/ junior secondary and senior/upper secondary)	–	Specific curriculum	2
Namibia	Secondary level (no distinction as in lower/ junior secondary and senior/upper secondary)	–	Specific curriculum	2
Niger	Secondary level (no distinction as in lower/ junior secondary and senior/upper secondary)	–	Specific curriculum	2
South Africa	Secondary level (no distinction as in lower/ junior secondary and senior/upper secondary)	–	Specific curriculum	2
Burkina Faso	Secondary	–	Integrated	9
Togo	Secondary	–	Integrated	9
Congo	Secondary	–	Integrated	9
Gabon	Secondary	–	Integrated	9
Mali	Secondary	–	–	Over 10
Côte d'Ivoire	Secondary	–	Integrated	9
Cameroon	Secondary	–	Integrated	Over 10
Uganda	Secondary	–	Integrated	9

Source: Based on Oketch (2007).

following: (1) private provision is experiencing phenomenal growth and in some countries, such as Mali, it is dominant to government provision; (2) the provision is varied in terms of ownership, where some are operating as individual enterprises and others are organized regarding their institutional framework, legal status, objectives, and ways of financing themselves – however, detailed information is often difficult to obtain; (3) the majority of the private providers cater to students who come from low socio-economic backgrounds; (4) many of the private providers operate illegally because they cannot be traced in government registration books; (5) commercial trade courses are dominant among private providers; (6) They are totally tuition-based, market-driven, flexible, and can change courses easily to respond to demand; (7) they are not coordinated in any way to work closely with enterprises, but the students themselves make choices which they think respond to labour market skills demand; and (8) overall, the private providers offer better prepared, relevant courses than the government, but they also have greater quality variability because they are commercially-driven, rather than being guided purely by merit as institutions.

Like all the other provisions, there is no pathway of access into higher levels of education, even for those who access private TVET provision. Nonetheless, the commercial private provisions are thriving and meeting the labour market skills demand for those able to afford them. There is potential that private sector provision can be strengthened, and this will require a clear policy framework that allows the government to take an inspection role. In some cases, the government can even fund the commercial TVET provision to train the youth in specific skills. The fact that they are flexible and respond to the labour market needs means they would offer value for money to the governments and at the same time meet the educational demand. In fact, in some cases, these commercial provisions have shed off the low perceptions associated with TVET. For example, many that specialize in community- and technology-related training have thrived and attracted those from the general education strand. They have also thrived because they have modeled their courses in such a way that it does not generate or lead to dead end careers.

TVET financing is also an important aspect that varies in pattern across different countries. It ranges from less than 1 percent in some countries and over 12 percent in others as a proportion of total educational expenditure. Like provision, this low investment in TVET signals that it is not an area of priority, yet the rhetoric in public documents highlights the strategic role that TVET is supposed to play in the development of relevant skills among the youth in SSA. However, the financing in the private sector is much harder to obtain, and the data that is normally cited is only that which is official within government provision.

Oketch's (2007) discussion concluded the following: (1) over the years, TVET has more or less maintained a business-as-usual trend, with piece meal policies here and there, leaving the TVET framework untouched and guided by the traditional mould. This has relegated it to a second-class pathway in the education system. This is problematic and policies have not been bold enough to address this; (2) TVET is entrenched in either junior or senior secondary levels but even here, it forms a marginal position and is not fully desirable education. Consideration should be given to proper TVET that is not an alternative pathway, but one equally rewarding pathway in the education system that is well-synchronized with the general education model. The US community college model is one that is less costly and can be easily adopted in the African contexts; (3) the conversion of polytechnics into universities has simply sent another strong message that TVET is not as valued. While some of these have referred to themselves as technical universities, they have rebranded and taken on a general education outlook rather than promoting high level TVET. This is yet again an example of the policy contradictions within governments whereby on the one hand TVET is praised for its relevance and on the other, stronger TVET institutions such as polytechnics are converted into universities with clear preference for general education; (4) the image of TVET as last resort pathway of education requires addressing within policies. This has not happened and Foster's view that TVET benefits are a myth still remains. The demand continues to be in general strand; (5) the existence of a dual track system which tracks pupils into ability groupings does not auger well for TVET policy and transformation. Such tracks need to be dismantled and TVET and general education integrated in one way or another; (6) the potential benefits associated with private provision should be tapped into and encouraged as they appear better able and prepared to offer flexible and alternative provision to government. Expanding private sector provision through close partnerships with government and enterprises is worth supporting by governments in SSA.

From the general review, there is no doubt about the strategic role that TVET can play in meeting skills needs amongst the youth in SSA and contributing to their employability. However, TVET requires transformation, beginning with shedding off its traditional mould, and making it relevant to the skills needs and demands of the labour market (Oketch 2007). On the basis of these general observations and reviews, the next section assesses TVET policies and youths in Ghana, Kenya, and Botswana.

Case studies of TVET in Africa

TVET in Ghana

Ghana is one of the peaceful countries in SSA. In the recent years, it has made tremendous progress in political reforms through the strengthening of its democratic space and freedom of expression. A multi-party political system has taken root in the country and is thriving. This has enabled an environment for economic growth. According to the World Bank (2013a), Ghana's population in 2011 was approximately 25 million and GDP growth in 2010 was 8 percent and this shot up to double digit growth of 14.3 percent in 2011.

TVET forms an integral part of the Ghana education system and had been so since it attained independence in 1957. Several reforms have been implemented in Ghana to align the education system with the needs of the society. One of the main reforms was the 1987 reform focusing on TVET which also changed the structure of the education system. Before the 1987 reform, the dominant provision at the secondary level was general education. Whatever existed as TVET was minimalist. The education system was cast to promote progression into the university. The existing TVET was at middle school level which prepared participants to enter technical institutes and later on national polytechnics, but as noted earlier, the entire system was basically geared toward promoting general education. The 1987 reform introduced pre-vocational skills programme made up of 12 subjects, and a pre-technical skills programme made up of five subjects (Akyeampong 2005).

TVET was embedded within the Junior Secondary School (JSS) which now had a dual function: (1) preparation of students for further Senior Secondary School (SSS); and (2) terminal qualification for entry into the labour market or self-employment. Greater diversification nonetheless was at the SSS level. Akyeampong (2005) has noted that the reforms were so extensive and with significant teaching ramifications, and yet the consultation process leading to the reforms was not inclusive. He notes that the 1987 reforms were politically motivated reforms because there were no consultations with key stakeholders or driven by clear empirical evidence, although he also acknowledges that the noble goal was expanding educational opportunity (Akyeampong 2005: 167–169). A significant feature of the diversified SSS curriculum was and still remains the case, the opportunity it accorded students studying different pathways to also select from other pathways. The combination was such that students in the TVET pathway could also select one or two elective subjects in science or languages such as French. In other words, it requires students to mix subjects as between general core subjects and TVET-related subjects. Elective subjects were as follows (Akyeampong 2005: 171, Table 5.2):

- Science (physics, chemistry, biology, math/technical drawing)
- Technical (technical drawing, physics, maths, applied electricity/metalwork)
- General arts (e.g., geography, economics, French, maths)
- Visual arts (general knowledge in art, graphics, ceramics, economics/French)

The reformed education system and the diversification introduced in the SSS was to address some of the challenges that had beset TVET in Ghana and to remove the dual track model by integrating TVET with general education, under what was referred to as a diversified secondary system. The merit of this was to encourage or allow those in the TVET pathway subjects to have the opportunity for progression into further education, similar to those who were in the general pathway. Soon, however, the universities came up with their own criteria, which considered some of the SSS pathways as inadequate preparation for university entrance. As noted by Akyeampong (2005), this was a reflection of preference for general education that had entrenched itself within the psyche of Ghanaians, including the university system, which had felt that this integration of TVET and general pathways was ill-conceived and not adequately 'intellectual' for university education. In short, there was still the feeling that even under the integrated system with the combination of electives which allowed students to have knowledge of TVET and foundations in general education did not produce university material students.

The reforms expanded access as had been intended and helped to remove the impediments that had previously existed for TVET. At the JSS level, there was clear input into TVET and at the SSS level, there was diversification based on areas of strength and interests that students brought with them from the JSS. What was clear was that in the SSS, if one was strong in general subjects, they were compelled to also select subjects that were related to TVET and vice versa; for those that preferred TVET at JSS, they would follow that path into SSS but had to select some general subjects as part of the study/curriculum composition. But even this attempt to integrate TVET and general education did not do the trick of amending the negative perceptions that had been associated with TVET subjects. It became more or less window dressing as a majority of students did not like the TVET subjects at JSS. As noted by Akyeampong (2005), TVET remained unpopular with students (175). TVET subjects were seen as inferior and only suitable for academically weak students, and this was a view that even the teachers held.

Agriculture and business which were classified as TVET were acceptable and enrolled the most students under the TVET subjects cluster. There was also a gender dimension to the reformed JSS and SSS. Girls tended to be the ones who enrolled the most in the pre-vocational subjects at JSS. Still even at this stage, Foster's (1965) views presented earlier on regarding TVET in Ghana, played in the minds of students as many considered TVET subjects at JSS as less likely to lead to better employment in the future. Again, this was now a clear reflection of the mismatch between what policy advocated and the reality and actual choices that students made in their areas of study. Citing King and Martin (2002) in their follow up study on TVET in Ghana, Akyeampong (2005) concluded that curriculum reforms in Ghana aimed at integrating TVET and general pathways as was intended did not achieve their goal. This is because the labour market reward system still valued general education and students could see this for themselves. The analysis presented by Ampiah and cited by Akyeampong (2005) reflects that the diversified model in Ghana did not address the TVET dilemma. Pre-vocational subjects at JSS were still considered inferior and more specialized TVET at SSS level while useful had already suffered the negative perceptions that were associated with the JSS-prevocational programme. They therefore recommend a liberal arts and science model at JSS, more or less following the American model, which in many respects does not start from the premise that there are dual paths, but rather that the foundation of functional TVET is well-grounded general education.

The attempt to introduce TVET early on in the system creates an undesirable dual track and the attempt to diversify does not offer a strong solution. The recommendation then is to strengthen liberal arts and science in the early years and allow for different pathways later on, with the possibility for lateral and vertical movement. This does mean that the agenda for TVET in Ghana has to shift away from considering it as a means of coping with youth pre-vocational skills and those unable to transit into SSS, but rather that the foundation of all education up to JSS should be general arts and science and at SSS, serious TVET can be introduced. This would also mean that JSS is not terminal as such, but is the preparation for SSS where proper TVET skills can be instilled, and those willing to proceed to university from the TVET strand can do so, and those wanting to join the labour market will also feel rather adequately prepared to do so. This is more or less similar to the model that Botswana followed and strengthened, in which everyone selected to join TVET is not from a pool of those perceived as inferior in terms of their prior education preparation but rather that the general pathway and the TVET pathway at the SSS select from the same pool of students from the JSS. This might do a blow to the perception that TVET is inferior. Indeed, the reform in Ghana missed this opportunity because by introducing pre-vocational skills at JSS and making it terminal, it did not address the negative perceptions of TVET engrained for many years in Ghana, and these were carried forward even at the SSS level.

Kenya case study

Before the ugly 2007 post-election violence, Kenya was regarded as one of the promising countries in SSA. It had managed to lead a peaceful transition of power in the 2002 election, but this good image was destroyed in 2007. Corruption was also rampant in the government and tainted all the hope that had been associated with the 2002 elections. According to World Bank (2013b), Kenya's population in 2011 was approximately 41.6 million, and GDP growth was 4.3 percent in 2011, far below its potential. Much of this has been due to political apprehension before the elections, which also led to a decline in the number of tourists, one of Kenya's previously vibrant foreign exchange earner sectors. The impact of the images of corruption in government and the aftermath of the 2007 post-election violence hampered economic growth. It is hoped that in the coming years, and with now stable political transition, the economy will be transformed to attain double digit growth.

Youth unemployment remains one of the challenges that Kenya faces, and the youth population makes a significant number of the country population and remains the most unemployed and most vulnerable. Since its independence in 1963, TVET has been central in addressing the issue of youth employment. As noted by Mwiria (2005: 227), 'interest in vocationalizing the secondary school curriculum dates back to the mid-1970s and early 1980s following the recommendations of two government-appointed commissions. However, it was not until 1986 that the current system of vocationalizing school curriculum was institutionalized with the implementation of a new national system popularly known as the 8-4-4 system.' This new system restricted the education system to entrench the vocational curriculum right at the primary and secondary level, mainly to equip youth with pre-employment vocational skills. The system was changed from what was previously an elite academic model of seven years of primary, four years of secondary, two years of advanced secondary schooling (also known as A level), and three years of university to eight years of primary, four years of secondary schooling and four years of university (8-4-4). There has been much expression that the 1986 reform was rushed without wider inclusive consultation and agreement.

In terms of the curriculum content, the TVET under the 8-4-4 system comprised core vocational subjects and those that were referred to as industrial subjects. The former included agriculture, accounting, commerce, etc., while the latter included building construction, electricity, metal work, etc. The aim was to instill among the learners skills for self-reliance in self-employment ventures. The various commissions, but notably the 1999 Koech commission, whose official title was 'Totally Integrated Quality Education and Training (TIQUET): Report of the Commission of Inquiry into Education System,' made recommendations which appeared to suggest that TVET should be made foundational, but rather the core subject areas should be the focus. It only emphasized information technology, and even went further to recommend the scrapping of the 8-4-4 system, indicating its vocational idea was a waste of time. This did not auger well with the then-President Moi, who championed the idea of the 8-4-4 system, and much of the commission's recommendations were rejected. There were nonetheless several recommendations relevant to TVET, but these were policy statements in broad terms, not any different from what had been there before and repeated thereafter in several documents. These included the following: (1) increased training opportunities for those leaving school. This meant pre-employment vocational training opportunities; (2) focus on training in agriculture, industry, and commerce; (3) promotion of vocational entrepreneurship skills; (4) increasing the number of artisans, technicians, and technologists; (5) exposure of students to scientific and technological trends, skills, ideas, and promotion of lifelong skills that enable learners to better adjust to their work and domestic worlds through inculcation of competencies that promote creativity, communication, cooperation, innovativeness, and problem-solving abilities; and (6) promoting and preparation of TVET students for post-secondary middle level institutions, as well as university. It appears that policy recommendations (5) and (6) are in tandem with what can lead to functional TVET. But the downside of these policy recommendations is that they did not go a step further to recommend a national qualification framework that would make TVET a rewarding educational pathway. It had the right ideas in the last two recommendations, but stopped short in articulating how they would be operationalized.

It is not surprising that nothing actually changed and TVET continued more or less with business as usual. This was a missed opportunity to chart a different path for TVET and bring it at par with general education. However, the recommendation that there were to be core competencies that precede TVET is an important one. As noted earlier, one of the moulds that TVET needs to shed off is that idea that it recruits from a lesser ability pool of learners. This is the first transformation that TVET needs to address, and this also has an implication on the level where

TVET should start – either at junior secondary or senior secondary, leading to post-secondary training. Mwiria (2005) offers extensive review of the 8-4-4 system and its TVET character, looking at specific examples. He concluded with depressing comments. The whole policy change, including restructuring the education structure, was ill-conceived to address the crisis problem of youth unemployment. He agreed with Psacharoupolos's (1997) earlier argument that education is not the solution to an unemployment problem. Here is how Mwiria put it: 'By blaming education for this [unemployment] crisis, education was made a victim for a problem it is incapable of resolving' (Mwiria 2005: 294). The main concern was that the causes of unemployment were not well understood, and believing that TVET was the solution without first understanding the problem was in and of itself misplaced. The 8-4-4 system has been much criticized and many parents objected to it. Indeed the super elite simply did not want to follow the system and enrolled their children in international schools that basically maintained the elite British model. In the end, the system was watered down so much that its initial vocational orientation has all but disappeared. Today, the system mainly promotes general education and the combinations that made it vocational are no longer discussed. Subjects such as computers are readily accepted, and so is business and commerce, whereas the core and real TVET subjects such as agriculture, metal work, and so forth have become less visible and less studied.

To make things even more difficult, the Kibaki administration that came to power in 2004 did not change the 8-4-4 system, but seemed even less enthusiastic about promoting vocational learning. Once Free Primary Education was introduced as a policy it consumed the attention, rather than the TVET curriculum. The government in fact moved away from addressing youth unemployment through the education system and instead focused on offering the youth manual employment through a government scheme supported by the World Bank. The scheme, known as *Kazi Kwa Vijana* (Swahili for 'jobs for the youth'), was to employ youth in government projects such as road maintenance, cleaning, etc., and in the process enable them to earn a minimal wage. It was hoped that free primary education would encourage completion of primary education. The next stage was the completion of secondary and thus the introduction of free day secondary education policy. The Kibaki administration thus simply 'ignored' TVET.

As noted by Mwiria (2005), the simplicity notion of TVET has not helped. What is needed is recognition that TVET must start with teaching analytical skills, communication skills, democratic values, and environmental awareness. These, he reckons, are what can form strong foundation for TVET. Examination should not be about memorization, but rather applicability of skills and knowledge.

The Kenya Vision 2030 that sets priorities to make Kenya a middle-income country by 2030 does not seem to have simple TVET ideas. It is promoting innovation and high level technical skills. It recognizes the fact that the youth are Kenya's potential for development. It recognizes rapid urbanization and the need to create better jobs, to professionalize and expand the informal sector. This is much different from the 8-4-4 vision of TVET, which was aimed at containing the youth in the villages and teaching them to appreciate agriculture.

Botswana case study

Due to its political stability, democracy (since its independence in 1966), and freedom from corruption, Botswana is often considered Africa's shining success story. It has experienced sustained economic growth over the years. Botswana is also considered to have been successful in its implementation of TVET. Weeks (2005) attributes this success to Botswana's resistance to implement a full vocationalized secondary school curriculum as the reason for its success. The approach that Botswana implemented was to opt for only providing some pre-vocational education through a limited number of practical subjects. Full vocationalization, which Weeks (2005) defines as 'the devotion of more than three to five hours a week to master trade of secondary schools is not possible in Botswana, nor has the government endorsed it' (Weeks 2005: 136). The other aspect is that initially Botswana had to import teachers, but it also made deliberate efforts to train its own teachers. It also invested heavily in TVET infrastructure, mainly because it had adequate resources and a small population to do so (Weeks 2005).

Education structure

From the time of its independence, Botswana has changed its education structure severally. Before independence in 1966 it was a 8–3–2 structure. It changed to 7–3–2 on the eve of independence, and in 1986 this was again changed to 7–2–3 as an interim step to 6–3–3 structure (Weeks 2005).

Reforms

In 1977 and 1979 the first national commission on education stated: 'The purpose of the schools at all levels will be to prepare children for useful, productive life in the real world. They should have the basic skills of literacy, numeracy, and the knowledge that will make them self-reliant later in life, whether they continue full-time schooling, study on their own, find employment, or become self-employed' (Weeks 2005: 100). The first commission recommended that in senior secondary schools students should not take more than one practical subject. There was the clear belief that to take more than one practical subject might disadvantage a student when it came to tertiary selection (Weeks 2005: 100).

The second commission came about in 1993–94 and it simply re-affirmed the need to return to the 7–3–2 structure. It was aimed at guaranteeing universal access to basic education whilst consolidating vocationalizing the curriculum content at the basic education level (Weeks 2005: 100). The following comment from the second commission explains how Botswana is unique, and responds to criticism that it had not vocationalized enough:

> However, in terms of international trends it could be said that Botswana enjoys the advantage of having a senior secondary curriculum, which may

be regarded as contemporary among middle-income developing countries as it has not suffered from, misdirected 'vocationalization' efforts. The trend among middle-income countries is that emphasis should be placed on cognitive development, language, mathematics, and science at the secondary level. Training for employment should begin after education. Botswana is therefore correctly aligned in concentrating on the academic disciplines. At the same time the key workplace-related subjects like Commerce and Design and Technology are being introduced.

(Weeks 2005: 100)

Botswana's success is also linked to real investment in the education sector and an emphasis on practical subjects that is incomparable to other African countries (Weeks 2005: 115). Schools were rebuilt after 1994, and nearly all the junior schools were equipped with laboratories.

As Weeks noted, it is recognized in Botswana that three to five hours a week on a practical subject will not usually lead to the mastery of what is required on the job or in self-employment. This is very different to what is happening in other countries where practical subjects were simply 'sold' to students and parents on the grounds that they will lead to employment, or if no jobs are available, at least to self-employment (Weeks 2005: 138).

Weeks defined pre-vocational preparation 'as a general education that combines knowledge, skills, values and attitudes in a form that prepares learners on how to investigate, develop and apply concepts learned in real life situations e.g., the home, community, recreational, social and work environments. Pre-vocational preparation should form a sound basis for further education and training. It should also stimulate innovativeness, problem solving and quality performance in a methodological manner in order to produce self-confident learners who would in turn lead successful lives' (Weeks 2005: 138–139).

Botswana remained committed to systematically promoting its pre-vocational education 'instead of trying to vocationalize its secondary schools.' It also invested well in the facilities and human resources that supported this commitment. Even Foster, who has been famous for writing the vocational school fallacy, agreed in 2002 that Botswana had it right, noting that Botswana has achieved 'an appropriate structural and institutional environment' to support pre-vocational education in secondary schools (Weeks 2005: 139).

Conclusion

This chapter has reviewed TVET environment in SSA in general and used the cases of Ghana, Kenya, and Botswana to highlight policy mistakes and the success of Botswana's approach. It is clear that overall, SSA youth are its potential, and yet there is no clear policy focus on how TVET can be harnessed to support youth skills. TVET remains marginalized in the education system, and it seems to select from a pool of low ability learners rather than a parallel and high quality pathway of education to the general education. General education remains dominant. The finance of TVET is also weak, and the Kenyan government's 2012 draft framework for education under its 2010 new constitution acknowledges that the government has paid and continues to pay low attention to TVET (MoE 2012). There is, however, a clear view that private providers are more innovative and can offer more functional TVET than governments. However, they have been left to operate without government support and supervision, and therefore there are large variations in the quality of what is offered. Some countries, such as Botswana, have some working framework for TVET. They seem to have a better integrated plan for using TVET to address youth employment or the approach is one that has integrated TVET. Botswana has also placed greater resources in TVET and seems to have well thought through the TVET they wanted. For a majority, TVET has remained desperately dysfunctional and nearly useless to address youth unemployment. Policies are prescriptive with general statements about the potential of TVET, but these are immediately countered by systemic weaknesses, threats, and conclusions that simply render governments capability in so far as mounting functional TVET meaningless and weak.

The Ghana and Kenya case studies have offered opportunity to present comparison of two countries similar in some aspects and how they have grappled with the youth unemployment and the policies they have put in place to address it. Both followed the same path, Ghana in 1987 and Kenya in 1985–86, with restructuring the education system and introducing heavy TVET pathways. Ghana's aim was to instill pre-employment vocational skills at junior secondary, which is then followed at senior secondary. In a way it created a track system where once one is engaged in TVET at junior secondary, they go on to TVET at senior secondary, then on to a dead-end job prospect. Those who did not make it to senior secondary had rudimentary pre-employment TVET that did not offer them the confidence to face the world of work. They remained desperate and weak to solve their unemployment situation. In the end, general education continued to thrive and the reforms have not helped to position TVET as a pathway that can address the youth unemployment problem.

Kenya's case is not much different than Ghana's. TVET started in primary, equivalent to Ghana's juniors secondary. But when learners completed the grade eight under the 8-4-4 system, what they had been taught such as building grass-thatched huts, and how to dig using a hoe did not make meaningful difference in their lives. Here again the pre-employment skills intended by the policy did not produce desirable outcome. TVET at the senior secondary level was less structured compared to Ghana's, and students simply continued as though there was general education with one subject in TVET chosen to make the combination requirements. Overall, the majority just wanted to gain the qualifications that could lead them to university. Once they completed the secondary level, they were unprepared to create jobs or address the youth unemployment through the so called 8-4-4 skills. No wonder, youth unemployment has remained. In the end, policies in both countries, similar in many respects, have not produced TVET that can equip youth with competencies to face the challenges of employment and deal with youth unemployment. Youth unemployment, therefore, remains a crisis, and the current approach seems to emphasize TVET less. The newly elected Kenyan government focused on other areas to address youth unemployment. This is perhaps recognition that the TVET path has not worked, because even the youth with general education have now failed to find employment. Expansion of manufacturing, focusing of youth funds to help them in start-ups, and accepting and promoting small scale enterprises are now given greater policy priority than the simple notion that TVET in the education system will address youth unemployment.

Recommendation

All is not lost, and TVET is still a strategic educational pathway that can address youth unemployment. TVET has been misinterpreted as a programme for low ability learners. It has maintained its colonial mould. Some of the key areas that need to be addressed to make relevant TVET policies include the following: (1) Making TVET select from the same pool as general education. Any policy that does not address the second class type of education tag that TVET has carried all along is bound to not be as transformative. TVET has to be seen as a viable pathway that along the way can join with general education and vice versa. The Botswana model, where there is limited TVET track, is worth considering.

(2) Instilling general competencies. TVET has to start with a focus on key general competencies that would build the foundation for TVET. These should include instilling analytical skills, communication skills, and numeracy skills, as is the case in Botswana. It may be said that the foundation of TVET is a strong general education. This is linked to the first point above, because it will enhance the pool upon which TVET selects its participants.

(3) Focus on skills that are of lifetime in nature rather than dead end skills. This is related to key competencies that can lead to easy retraining. Transferrable skills, rather than static skills, require that analytical skills are enhanced.

(4) Developing a National Qualifications Framework (NQF) and aligning it to the discussions around youth dividend and development in SSA is an important step towards transforming TVET. Young and Allais (2011) have written extensively on this notion, noting that an estimated 100 countries have embraced the NQF idea. Adams (2011) further noted that NQFs empowers the workforce and encourage lifelong learning. Dealing with containing the youth in the rural areas and addressing run-away unemployment through low level skills is not what SSA requires. TVET policies need to address qualification transferability and the reward system. It needs to be made one of the strands for education economic pillars rather than a system for those perceived as less capable of entering general education and its reward system. It also needs serious investment that will lead to its graduates being equipped with requisite skills to support industrial growth and related technology in Africa.

References

Adams, A. V. (2011). 'The Role of Skills Development in Overcoming Social Disadvantage'. Paris: UNESCO.

African Economic Outlook. (2013). 'Promoting Youth Employment in Africa.' Available at: http://www.africaneconomicoutlook.org/en/in-depth/youth_employment (accessed on 20 December 2013).

Akyeampong, K. (2005). 'Vocationalisation of Secondary Education in Ghana.' In J. Lauglo and R. Maclean (eds.), *Vocationalisation of Secondary Education Revisited.* Dordrecht: Springer.

Atchoarena, D., and Delluc, A. (2001). 'Revisiting Technical and Vocational Education in Sub-Saharan Africa: an Update on Trends, Innovations and Challenges.' Paris: UNESCO, IIEP.

Atchoarena, D., and Esquieu, P. (2002). 'Private Technical and Vocational Education in Sub-Saharan Africa: Provision Patterns and Policy Issues.' Paris: UNESCO, IIEP.

Blaug, M. (1973). 'Education and the Employment Problem in Developing Countries.' Geneva: ILO.

Foster, P. J. (1965). 'The Vocational School Fallacy in Development.' In C.A. Anderson and B. J. Bowman (eds.) *Education and Economic Development.* Chicago: Aldine.

International Labour Organization (ILO) (2012). 'The Youth Employment Crisis.' Highlights of the 2012 Report. Geneva: ILO.

King, K., and Martin, C. (2002). 'The Vocational School Fallacy Revisited: Education, Aspiration and Work in Ghana 1959–2000.' *International Journal of Educational Development*, 22(1): 5–26.

Lauglo, J. (2010). 'Revisiting the Vocational School Fallacy: A Tribute to Philip Foster.' *Comparative Education*, 46(2): 223–35.

Middleton, J., Ziderman, A., and Adams, V. A. (1993). *Skills for Productivity: Vocational Education and Training in Developing Countries.* New York: World Bank and Oxford University Press.

Ministry of Education (MoE) (2012). 'Task Force for the Re-alignment of the Education Sector to the Constitution of Kenya 2010: Towards a Globally Competitive Quality Education for Sustainable Development. Report of the Task Force.' Nairobi: Republic of Kenya.

Mwiria, K. (2005). 'Vocationalisation of Secondary Education; Kenya Case Study.' In J. Lauglo and R. Maclean (eds.) *Vocationalisation of Secondary Education Revisited.* Dordrecht: Springer.

Oketch, M. O. (2007). 'To Vocationalise or Not To Vocationalise? Perspectives on Current Trends and Issues in Technical and Vocational Education and Training (TVET) in Africa.' *International Journal of Educational Development*, 27: 220–34.

Oketch, M. O. (2008). 'Vocationalisation of Secondary Education Revisited.' Review on J. Lauglo and R. Maclean (eds.) *Technical and Vocational Education and Training: Issues, Concerns and Prospects*) New York: Springer. *Comparative Education Review*, 52(1): 135–38.

Psacharopoulos, G. (1997). 'Vocational Education and Training Today: Challenges and Responses.' *Journal of Vocational Education and Training*, 49(3): 385–94.

Tilak, J.B.G. (2002). *Vocational Education and Training in Asia.* Dordrecht: Kluwer Academic Publishers.

Weeks, G. Sheldon. (2005). 'Pre-vocational Secondary Education in Botswana.' In J. Lauglo and R. Maclean (eds.), *Vocationalisation of Secondary Education Revisited.* Dordrecht: Springer.

World Bank. (2013a). 'Ghana Overview'. Availabe at: http://www.worldbank.org/en/country/ghana/overview (accessed on 20 December 2013).

———. (2013b). 'Kenya Overview.' Available at: http://www.worldbank.org/en/country/kenya/overview (accessed on 20 December 2013).

Young, M. and Allais, S. (2011). 'Options for Designing and Implementing an NVQF for India.' Draft Report. Geneva: International Labour Office and The World Bank.

8 The success of learnerships?

Lessons from South Africa's training and education programme

Neil Rankin, Gareth Roberts, and Volker Schöer

Introduction

Technical and vocational education and training (TVET) is viewed by many countries and multi-lateral organizations as a key requirement for developing skills, increasing productivity, improving employability, and creating 'decent work' for young people. The African Development Bank's High Level Panel recommendation on skills development concludes that 'Well targeted vocational training will better align worker skills with the demands of the job market. A key goal would be to increase the percentage of secondary students receiving vocational and technical training in Africa, currently the lowest in the world' (AfDB and OECD 2008: 58). This enthusiasm for TVET is also visible at a country level – almost all African countries do have formal TVET programmes in place and, at the time of writing, seventeen countries in sub-Saharan Africa (SSA) had draft, comprehensive, sector-wide education plans for TVET.

Most TVET programmes in SSA countries are relatively small. One of the largest and best established is South Africa's learnership programme which combines classroom learning with on-the-job training. This programme is large-scale, well-funded, and has been an official government initiative for over 10 years. Its primary aim is to train low-skilled young people in the skills which firms require, and facilitate their entry into jobs. Firms collaborate with Sector Education and Training Authorities (SETAs) and training providers to design programmes to suit their needs. The wages of learners are subsidized and firms have no obligation to hire the participants after a learnership. This means that firms can trial potential future employees in order to ascertain their productivity, employability, and fit with the job.[1] The programme is neither targeted at specific sectors, although the SETAs operate at the sector level, nor at specific firms and the types of training provided is driven by the needs of firms.

At face value learnerships seem like a good solution to South Africa's high rates of youth unemployment. Those without jobs usually have low levels of skills and limited previous work experience and firms complain that a lack of skills is a constraint to their growth. Learnerships tackle these issues by providing useful skills (since the type of training is demand-driven by the firm) and work experience, and firms do not pay the full costs of training or employment. However, despite its longevity and cost there is very little research which investigates whether the programme is meeting its goals and what the consequences of the structure of the programme and its funding are.

The most comprehensive study to date is by the Human Sciences Research Council (HSRC). This study surveyed a cohort of people who had enrolled in a learnership in 2005 and then interviewed them in 2007 and 2010 (Kruss et al. 2012). This chapter complements the HSRC study in that it follows a group of young people over four years from 2009 to 2012, some of whom were enrolled in learnerships. We are thus able to compare the outcomes of those who took part in learnerships and those who did not (unlike the HSRC study which only follows those who enrolled in a learnership). Using this data we attempt to determine the impact of completing a learnership on young people through matching those who took part in learnerships to those with observably similar characteristics who did not. In addition to investigating the outcomes of individuals we also use firm level data which includes information on general and SETA-accredited training (which we use as a proxy for learnerships), to investigate the types of firms which take part in training. This allows us to ascertain how the potential costs and benefits of learnerships may be distributed across firms.

The findings of this research indicate that learnerships are not effective in achieving the stated goals of the programme. Although those completing learnerships are more likely to be in employment than others soon after completion, this benefit fades rapidly. Learnerships do not seem to target those with the lowest skills levels but favour those with higher levels of skills and education. There is no evidence that firms which participate in SETA training expand employment more rapidly than those who do not. Lastly, given that larger firms are much more likely to participate in this type of training but that the training is paid for by a 1 percent payroll tax (which as a proportion of revenue is higher on average for small firms), learnerships are a cross-subsidization of training and wages in bigger firms by smaller firms. The current structure of the programme raises the relative cost of employing lower skilled workers in smaller firms. These results provide valuable lessons for the design of similar TVET programmes in other African countries, particularly in terms of how these programmes are funded.

This chapter is structured as follows: Section 2 discusses the role of learnership-like programmes in other countries; Section 3 summarizes the challenges of youth unemployment in South Africa and how the learnership programme attempts to address these challenges; Section 4 investigates the relationship between learnerships and individual level outcomes; Section 5 examines the relationship between SETA-accredited training and firm level outcomes; and Section 6 concludes and draws policy lessons for other African countries.

The role of learnership-like programmes in other countries

Vocational education and training programmes, which combine theoretical instruction with practical firm-based experience, are often seen as an important solution to get young people into jobs. This is especially the case for young people who do not complete formal schooling or who are unable or unwilling to continue into other forms of higher education. These types of programmes are often demand-driven and align the skills taught with the requirements of the job, helping to improve the match between workers and firms and the lack or mismatch of skills which is often given as an explanation for unemployment in developing countries (Almeida et al. 2012).

The well-established programmes of central Europe (including Austria, Denmark, Germany, and Switzerland) are often used as the model for these types of interventions (Eichhorst et al. 2012). However, despite their prominence Eichhorst et al. (2012) argue that, once selection is taken into account, these types of programmes generally improve early labour market transitions, but the benefits of these programmes diminish with time as non-participants begin to gain a foothold in the labour market. The nature of the training, types of jobs transitioned into, and country-specific characteristics also seem to matter. Eichhorst et al. (2012) note that in countries where these types of programmes are not seen as the last resort option for low-skilled individuals, an apprentice system can negate the impact of low school performance on labour market outcomes.

Although almost all African countries have some formal TVET programmes in place and at least seventeen countries in SSA have draft, comprehensive, sector-wide education plans for TVET (AfDB and OECD 2008), Rother (2007) finds only six countries which provide formal vocational training and apprenticeships for young people. These include programmes in Côte d'Ivoire, Namibia, and Zimbabwe. In Benin and Mali, these types of programmes are relatively small and have been tied to the traditional craft sector and participants spend between 15–20 percent of their time in formal training and the rest gaining practical experience. Countries like Gambia and Ethiopia have also implemented these types of TVET programmes in the last 20 years but the scale remains small (Eichhorst et al. 2012). On the whole, most of these types of programmes in SSA are limited in scale and many are pilot projects and collaborations with NGOs. South Africa's learnership programme thus stands out – it is relatively large-scale, well-funded, and has been an official government initiative for over 10 years.

Evaluation of these programmes, and thus any indication of their success, is generally limited. Of the six programmes Rother (2007) surveys only two have any information on the gross outcomes of the interventions, including statistics like numbers who found a job and improvements in earnings, and none conduct any more rigorous impact evaluation to determine net benefits compared to a control group or cost-effectiveness.

Informal training systems, such as apprenticeships, are relatively more common in SSA. In these arrangements, young people generally enter a period of training with a 'master' or 'mistress' – an experienced person in the field, at no or low rates of pay. This arrangement is mostly negotiated between the parents or guardians of the potential apprentice and the master/mistress and may involve paying a fee to the master/mistress. The training can last several years and is fairly specific to the firm or the products or services which the firm produces. Many apprentices indicate that they wish to start their own businesses once their training is completed but this requires access to a substantial amount of start-up capital (Monk et al. 2008). There is evidence from Ghana, where apprenticeships follow a model typical in West Africa, that there is selection into apprenticeships but the currently employed who have completed apprenticeships but with no formal education, earn 50 percent more than similar employed people who have not undertaken apprenticeships (Monk et al. 2008). Since selection into this type of training may be important, it does not necessarily follow that scaling-up apprenticeships of these types will lead to higher wages. However, given that the apprenticeship system is the most widespread form of training and continues with no government support suggests that it is playing a crucial role in the labour market.

The South African employment challenge and the learnership programme

Unemployment rates for young South Africans are high – more than half of those aged 20–29 years who want to work do not have a job. Although unemployment has increased since 2008 due to the knock-on effects of the global financial crisis as young people have struggled to get into jobs (Rankin et al. 2012), youth unemployment has historically been very high in South Africa. Yu (2013) shows that since 2000 broad unemployment rates were never below 40 percent and were above 50 percent for most of the 2000–11 period. In addition to youth unemployment being high, labour force participation by young people is low. This means that in South Africa, approximately one person in eight below the age of 25 is employed, compared to an average of about two in five in other emerging countries (National Treasury 2011).

A strong correlate with unemployment is low levels of education (generally incomplete secondary school or lower) and low skills. The unemployed are also less likely to have any previous work experience. Firms, on the other hand, report that a shortage of skills is one of their most pressing constraints.[2] South African unemployment is thus characterized by the twin dilemmas of large numbers of unemployed individuals with low-skilled levels but demands from firms for more skilled workers.

In addition to the mismatch between the low levels of skills among the unemployed and the demand for skilled employees from firms, weak employability signals given by school qualifications also create uncertainty. This is particularly the case for young people with no job experience to act as a productivity signal. A wage floor in South Africa means that wages cannot fall to compensate for this uncertainty. This wage floor is a result of institutional factors including the structure of collective bargaining which sets minimum wages and labour regulations, and the spatial legacy of apartheid which means that most of the unemployed and low-skilled are located far from jobs and consequently transport costs are high. Firms are thus unwilling to employ young people since at current wage rates it is difficult and costly to ascertain whether they will contribute positively to the firm. An initiative introduced in late 2013 to compensate firms for employing new young workers is a wage subsidy through a tax incentive, formally known as the Youth Employment Tax Incentive.

South Africa's learnership programme is a long running intervention which aims to address the low levels of skills and weak productivity signals which characterize the unemployed. This programme was implemented in 2001 as part of the National Skills Development Strategy and combines classroom learning with on-the-job training, practical experience, and a path to a formal qualification. Learnerships usually take a year to complete but the time length can vary, based on the nature of the programme and the previous experience and qualifications of the individual.

Learnerships are administered and managed, currently, by SETAs. These SETAs are sector-specific and have a board comprised of representatives from organized business, organized labour, and the Ministry of Higher Education. Firms and workers who are not formally organized, or whose organizations do not have formal recognition, are thus unlikely to be represented at the board level. It is estimated that the learnership system caters for between 44,000 and 55,000 people per year (Kruss et al. 2012).

The learnership programme is expected to both facilitate skills development in the formal sector, through a demand-led process, and assist new entrants into employment (Visser and Kruss 2009). It was not intended to target a specific group but rather to be open to all skill levels, sectors, and ages, but also to address specific vulnerable groups – the youth, women, and the unemployed (Visser and Kruss 2009). In practice though, learnerships are only available to those aged 16–35 years and many SETAs, such as the HWSETA, report the primary aim of a learnership as a 'provision of skills to unemployed or employed but unskilled individuals' (HWSETA 2013). Visser and Kruss (2009) also acknowledge that the learnership system is increasingly prioritizing employment creation, especially through providing skills development for young Africans with low levels of skills.

The funding for this programme is derived from a payroll tax of one percent on employers. Eighty percent of this revenue is then channeled through SETAs to fund demand-led development and training. In the 2011–12 tax year, the South African Revenue Service (SARS) collected approximately R10 billion (approximately US$1.4 billion) in payroll and workforce taxes – an increase of 17 percent over the previous tax year (National Treasury and South African Revenue Services 2012). This is a substantial real increase, given that inflation in 2012 was approximately 5.6 percent compared to 2011.

The learnership programme is intended to be demand-driven – firms identify the skills which they need and they approach the SETA for their sector to initiate the learnership.[3] The SETA will provide a grant for the learnership provided the firm meets certain criteria. The firm then identifies a SETA-accredited training provider and advertises for candidates for the learnership who go through the company's recruitment process. The Department of Labour does have a database on which prospective candidates can register; candidates are supposed to be notified when appropriate learnerships become available. This is one of the functions which the Department of Labour's Labour Centres carry out. Once suitable candidates have been identified the learner, employer, and training provider sign the agreement and the firm must register the position with the requisite SETA in order to claim tax back. The learner undergoes a number of assessments during the learnership, and if completed successfully receives a nationally accredited qualification. The employer does not have an obligation to employ the learner upon completion of the learnership.

Despite the importance of learnerships as a policy initiative in South Africa, there has been relatively little work on the effectiveness of the programme. The HSRC has conducted a large study of learnerships and apprenticeships, surveying a cohort of people who had enrolled in a learnership in 2005 and then interviewing them in 2007 and 2010 (Kruss et al. 2012). Whilst this provides considerable information on the trajectories of people who have been exposed to learnerships, it does not allow for any comparison between these individuals and those who have not undertaken learnerships. This means that nothing can be said about whether the trajectories of those who come through learnerships are any different to those who do not.

The HSRC study shows rates of completion of learnerships of 65 percent two years after enrolment, with 15 percent dropping out without completion, typically during the first six months of the programme, and the balance still enrolled in longer programmes. Transitions from learnerships to employment were high – 86 percent of those surveyed who had completed learnerships were employed (not necessarily in the company where they completed their learnership) and 90 percent of these were in permanent positions. The HSRC work also indicates that those who have completed learnerships experience 'uncomplicated' trajectories into work, mostly experiencing only a single transition into work after completing the programme. Successful transition into employment after the learnership differs by the level of qualification (Visser and Kruss 2009). However, for those learners who were unemployed prior to the programme, only 43 percent of those who registered for a low-skills qualification (National Qualification Framework, NQF 1–3) found employment, compared to 76 percent of those in the medium-skills group (NQF 4) or 64 percent for the high-skills level (NQF 5–8). Enrolment in low-skills programmes is significantly larger than for the other groups and this low conversion rate is, according to Visser and Kruss (2009), a 'significant failure.'

The existing work in South Africa indicates that learnerships may most benefit those with previous work experience and with higher skills. This work also does not indicate whether the individuals who participated in a learnership are any better off than observably identical individuals who did not. To do this requires data on both those who participated in learnerships and those that did not.

In order to evaluate the learnership programme we need to identify indicator variables for the two broad goals of the programme: (1) skills provision and (2) increased entry into jobs. If the learnership programme is successful we should observe higher skills levels among firms and better firm performance – if a lack of skills is a limiting constraint for those firms benefiting from the programme – faster transitions into employment and better labour market outcomes for those people taking part in learnerships. Since many SETAs also state that an aim of the programme is the provision of skills to those with low skills levels, we anticipate that a successful programme would target these types of individuals and improve their outcomes. In the next two sections we compare the outcomes of individuals for those taking part in learnerships, and those not, in terms of labour market status and other measures, and the outcomes for firms who undertake SETA-accredited training and those who do not. We also attempt, where possible, to differentiate outcomes by skills group.

Learnerships and young people

The data used

In order to understand the impact of learnerships on labour market outcomes for young people in South Africa we use a unique dataset which tracks African individuals initially aged between 20 and 24 years. The first round of the Labour Market Entry Survey (LMES) was collected in 2009 and individuals were re-interviewed every year until 2012. Individuals were selected based on a stratified random sample drawn from areas in Johannesburg, Durban, and Polokwane and surroundings and were followed even if they moved out of these areas. The sample is predominantly urban but some individuals in the rural areas surrounding Polokwane were interviewed. Approximately one-third of the sample was drawn from databases of young people looking for work provided by the Department of Labour's Labour Centres in these areas (see Levinsohn et al. 2013, for more detail on the sampling). One function of these Labour Centres is to advertise learnerships and this, together with the urban nature of the sample, means that it is likely that learnership participation in the sample is over-represented compared to the population as a whole. The LMES dataset differs from the data used by Visser and Kruss (2009) since it is a sample of the broader youth population and not only of those who have chosen to enrol in learnerships. As such we are able to compare the outcomes of those who participated in learnerships to the outcomes of those who did not.

In 2010 a randomly chosen subset of the individuals were allocated vouchers which entitled any firm which employed them to claim back up to half their wages for a period of six months. Levinsohn et al. (2013) show that these vouchers did increase employment probabilities both one-year and two-years after allocation. Thus the dataset we use includes this employment improving intervention, however, the focus of this chapter is not on the impact of this intervention. We have chosen to keep those individuals who were part of this experiment in the sample for two reasons: first, dropping them cuts the sample size in half and makes the number of those with learnerships relatively small; and second, our analysis indicates that this intervention did not affect the probability of young people undertaking learnerships. In addition to this, when we undertake our analysis we use control variables for characteristics prior to the wage subsidy voucher allocation.

Table 8.1 Sample descriptive statistics

Statistics	Age	Male (%)	Complete matric (%)	Wage voucher (%)	Employed (%)	Started and completed learnership between 2009 and 2011 (%)	Ever enrolled in learnership (%)	Ever completed learnership (%)
2011								
Mean	24.18	0.44	0.71	0.51	0.34	0.02	0.08	0.05
Std. dev.	1.51	0.50	0.45	0.50	0.47	0.15	0.26	0.21
n	2358	2358	2358	2358	2358	2358	2357	2357
2012								
Mean	25.16	0.43	0.72	0.51	0.33	0.03	0.03	0.01
Std. dev.	1.51	0.49	0.45	0.50	0.47	0.16	0.16	0.10
n	2106	2107	2107	2106	1866	2107	1762	1762
Total								
Mean	24.64	0.43	0.72	0.51	0.33	0.02	0.06	0.03
Std. dev.	1.59	0.50	0.45	0.50	0.47	0.16	0.23	0.18
n	4464	4465	4465	4464	4224	4465	4119	4119

Source: Authors' calculations.

Table 8.1 shows the descriptive statistics from the sample for the last two rounds of the survey, 2011 and 2012. We confine our analysis to these rounds since these were the rounds where the bulk of the learnership questions were asked, and during these rounds individuals were older and more likely to have completed education and be transitioning into employment. These statistics show that the average age of those in the sample was 24 years in 2011 and 25 years in 2012, that almost 60 percent of the sample are female, and more than 70 percent have completed secondary school (matric). Half the sample took part in the wage voucher experiment and approximately one-third were in employment in each round.

These statistics show the limited reach of the learnership programme among young people. Only 2.5 percent of our sample enrolled in and completed a learnership during the period between the first round of the survey (in 2009) and the third round (in 2011). Figures for enrolment and completion of learnerships outside this period are higher – 8 percent of the sample claimed to have ever enrolled in a learnership prior to 2011 and 3 percent in 2012, and 5 percent claimed to have completed a learnership prior to 2011 and 1 percent in 2012. Despite the relatively small proportions undertaking learnerships, if these are scaled by the number of young people in these age groups in South Africa this indicates that approximately 50,000–200,000 young people complete a learnership every year. These estimates are higher than Visser and Kruss (2009) for at least two reasons. The first is the inherent bias in the sample towards those types of individuals who are most likely to be enrolled in learnerships and the small sample sizes means that these overestimates at the sample level are magnified once scaled-up to the aggregate level. The second is that actual numbers of enrolments in learnerships have increased since the HSRC study.

What characteristics are associated with participating in a learnership?

The first question we ask is whether those who participate in learnerships are different from those who do not and what characteristics are associated with participating and completing a learnership? The HSRC study suggests that learners may have different characteristics to those in the general population but they do not systematically compare the two groups. In Table 8.2 we investigate whether those who have enrolled in a learnership are different in terms of age, gender, and education.

A robust finding is that those with matric (completed grade 12), the South African school leaving certificate, are more likely to participate in, and complete a learnership compared to those who have not completed secondary school. The size of the effect varies by 2.3 percentage points for enrolling and completing a learnership during the 2009–11 period to 5.8 percentage points for ever participating in a learnership. This relationship between education and learnerships is despite the fact that learnerships are, at least in theory, available to those with less than grade 12 and that Visser and Kruss (2009) show that approximately two-thirds of their sample are enrolled in learnerships with NQF levels less than

Table 8.2 Characteristics associated with participating in a learnership, OLS regressions

	(1)	*(2)*	*(3)*
	Ever enrolled in learnership	*Ever completed learnership*	*Enrolled and completed learnership (2009–11)*
Age	–0.000854	0.00424**	–0.00183
	(0.00239)	(0.00184)	(0.00156)
Male	0.00141	–0.00138	–0.00597
	(0.00721)	(0.00557)	(0.00471)
Matric	0.0576***	0.0336***	0.0227***
	(0.00823)	(0.00636)	(0.00538)
Wage voucher experiment	0.000793	0.00367	–0.00446
	(0.00704)	(0.00545)	(0.00460)
2011 wave	0.0489***	0.0424***	–0.00189
	(0.00743)	(0.00574)	(0.00481)
Observations	4,118	4,118	4,464
R-squared	0.058	0.048	0.061

Source: Authors' calculations.

Note: Standard errors in parentheses, sampling cluster controls included but not reported; ***$p <$ 0.01, **$p < 0.05$, *$p < 0.1$.

matric. There may be a number of reasons why our results differ. One may be that enrolments have changed since 2007 and that now fewer learnerships are offered for those with lower levels of education. The lower likelihood of becoming employed for these individuals, when compared to other higher level learnerships, as shown by Visser and Kruss (2009), could be a factor contributing to that. The second reason may be that these types of learnerships are concentrated in geographical areas where the participants in the LMES are not drawn from. The third is that those who take part in these types of learnerships are less likely to report them as learnerships. At this stage it is difficult to disentangle which of these explanations are correct. What this data does illustrate is that, certainly in this sample, learnerships are not undertaken by the least educated, who arguably could be the most in need of this type of intervention.

There is no evidence that learnership participation differs by gender or age and no indication that individuals who were part of the wage subsidy voucher experiment discussed earlier were more likely to enroll in a learnership. The data does indicate that older individuals in the sample were more likely to have completed a learnership. This is expected since many of the younger individuals enrolled in learnerships may still be busy with them.

Are learnerships associated with a higher probability employment and better labour market outcomes?

The key question to answer in order to understand whether learnerships are an effective intervention to get young people into jobs is whether those who have undertaken a learnership are more likely to be employed. In order to do this we use two analytical approaches. The first is to estimate the following specification using ordinary least squares (OLS):

$$Employment_{it} = \alpha_t + \beta_1 Learnership_i + \beta_2 Learnership_i \times 2012 + X'_{it}\delta + \varepsilon_{it}$$

where: $Employment_{it}$ is a dummy variable which captures whether the individual (i) is in wage employment during period t; α_t is a constant term which varies with time; $Learnership_i$ is a dummy variable which captures whether the individual participated in and completed a learnership between 2009 and 2011; $Learnership_i \times 2012$ is an interaction variable between completing the learnership and the 2012 round of the survey; X'_{it} is a vector of control variables including gender, age, education, and controls for the area in which the individual was sampled; and ε_{it} is a standard error term.

The coefficient estimates of interest are β_1, which measures the relationship between learnerships and the probability of being in wage employment, and β_2, which measures whether this relationship continues into 2012.

The second approach is a propensity score matching (PSM) method which balances the covariates between a treatment (in this case learnership) group and a control group based on their predicted probabilities of being in the treatment group (Rosenbaum and Rubin 1983). Essentially this technique creates an observationally similar group of individuals to serve as a control group for those who enrolled in a learnership and then compares the outcomes between these two groups. We use a set of characteristics for the individuals obtained from the 2009 round of the survey which pre-dates their participation in a learnership. These characteristics are:

- their employment in 2009;
- gender;
- education level;
- age;
- how many earners they lived with the in 2009 (to proxy for connection to the labour market);
- the province they were sampled in;
- whether they were sampled from a Labour Centre database;
- and whether they took part in the wage subsidy voucher experiment.

Individuals are matched using a kernel matching method and only one individual is not matched since they differ substantially from the others.

The results obtained from both methods are similar. Table 8.3 presents the OLS regression results, Table 8.4 the first stage of the PSM method, and Table 8.5 presents the average differences in outcomes between the matched groups. These differences are summarized in Figure 8.1. Although both methods indicate an effect of an increase in employment probability by 4–5 percentage points in 2011, neither of these estimates are significant at the 10 percent significance level. Both methods also indicate that by 2012, at least one year after completion of the learnership, those who completed a learnership are no more likely to be in wage

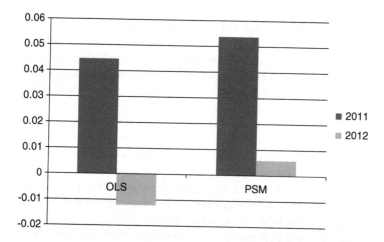

Figure 8.1 The difference in employment probabilities between those who participated in and completed a learnership between 2009 and 2011

Source: Authors' calculations.

Table 8.3 Learnerships and wage employment, OLS regressions

	(1)	(2)	(3)	(4)
Ever enrolled in learnership	0.186*** (0.0321)			
Ever completed learnership		0.0893** (0.0417)		
Enrolled and completed learnership (2009–11)			0.0190 (0.0468)	0.0445 (0.0622)
Enrolled and completed learnership (2009–11) × 2012				−0.0566 (0.0910)
Age	0.0229*** (0.00488)	0.0224*** (0.00490)	0.0223*** (0.00486)	0.0223*** (0.00486)
Male	0.104*** (0.0147)	0.105*** (0.0148)	0.112*** (0.0147)	0.112*** (0.0147)
Matric	0.0997*** (0.0169)	0.107*** (0.0169)	0.105*** (0.0168)	0.105*** (0.0168)
Wage voucher experiment	0.0490*** (0.0144)	0.0489*** (0.0145)	0.0512*** (0.0143)	0.0511*** (0.0143)
2011 wave	0.0352** (0.0153)	0.0405*** (0.0153)	0.0337** (0.0151)	0.0322** (0.0152)
Observations	4,118	4,118	4,223	4,223
R-squared	0.071	0.065	0.063	0.063

Source: Authors' calculations.

Note: Standard errors in parentheses, sampling cluster controls included but not reported; *** $p <$ 0.01, ** $p < 0.05$, * $p < 0.1$.

Table 8.4 Probit estimates of determinants of participation in a learnership, first stage of PSM

	(1)	(2)
Wage voucher experiment	−0.0547 (0.117)	−0.0873 (0.123)
Employed in 2009	−0.261 (0.236)	−0.687* (0.364)
Male	−0.00992 (0.118)	−0.0462 (0.124)
Age	−0.0350 (0.0403)	−0.0313 (0.0422)
Number of individuals employed in household in 2009	0.0143** (0.00678)	0.0132** (0.00668)
Matric	0.644*** (0.192)	0.511*** (0.184)

Table 8.4 (Continued)

	(1)	(2)
Labour Centre sample	0.330***	0.365***
	(0.123)	(0.130)
KwaZulu-Natal	−0.600***	−0.553***
	(0.209)	(0.213)
Limpopo	−0.397***	−0.410***
	(0.137)	(0.143)
Constant	−1.609	−1.513
	(0.982)	(1.062)
Observations	2,358	2,106

Source: Authors' calculations.

Note: Standard errors in parentheses; *** $p < 0.01$, ** $p < 0.05$, * $p < 0.1$.

employment compared to others. This indicates that learnerships have no impact on employment probabilities except for during and potentially immediately after completion of the learnership.

A change in the probability of being employed is only one potential way to measure the success of a learnership from an individual's perspective. In order to investigate other aspects of success we consider three other outcomes: whether (1) the individual reports being happy in their job; (2) whether they have had any promotions; and (3) their monthly earnings. These results, presented in Table 8.6, indicate that there is a relationship between happiness in the job and completion of a learnership although this relationship diminishes with time. There is no evidence that undertaking a learnership increases the probability of being promoted and there is some evidence that those who completed a learnership may have higher levels of earnings in 2012, although this estimate is not significantly different from zero. Taken together, these results indicate that the benefits of a learnership to an individual are relatively short term.

Table 8.5 Impact of a learnership on the probability of being in employment, PSM

	(1)	(2)
Average treatment effect on the treated (ATT)	0.0768	0.00532
	(0.0629)	(0.0687)
Observations	2,358	1,865

Source: Authors' calculations.

Note: Standard errors in parentheses; *** $p < 0.01$, ** $p < 0.05$, * $p < 0.1$.

Table 8.6 Other measures of success and learnerships, OLS regressions

	(1)	(2)	(3)
	Happy in job	Promotion	Ln (monthly earnings)
Enrolled and completed learnership (2009–11)	0.300***	–0.0558	–0.0401
	(0.0887)	(0.0487)	(0.140)
Enrolled and completed learnership (2009–11) × 2012	–0.163	–0.00932	0.285
	(0.145)	(0.0798)	(0.242)
Observations	1,728	1,728	1,667
R-squared	0.063	0.051	0.133

Source: Authors' calculations.

Note: Standard errors in parentheses, sampling cluster controls included but not reported, regressions also control for age, gender, matric, wage subsidy voucher, and year; *** $p < 0.01$, ** $p < 0.05$, * $p < 0.1$.

Learnerships and firms

The funding for, and implementation of learnerships happens at a firm level. It is therefore important to consider how the costs and benefits of the programme differ across firms of different characteristics. To do this we use firm level data collected by the World Bank in 2007–08 as part of their Investment Climate Assessment Survey. This survey collects information on firm characteristics including output, labour costs, employment, and training from predominantly manufacturing firms in the major metropolitan areas in South Africa. With this data we can examine whether certain firms are likely to contribute more to learnerships through payroll taxes and which types of firms are likely to benefit most from SETA-accredited training. By so doing we can get an indication of how the costs and benefits of the programme are distributed across firms.

Do labour costs, and therefore the relative cost of a payroll tax, differ across firms?

To ascertain whether labour costs differ by firm characteristics we regress labour costs as a proportion of firm level output on employment, the capital-labour ratio, the proportion of non-production workers employed (a proxy for high-skilled workers), and sector and location controls. Table 8.7 shows these results. Smaller firms have a significantly larger share of labour costs to output than larger firms, even after controlling for capital intensity, the skills composition of their workforce, and their sector and location. This relationship is of relatively large magnitude – a firm which employs 100 people has 2 percentage points (9 percent) lower labour costs as a share of output than a ten employee firm, and the difference between a 500 employee firm and a ten employee firm is 3.8 percentage points (15 percent). Payroll taxes add 1 percent to labour costs and thus fall proportionally more on smaller firms given these firms have higher relative

Table 8.7 Labour costs as a proportion of output, and firm characteristics, OLS regressions

	(1)	*(2)*	*(3)*	*(4)*
Ln (employment)	−0.0113***	−0.0109***	−0.00886***	−0.00970***
	(0.00309)	(0.00311)	(0.00301)	(0.00308)
Ln (capital/employment)			−0.0181***	−0.0172***
			(0.00247)	(0.00255)
Non-production workers/ employment		−0.0321	−0.0275	−0.0173
		(0.0287)	(0.0277)	(0.0288)
Sector controls:	No	No	No	Yes
City controls:	No	No	No	Yes
Observations	680	680	677	672
R-squared	0.019	0.021	0.093	0.121

Source: Authors' calculations.

Note: Standard errors in parentheses; *** $p < 0.01$, ** $p < 0.05$, * $p < 0.1$.

labour costs. Although the magnitude of this effect may appear small it is a regressive tax on smaller and more labour-intensive firms and changes relative prices, making labour more expensive relative to capital. This raises the costs of smaller firms and makes it more difficult for them to compete against larger firms. It also encourages the substitution of labour with capital if this is possible.

Are certain types of firms more likely to engage in learnerships than others?

Smaller firms pay a higher proportion of their output to fund learnerships but this would balance out if they were more likely to engage in learnerships or other SETA-accredited training and thus claim some of these funds back. Figure 8.2 shows that this is not the case – larger firms are much more likely to engage in training in general and SETA-accredited training in particular. Only 13 percent of firms in the 10–19 employee category partake in SETA-accredited training, compared to 44 percent in the 200–999 employee group. Furthermore, smaller firms are much less likely to engage in SETA-accredited training even if they engage in training. There are a number of reasons why SETA training favours larger firms. The first is that smaller firms may not have the resources to implement or administer these programmes. The fixed costs associated with these programmes may require a certain sized firm to achieve economies of scale. The second is that the content or recognition of learnerships and other SETA training programmes may be biased in favour of large firms. This is likely to be the case where business organizations and organized labour, which predominantly represent larger firms, are strongly involved with the SETAs.

As the individual data illustrates, those at the bottom of the skills distribution are the least likely to enrol in learnerships. The firm data also indicates a bias against lower skilled workers. Firms with higher proportions of production workers,[4] a proxy for low-skilled workers, are less likely to engage in SETA-accredited

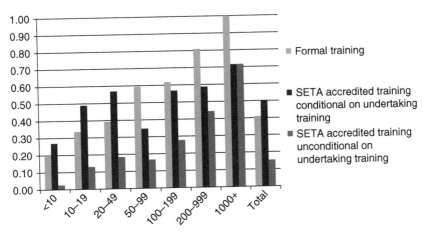

Figure 8.2 Proportion of firms engaged in training
Source: Authors' calculations.

Table 8.8 Change in Ln (total employment) between 2005 and 2008 and SETA-accredited training, OLS regressions

	(1)	(2)
Ln (total employment$_{2005}$)	−0.0473***	−0.0624***
	(0.00764)	(0.00811)
SETA-accredited training	0.0102	0.0341
	(0.0307)	(0.0308)
Constant	0.375***	0.354***
	(0.0245)	(0.0525)
Sector controls:	No	Yes
City controls:	No	Yes
Observations	747	746
R-squared	0.053	0.126

Source: Authors' calculations.
Note: Standard errors in parentheses; *** $p < 0.01$, ** $p < 0.05$, * $p < 0.1$.

training. A firm where 65 percent of its workforce are production workers (this is approximately the 25th percentile in the sample in terms of the ratio of production workers to total employment) is approximately six percentage points more likely to train than one with 85 percent production workers (the 75th percentile).

One further argument for SETA-accredited training is that it may help firms overcome a shortage for skills and thus expand employment. There is no indication in this dataset that firms which undertake SETA-accredited grow employment faster than those that do not, once the initial level of employment is controlled for. These results are reported in Table 8.8.

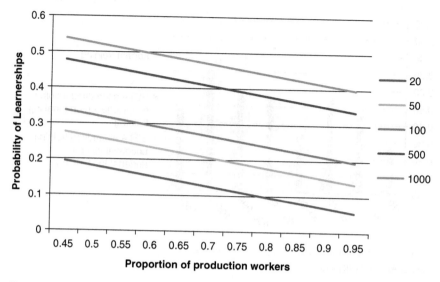

Figure 8.3 Predicted probability of engaging in SETA-accredited training by firm size and the proportion of production workers

Source: Authors' calculations.

Notes: Predicted values based on an OLS regression of whether a firm engages in SETA-accredited training or not on ln (firm size) and the proportion of production workers in the total workforce. All coefficient estimates are significant at the 1% level.

These firm level results indicate that the system of funding learnerships is biased against smaller and more labour-intensive firms. In addition to this, it is precisely these types of firms and those with higher proportions of production (low-skilled) workers which are less likely to engage in SETA-accredited training (see Figure 8.3). Small firms are thus disadvantaged twice by the programme – they pay relatively more through the payroll tax and they are less likely to benefit. The design of the current learnership programme is thus regressive and amounts to a subsidy of training of higher skilled workers in larger firms by smaller more labour-intensive firms. In addition to this redistributive (in the wrong way) aspect, the way the programme is funded through a tax amounting to a fixed proportion of wages changes the relative prices of labour and capital. As Behar (2010) has shown, capital and labour are substitutes in South Africa and an increase in the price of labour, caused by this tax, reduces its demand relative to capital. The programme design is thus wrong if it wants to encourage training and employment of the lower-skilled in smaller firms – the type of employment South Africa needs if it is to create jobs for the currently unemployed.

Conclusions and lessons for other countries

Africa is likely to face a growing bulge of youth unemployment in the future as the rate of formal job creation does not keep pace with the entry of young people into the labour market (see Filmer and Fox (2014) and Thurlow, this volume).

South Africa is already facing this challenge with high and rising rates of youth unemployment. The outcomes of its policies to reduce youth unemployment can thus provide lessons for the rest of the continent.

A potential reason why young people remain unemployed is that they lack the practical skills and work experience required in a job. Uncertainty about the productivity of young people and wages which do not or cannot fall to compensate for this uncertainty results in unemployment. One type of intervention which could overcome this market failure would be a combination of class-based learning, practical training, and work experience. In these types of programmes individuals learn practical and relevant skills, are better able to signal their actual productivity to firms since they are working in an actual firm environment and may also get a certificate upon completion which would signal their abilities to other firms. Firms get subsidized training which may enable them to train individuals in skills specific to the sector or firm and have an opportunity to assess the match between them and a potential employee at a lower cost and with limited costs should the match not work. The TVET programmes of central Europe (including Austria, Denmark, Germany, and Switzerland) are often used as the model for these types of interventions (Eichhorst et al. 2012). South Africa's learnership programme provides an example of this type of programme in Africa.

Using data from both a longitudinal survey of young people initially aged 20–24 years and firms in the manufacturing sector we are able to investigate whether those who participate in and complete learnerships are any better off in the labour market than those who do not, and how the costs and benefits are distributed across firms. Our results suggest that there is a selection of people with school leaving certificates (matric) into these learnership programmes and thus those at the lower end of the skills and education distribution may be left out. This might be because firms want the types of skills which require at least secondary school education, it could be that those with matric have other characteristics (such as motivation) which are also associated with applying for a learnership, or it might be that firms use a matric qualification as a sorting mechanism to reduce the number of applicants for a position to a tractable number. Regardless of the reason, these results suggest that those with low education levels are less likely to benefit from the programme which is contradictory to the stated aims of the intervention.

Learnerships do seem to facilitate the transition into jobs, another goal of the programme. Those who complete a learnership are more likely to be in employment directly after completion than those who do not enrol in learnerships but, similar to the research summarized by Eichhorst et al. (2012), this advantage fades with time. We find that, at least within the time period we surveyed these young people, completing a learnership is not associated with a better job, in terms of income or promotion, compared to those who did not participate.

A major flaw in the learnership system is the way it is funded. Learnerships are administered by SETAs, which received funding from a payroll tax on companies. This payroll tax of 1 percent of wages is regressive since smaller and more labour-intensive firms spend a larger relative proportion on wages than larger firms. In addition to the regressive nature of the tax it also changes the relative costs of inputs making labour relatively more expensive compared to capital and thus encouraging substitution away from low-skilled labour.

Not only do the costs of the programme fall disproportionally on smaller and more labour-intensive firms, but these types of firms are also least likely to benefit. Firm size is positively associated with taking part in SETA-accredited training as is the proportion of non-production (higher skilled) workers. The unequal distribution of costs and benefits means that this programme, and SETAs more broadly, act to redistribute resources from smaller to larger firms, from more labour-intensive firms to less, and from lower skilled workers to higher. This is the wrong direction of redistribution of resources required in the South African economy to create jobs for the currently unemployed, most of whom are young people.

These results suggest a number of lessons for other African countries hoping to implement programmes of this nature. First, the way the programme is funded matters. Funding these types of interventions through a payroll tax is distortionary – it raises the relative cost of labour and falls most heavily on smaller firms whose labour costs are a larger proportion of output than larger firms. A potentially better way of funding would be from the general tax pool or as a tax incentive for those firms who undertake training of this nature. Second, these types of programmes may be subject to institutional capture by those constituencies, such as larger firms and more skilled workers, who will benefit the most. This is not necessarily a bad thing if these are the types of firms and workers an economy is lacking, or if this reduces the coordination costs, which may be associated with programmes of this nature, but these types of firms may be training anyway. Third, these interventions by themselves are unlikely to create the large numbers of new jobs for young people who African economies will need to reduce unemployment and raise incomes significantly. Evidence for South Africa and more broadly suggests that they do facilitate entry into jobs for young people but that this impact wears off relatively rapidly. This suggests that these programmes may be just pushing their participants to the front of the job queue and not creating many new jobs.

Notes

1 Many firms view South Africa's labour regulations as a constraint to hiring since getting rid of employees who are bad fits is viewed as difficult – see Rankin (2006) for a discussion.
2 For example, lack of skilled staff was ranked third as a constraint by respondents in a 2012 survey of small and medium firms (SBP 2013) and third in the World Bank's 2007 Investment Climate Assessment survey (World Bank 2011).
3 This information is taken from a number of SETA, and the Department of Labour's websites. For example www.merseta.org.za/SkillsDevelopment/LearningProgrammes/Learnerships.aspx; www.labour.gov.za/DOL/find-more-info/all-about-learnerships/.
4 Production workers are those who are actually involved in the production process and does not include management or support workers.

References

AFDB and OECD (2008). *African Economic Outlook 2008*. Paris: OECD.
Almeida, R., Behrman, J., and Robalino, D. (2012). *The Right Skills for the Job? Rethinking Training Policies for Workers*. Washington, DC: World Bank.

Behar, A. (2010). 'Would Cheaper Capital Replace Labour?' *South African Journal of Economics*, 78(2): 131–51.

Eichhorst, W., Rodríguez-Planas, N., Schmidl, R., and Zimmermann, K. F. (2012). 'A Roadmap to Vocational Education and Training Systems around the World.' IZA Discussion Paper 7110. Bonn: Institute for the Study of Labour.

Filmer, D., and Fox, L. (2014). *Youth Employment in Sub-Saharan Africa*. Washington, DC: World Bank.

HWSETA (2013). 'Health and Welfare Sector Education and Training Authority: Learnerships.' Available: http://www.hwseta.org.za/welcome.asp?page=category_display. asp&category=267&P_Category=59&name=Learnerships%20&action=view (accessed 20 December 2013).

Kruss, G., Wildschut, A., Janse van Rensburg, D., Visser, M., Haupt, G., and Roodt, J. (2012). *Developing Skills and Capabilities through the Learnership and Apprenticeship Pathway Systems*. Pretoria: Human Science Research Council.

Levinsohn, J., Rankin, N. A., Roberts, G.A., and Schöer, V. (2013). 'Wage Subsidies to Address Youth Unemployment in South Africa'. Department of Economics Working Papers. Stellenbosch: Stellenbosch University.

Monk, C., Teal, F., and Sandefur, J. (2008). 'Does Doing an Apprenticeship Pay Off? Evidence from Ghana.' Working Paper. Oxford: University of Oxford, Centre for the Study of African Economies.

National Treasury (2011). 'Confronting Youth Unemployment: Policy Options for South Africa.' Discussion Paper. Pretoria: National Treasury.

National Treasury and South African Revenue Services (2012). 'Tax Statistics 2012.' Pretoria: National Treasury and SARS.

Rankin, N. (2006). 'The Regulatory Environment and SMMEs. Evidence from South African Firm Level Data.' Development Working Papers. Cape Town: University of Cape Town, Policy Research Unit.

Rankin, N. A., Roberts, G. A., Schöer, V., and Shepherd, D. (2012). 'The Financial Crisis and its Enduring Legacy for Youth Unemployment.' In J. Hofmeyr (ed.), *2012 Transformation Audit. The Youth Dividend: Unlocking the Potential of Young South Africans*. First Edition. Cape Town: Institute for Justice and Reconciliation.

Rosenbaum, P. R., and Rubin, D. B. (1983). The Central Role of the Propensity Score in Observational Studies for Causal Effects. *Biometrika*, 70(1): 41–55.

Rother, F. (2007). *Interventions to Support Young Workers in Sub-Saharan Africa. Regional Report for the Youth Employment Inventory*. Washington, DC: World Bank.

SBP (2013). *Headline Report of SBP's SME Growth Index*. Johannesburg: SBP.

Visser, M., and Kruss, G. (2009). Learnerships and Skills Development in South Africa: a Shift to Prioritise the Young Unemployed. *Journal of Vocational Education & Training*, 61(3): 357–74.

World Bank (2011). 'Improving the Business Environment for Growth and Job Creation in South Africa: The Second Investment Climate Assessment.' Report. Washington, DC: World Bank.

Yu, D. (2013). 'Youth Unemployment in South Africa since 2000 Revisited.' Working Papers 04/13. Stellenbosch: University of Stellenbosch.

9 Conclusions

Moving beyond conventional wisdoms

Danielle Resnick and James Thurlow

Jon Abbink (2005:7) has observed that 'To be young in Africa came to mean being disadvantaged, vulnerable and marginal in the political and economic sense.' Yet, how African youth are more marginalized than young people elsewhere, or more so today than in other eras of history, is often not well-specified in the broader scholarly and policy literature. This volume has therefore aimed to achieve two main objectives. First, it has focused on the confluence of life cycle and generational effects in order to help contextualize the circumstances facing contemporary African youth. More specifically, the authors linked Africa's perceived youth crisis with broader economic development trajectories in the region, highlighting similarities and distinctions from the pathways experienced by other regions. At its root, the concern about youth is rooted in the demographic challenge created by the youth bulge. Every region of the world has gone through a similar demographic transition process as high fertility rates slowly adjusted to lower child mortality rates. The main difference is that Africa is undergoing this change at a much later period. Since it is a 'late-late economic developer' on the global scene (see Kohli 2004), Africa has few areas of comparative advantage in the labour-intensive industrial and manufacturing sectors that could contribute to higher rates of formal sector employment (see Rodrik 2014). At the same time, today's young Africans have not only higher rates of education than previous generations, but also greater access to cell phones, the Internet, and television, allowing them to learn how their experiences compare with young counterparts elsewhere. As such, the gap between youth realities and aspirations has the potential to be much larger than in other regions of the world, which mostly reached their youth bulge peak in the mid-1970s.

Secondly, it aimed to add greater nuance to extant conventional wisdoms related to the marginalization of Africa's youth, many of whom are closely tied to fears about unemployed youth in particular. In Chapter 2, Thurlow emphasized the importance of recognizing that there are actually substantial disparities in youth unemployment rates across Africa. Moreover, as an aggregate, Africa's current level of youth unemployment is actually not higher than it is in other regions of the world. But, nevertheless, his projections show that in the coming decades, creating enough jobs in absolute numbers *and* at higher levels of productivity will be a formidable task, especially if economic growth cannot be sustained at its already very high levels in the region and if more labour-intensive structural transformation does not occur. Young African women will be especially disadvantaged, since they comprise a larger share of the unemployed within the region and compared to other regions, they make up a larger share of the labour force. Key public policy options in the areas of education and population planning could help achieve the more optimistic scenario projections.

In Chapter 3, Resnick interrogated the popular notion in both the media and the life cycle literature that disgruntled African youth head to the streets to protest their living conditions. At the absolute level, she finds that today's African youth actually protest very little and only marginally more so than their older compatriots. More revealing, however, is that the youth who do protest are not necessarily more likely to be unemployed or more economically deprived, but have greater social and human capital, indicated by greater participation in community and religious organizations, are more educated, and frequently access the news.

Both Hansen (Chapter 4) and Bryceson (Chapter 5) question the 'waithood' perspective in which unemployed African youth are essentially waiting in limbo for a better tomorrow. Focused on the urban context, Hansen notes that instead of seeing African cities as disorganized and underserviced, her fieldwork has revealed that young people claim that the 'the city was where life was happening.' She emphasizes that while African urban youth may be waiting for a better tomorrow, this is not equivalent to idleness. Instead, they pursue entrepreneurial outlets in the street economy, express their voices through innovative music lyrics, or build their social networks through religious organizations. Instead of always resorting to criminal activities or provoking conflict, she instead details the myriad means of social interaction in which they engage to foster relationships and seek job opportunities.

For Bryceson, Tanzanian youth are neither alienated by their circumstances nor dependent on the protection and services of older, 'big men.' Instead, she details their ability to gain greater autonomy through mining in artisanal gold mines, which predominantly attract rural migrants and then quickly expand into secondary towns as food stands, housing, and other amenities are established. But many youth in these communities also lament the trade-offs between furthering their education and working in the mines, the temporary nature of the mining lifestyle, and the negative externalities for young women and girls who have become dependent on relationships with miners for economic security. Her chapter is a useful reminder that while economic autonomy enables youth to escape the boredom and apathy that accompanies 'waithood,' it can sometimes result in a 'premature adulthood' that truncates the formative adolescent period when self-awareness and long-term planning for one's future begins to take shape.

Chapters 6 builds on Bryceson's observations by emphasizing that finding jobs for young people is not enough. Sumberg et al. note that while rural youth employment programmes are popular in Africa's policy arena, they tend to result in only 'protective' or 'preventative' work schemes rather than truly 'promotive' or 'transformative' initiatives that actually enhance incomes, capabilities, and social inclusion. Instead, Sumberg et al. stress that young people are not just seeking jobs but pursuing aspirations, which is why existing employment programmes focused on small-scale, low-paying farm work fail to keep the youth in the countryside. Instead, the authors stress that a notion of true entrepreneurship that fosters innovation and risk-taking needs to be better embedded in these programmes.

Aspirations also lie at the center of Chapter 7 where Oketch questions the conventional enthusiasm around technical and vocation education (TVET). While on the surface TVET is a practical solution for helping youth gain specific skills and technological know-how for a specific subset of jobs, it is often perceived by both African governments and the youth as a second-rate form of education. In turn, low levels of public resources are invested into the sector and only low-quality students are attracted to it, which reinforces the impression that TVET is substandard to general education. Graduates of general education are subsequently better remunerated than their TVET counterparts. Consequently, drawing on Botswana's relatively successful example, Oketch not only recommends that African governments commit to TVET the level of financial resources needed to match their rhetorical enthusiasm for this policy intervention but also notes that a strong general education in literary, numeracy, communication and analytical skills should constitute the basis of any TVET programme.

Oketch's findings are complemented by those of Rankin, Roberts, and Schöer (Chapter 8) who focus on a form of firm-sponsored TVET education in the formal sector, known as learnership programmes, in South Africa. Targeted specifically to 16–35-year-olds, South Africa's learnership programmes are the most extensive in Africa and are often cited as an example for the rest of the region. Aimed at creating jobs for young people, they are supposed to be focused more on those who lack the skills demanded by firms. However, Rankin, Roberts, and Schöer show that the programme not only has relatively low enrolment but also is more likely to attract those who have completed secondary schooling than those who have not, which is contrary to its initial aims to help those with minimal education. Most significantly, while young people who complete learnerships are more likely to find jobs in the short-term, the learnerships are not able to generate the level of jobs needed to meet the current and forthcoming employment challenge highlighted by Thurlow (Chapter 2).

Today's youth in a post-2015 world

By marshaling empirical evidence to critique some prevailing wisdoms in the academic and policy arenas, this volume hopes to push the discussion about African youth further as we move towards the conclusion of the Millennium Development Goals and look forward to the Post-2015 Development Agenda. Toward this end, and drawing on these collective studies, at least five key points bear mentioning. First, in an era of limited financial resources, including from the donor community, difficult trade-offs may be needed in terms of prioritizing interventions that would benefit African youth. This is potentially most obvious in the domain of education policy. On the one hand, Chapter 7 highlighted that the much touted benefits of TVET will not materialize unless substantially more resources are invested in the sector to avoid it appearing as a second-rate education option for those students with lower aptitude. On the other hand, Chapter 2 noted that Africa still lags globally in its enrolment rates at the secondary level, and has woefully low enrolment at the tertiary level. Therefore, the general education system is also in need of a boost in terms of both additional financial and human capital. While ideally investments should be made at both levels, this may not be realistic in many of the region's more low-income countries. Tax incentives for private sector companies, both domestic and multinational, to engage in technical and on-the-job programmes for low-skilled youth (see Chapter 8) could be one potential financing option in those African countries with governments that can effectively regulate such programmes.

Secondly, there is greater need in discussions on African youth to avoid generalizing to the continent from case study experiences or to draw conclusions about correlations that are unsupported by data. Youth bulges do not necessarily lead to high youth unemployment and high youth unemployment does not automatically result in a greater number of protests or civil conflict. In fact, southern Africa disproportionately has the highest rates of youth unemployment. Yet, much of the fear over unemployed youth resorting to conflict has emerged from focusing on cases in East and West Africa, including Cote d'Ivoire, Liberia, Rwanda, Sierra Leone, and Uganda, which have comparatively much lower youth unemployment rates. This disjuncture highlights that poor governance and sub-national socioeconomic inequalities are more to blame for youth engagement in conflict than just having a surfeit of young people in the population.

Thirdly and relatedly, the emphasis in international and regional initiatives on improving prospects for the economic advancement of African youth is not really sufficient for real change to occur. Complementary mechanisms are needed to incorporate the youth into the political and policy arenas and thereby ensure commitment to youth issues continues despite the emergence of new priorities and development fads. Indeed, while 36 of the AU's member states have ratified the Youth Charter, it is not clear how many young Africans actually know about the Charter or have access to mechanisms at the national level to enforce it. More broadly, opportunities are needed for a new generation of Africans leaders to be able to access key political positions to help shape and implement youth policies.[1] Currently, even where democracy is well-entrenched in Africa, the lack of transparent mechanisms within political parties for choosing leaders effectively closes off opportunities for younger competitors.

Fourthly, it is important to recognize that African governments are facing a double burden by dealing with the ramifications of the youth bulge today rather than three decades ago when many other developing regions did so. Specifically, they are operating in a period of 'late-late development' where options for large numbers of jobs for unskilled workers in competitive global industries already have been taken by Asia and Latin America. At the same time, international norms about 'decent' jobs have changed in recent decades. As discussed in

Chapter 1, the High-Level Panel (HLP) report on the Post-2015 Development Agenda advocates not only creating more jobs but also better paying jobs that are generated by growth processes that do not exacerbate inequality (UN 2013). As such, one of the HLP's illustrative targets is to 'increase the number of good and decent jobs and livelihoods by x' (see UN 2013: 46). At the same time, in the wake of the Rio+ 20 Conference on Sustainable Development in 2012, African governments are expected to create jobs for the youth that are 'decent,' 'inclusive,' and also 'green' (UN 2012). While such high level goals can be inspirational and aspirational, addressing them in practice will be extremely challenging, especially since Chapter 2 illustrated clear trade-offs between creating more jobs in Africa and fewer jobs that are nonetheless more productive and therefore better paid. International targets that ignore these trade-offs may set up Africa for a failure, as some have argued the MDGs did (see Easterly 2009).

Finally, there is a time inconsistency problem that results from focusing exclusively on today's youth crisis. Most policy discussions on youth are related to promoting education and jobs. Yet, there are long-term implications of Africa's youth bulge that extend beyond these two sectors. For instance, for all the talk about youth marginalization, the Global AgeWatch recently revealed that Africa is the worst region in the world in which to be old. African countries clustered at the bottom of its global index, which is based on four criteria: income security, health status, capabilities (including the employment and educational status of older people), and enabling environment, which fosters social connections, safety, civic freedoms, and access to public transport.[2] Only five African countries even provide old age pensions with universal coverage, including Botswana, Lesotho, Namibia, South Africa, and Swaziland.[3] Just as in other regions that passed their youth bulge in the 1970s and now face an aging crisis, there will be tremendous stress on African governments to provide financially sustainable social security options for this segment of the population. Consequently, in tandem to addressing the economic and political constraints faced by this cohort today, more concerted planning needs to also be directed toward the very slow process of establishing viable social protection systems in the coming decades.

Conclusions

The demographic problem of the youth bulge has created alarmist responses, particularly in the policy community. This is understandable given Filmer and Fox's (2014) reminder that each year, another 5 million Africans turn 15. Yet, while daunting, this is not unusual in historical terms when viewed from a global perspective. Instead, the youth bulge has only served to magnify the more longstanding social, economic, institutional, political, and policy constraints that have sidelined the youth's prospects for change. In navigating these constraints, this volume illustrates that the youth do indeed display a diversity of behaviours and preferences rather than being uniformly prone to conflict and instability or apathy, disengagement, and 'waithood.' In order to best harness their initiative and creativity in a post-2015 world, a key aim should be moving beyond just achieving outcome targets to also considering processes of youth empowerment that ensure greater voice for, and accountability to, this heterogeneous constituency.

Notes

1 In a region where the median age is 19 years old, only a handful of presidents are younger than 60. At the time of writing, these included Hailemariam Desalegn (Ethiopia), Joseph Kabila (DRC), Paul Kagame (Rwanda), Uhuru Kenyatta (Kenya), Felipe Nyussi (Mozambique), and Macky Sall (Senegal).
2 See http://www.helpage.org/global-agewatch/.
3 See http://www.pension-watch.net/pensions/country-fact-file/.

References

Abbink, J. (2005). 'Being young in Africa: The politics of despair and renewal.' In J. Abbink and I. van Kessel (eds.), *Vanguard or Vandals: Youth Politics and Conflict in Africa*. Leiden, The Netherlands: Brill.

Easterly, W. (2009). 'How the Millennium Development Goals are Unfair to Africa.' *World Development*, 37(1): 26–35.

Filmer, D. and L. Fox with K. Brooks, A. Goyal, T. Mengistae, P. Premand, D. Ringold, S. Sharma, and S. Zorya. (2014). *Youth Employment in Sub-Saharan Africa*. Paris and Washington, DC: Agence Française de Développement and World Bank.

Kohli, A. (2004). *State-Directed Development: Political Power and Industrialization in the Global Periphery*. New York, NY: Cambridge University Press.

Rodrik, D. (2014). 'An African Growth Miracle?' *The Ninth Annual Richard H. Sabot Lecture*. Washington, DC: Center for Global Development.

United Nations (UN) (2012). *The Future We Want-Outcome Document*. Rio de Janeiro, Brazil: United Nations Conference on Sustainable Development. http://www.uncsd2012.org/content/documents/727The%20Future%20We%20Want%2019%20June%201230pm.pdf

United Nations (UN) (2013). *A New Global Partnership: Eradicate Poverty and Transform Economies through Sustainable Development*. New York, NY: UN.

Index

For Product Safety Concerns and Information please contact our
EU representative GPSR@taylorandfrancis.com Taylor & Francis
Verlag GmbH, Kaufingerstraße 24, 80331 München, Germany